HUGH CASEY

HUGH CASEY

The Triumphs and Tragedies of a Brooklyn Dodger

Lyle Spatz

ROWMAN & LITTLEFIELD
Lanham • Boulder • New York • London

Published by Rowman & Littlefield
A wholly owned subsidary of The Rowman & Littlefield Publishing Group,
Inc.
4501 Forbes Boulevard, Suite 200, Lanham, Maryland 20706
www.rowman.com

Unit A, Whitacre Mews, 26-34 Stannary Street, London SE11 4AB

British Library Cataloguing in Publication Information Available

Library of Congress Cataloging-in-Publication Data

Names: Spatz, Lyle, 1937–, author.
Title: Hugh Casey : the triumphs and tragedies of a Brooklyn Dodger / Lyle Spatz.
Description: Lanham : ROWMAN & LITTLEFIELD, [2017] | Includes bibliographical refer-
    ences and index.
Identifiers: LCCN 2016039730 (print) | LCCN 2016041726 (ebook) | ISBN 9781442277595 (hard-
    cover : alk. paper) | ISBN 9781442277601 (electronic)
Subjects: LCSH: Casey, Hugh Thomas, 1913–1951. | Baseball players—United States—Biogra-
    phy. | Pitchers (Baseball)—United States—Biography.
Classification: LCC GV865 .C328 2017 (print) | LCC GV865 (ebook) | DDC 796.357092 [B]—
    dc23
LC record available at https://lccn.loc.gov/2016039730

∞ ™ The paper used in this publication meets the minimum requirements of
American National Standard for Information Sciences Permanence of Paper
for Printed Library Materials, ANSI/NISO Z39.48-1992.

Printed in the United States of America

In loving memory of Paul Spatz (1939–2016)

CONTENTS

PHOTOGRAPHS

FOREWORD

A player always remembers his first day in the big leagues. Mine was July 25, 1948, a Sunday at Pittsburgh's Forbes Field. I had just been called up from the Fort Worth Cats of the Double-A Texas League. While shagging fly balls during batting practice and trying to look like I belonged in the majors, the biggest Dodger on the team walked over to me. It was Hugh Casey. He welcomed me and proceeded to give me encouragement and also some sound advice.

As time passed, he took me under his wing and not only befriended me, but also included me in numerous Brooklyn off-the-field events. We fished at Sheepshead Bay and visited restaurants and private parties. He introduced me to Brooklyn. Hughie was a popular figure. His big Irish character was readily recognized wherever he went. This story of Hugh Casey will give you a glimpse and feel of a colorful Brooklyn era.

Carl Erskine

ACKNOWLEDGMENTS

Christen Karniski and Dan Levitt, of Rowman & Littlefield, were a source of support and encouragement throughout the writing of this book.

Maury Bouchard, of Schenevus, New York, served as my fact-checker, as he has done in the past and, as always, saved me from numerous potential embarrassments. Like Maury, Rick Huhn of Westerville, Ohio, and Tom Bourke of St. Petersburg, Florida, read the entire original manuscript. Rick, a first-rate biographer himself, made several suggestions to make this a better book. Tom, the former chief of the microforms division at the New York Public Library, was an enormous help with both the genealogical history of the Casey family and the geography of New York as it was during the 1940s.

Gabriel Schechter provided access to Casey's player files from the National Baseball Hall of Fame Library archive in Cooperstown.

Steve Steinberg took valuable hours away from his own research at the New York Public Library to supply me with articles pertaining to Casey.

Stephan Saks, formerly of the Reference and Research Services, New York Public Library, helped track down some difficult to find newspaper stories.

My friends and colleagues at the Society for American Baseball Research graciously responded to my questions concerning their areas of expertise and supplied answers to my most trivial questions.

The photographs that appear in this book come from John Horne, of the National Baseball Hall of Fame Library, and Hugh Casey's son, Michael Kocijan.

The season and career statistics for Casey and all other players and teams come from two indispensable online sources: Sean Forman's Baseball-Reference and Dave Smith's Retrosheet.

INTRODUCTION

Hugh Casey was among the most colorful members of baseball's most colorful franchise—the Brooklyn Dodgers. He is a link between two of that team's most storied members, both named Robinson. Wilbert Robinson, then retired but formerly the manager of the pennant winning 1916 and 1920 Brooklyn clubs, discovered him. And in 1947, he was one of the many Southern-born players on the Dodgers who welcomed Jackie Robinson, with mixed emotions, as the first black man to play in the major leagues in the twentieth century.

Casey, an unabashed son of the South, was an outstanding pitcher for the Dodgers in the 1940s. That famed and colorful team engaged in four great pennant races, the first National League playoff series, and two exciting World Series. Casey was very much a part of all those teams, peopled by outsized personalities, including executives Larry MacPhail and Branch Rickey; manager Leo Durocher; and players like Robinson, Pee Wee Reese, Dixie Walker, Eddie Stanky, Joe Medwick, Dolph Camilli, and Pete Reiser. Along the way, he helped redefine the role of the relief pitcher and threw the most famous "pitch that got away" in World Series history.

Casey twice led the National League in saves and twice finished second. Of course saves were not an official statistic during Casey's career, and no one tracked them. When they did become an official statistic, in 1969, baseball statisticians looked at pre-1969 box scores and game stories and awarded saves retroactively. For this book, I treat those retroactive saves as if they were being recorded at the time they took place.

The 1940s Dodgers were involved in numerous brawls and beanball wars, and Casey was often in the middle of them. His most famous altercation came not on the field and not with another ballplayer, but in the Havana, Cuba, home of Ernest Hemingway, at the time America's most celebrated novelist. Not surprisingly, heavy drinking by both men preceded the fight.

Casey was most likely an alcoholic, a condition that played a role in many of his myriad personal problems: separation from his wife; running over and killing a blind man; failure to pay taxes on a tavern he owned in Brooklyn; and being charged in a paternity suit. The paternity suit, which was decided against him, may have been the final blow that led to his suicide at 37. He did it the same way Hemingway would nine years later, with a shotgun.

I

THE BLOOD OF THE OLD SOUTH

In his rookie season with the 1935 Chicago Cubs, Georgia-born Hugh Casey was one of several southerners on a team that included fellow pitchers Lon Warneke from Arkansas and Bill Lee from Louisiana. The club also had Walter Stephenson, a little-used backup catcher from North Carolina. For all of them, the American Civil War was far from over. Stephenson was overly proud of his Southern heritage, so much so that it led to a fight in the dugout with shortstop Billy Jurges, a native New Yorker, before a game in Pittsburgh on July 30. The fight so upset manager Charlie Grimm that he banished Stephenson to the minor leagues. Grimm was later forced to recall Stephenson when Gabby Hartnett was injured and he was left with only Ken O'Dea behind the plate.

As part of the ongoing verbal battle, Hugh "Drummer Boy" Casey, as he was called by Ed Burns of *Sporting News*, got in a zinger of his own. Casey, wrote Burns, made a wisecrack about "shootings that have occurred *since* the War Between the States."[1] This was a reference to a July 6, 1932, incident in which Violet Valli, a showgirl with whom Jurges was romantically linked, tried to shoot him at Chicago's Hotel Carlos, where they both lived.[2] If Jurges had calmed down after the exchange with Stephenson, Casey's gibe had him steaming again, although no blows were thrown.

A year later, Casey found another opportunity to publicly voice his Southern pride. The Los Angeles Angels, where the Cubs had sent him for the 1936 season, had started poorly. On April 21, they were in last place and had won only seven games, and the day before had ended a six-game losing streak. Manager Jack Lelivelt chose the 22-year-old Casey to face the Sacramento Solons that night in an attempt to give the Angels their first two-game winning streak of the season.

"Ah'm ready," said Casey, in *Los Angeles Times* reporter Bob Ray's attempt to replicate the youngster's southern drawl. "All Ah ask is that they get me a run or two. If the Angels evah get in the lead today, Ah promise to protect that advantage with mah life's blood, which is the blood of the old South and the Confederacy, suh."[3]

The blood of the old South and the Confederacy did indeed run deep in Hugh Casey's veins. Genealogical research shows that as far back as the late eighteenth century, all of Casey's ancestors were natives of the South, overwhelmingly from Georgia.[4] His parents and all four grandparents were born in Georgia.

Hugh's maternal grandfather, Atlanta-born James Franklin Burdett (1840–1934), was twenty-one years old on March 4, 1862, when he enlisted as a private in the 9th Battalion Georgia Artillery. The battalion's nickname was "Buckhead," for the section of Atlanta where many of its soldiers had lived prior to the war.

Later in the war, Burdett and his unit were attached to General Robert E. Lee's Army of Northern Virginia. When Ulysses S. Grant became general in chief of the Union armies in March 1864, he opened a campaign in Virginia designed to wear down Lee and the Confederacy.

During the Siege of Petersburg in October, Burdett took part in the Battle of Boydton Plank Road. Later, he and his unit were in West Virginia when they learned General Lee had surrendered to General Grant on April 9, 1865, at Appomattox Courthouse in Virginia. With the war essentially over—and lost—Burdett and a companion made the long trek home to Atlanta by foot.[5]

Hugh's paternal grandfather, William M. Casey, was also born in Atlanta but was too young for military service in the war. It is highly likely, however, that his father, older brothers, or uncles would have served. William Casey was nine years old in November 1864, when he watched Atlanta being burned to the ground. Growing up, young Hugh undoubtedly heard endless stories of the "lost cause" and the laying waste of their beloved Georgia from his Confederate soldier grandfather and other relatives.[6]

Hugh's father, James Oliver Casey, was born in 1878, the son of William and Hester (Donaldson) Casey. His mother, Elizabeth, was the daughter of James F. Burdett and Martha (Martin) Burdett.

James Casey, or Buck, as most people called him, and Elizabeth Burdett, or Lizzie, as most people called her, were married in Atlanta, in 1898. Between 1899 and 1913, Elizabeth gave birth to nine children, of which Hugh was the youngest. Sisters Nellie and Rebie E. and brothers James Frank, William M., Ellis S., and Everett J. preceded him. The family also lost a male infant and a one-year-old daughter.

Hugh Thomas Casey was born October 14, 1913, in the Buckhead section of Atlanta. He spent his childhood there, with his father, a Fulton County policeman since 1907, his mother, and his surviving siblings at 56 Peachtree Avenue, NE.

Casey's father had frowned on baseball, so Hugh's prime recreation as a youth was hunting in the nearby fields or fishing along the banks of the Chattahoochee River. James began to change his mind about baseball when Hugh's older brother Ellis began starring for a local team.

Casey attended Monroe A&M and Technical High School, where he pitched for the school baseball team. When Rache Bell, a prominent Atlanta sandlot coach, organized an American Legion junior team called the Northside Terrors, some of Casey's high-school teammates urged him to try out. He made the team by impressing Bell with his fastball and his endurance. In one playoff series, he threw five complete games, displaying the "workhorse qualities that later brought him fame."[7]

He also played semipro ball for several years under Tubby Walton, an independent scout who had discovered and sent several Georgians to the major leagues. Casey was on Walton's 1930 team. Such future major leaguers as Marty Marion and Jim Bagby Jr. were on the 1932 and 1933 teams. By this time, Hugh's father had become a devoted fan and often rearranged his shifts to allow him to attend games.

"Dad started to work at 12 at night," Casey remembered. "He would work until 12 the next day, then he and mother would hop in the car and follow the team wherever we went. Often we played in Tennessee or Alabama, but still they'd go along."[8]

One afternoon in 1931, in Gainesville, Georgia, Casey, then 17, was near unhittable, fanning 18 opposing batters. He also hit two home

Figure 1.1.   A relatively thin and dapper Casey poses with some young admirers in 1935. *National Baseball Hall of Fame Library, Cooperstown, NY.*

runs. The next day, the Detroit Tigers signed him to a contract, which was actually signed by his father because Hugh was underage.

"I started with Wheeling [West Virginia] in 1931," Casey said in a 1947 interview with J. G. Taylor Spink of *Sporting News*. "You will not find any mention of my having been with Wheeling in any of the record books. But I pitched there, very briefly, as a Detroit farmhand. I hurt my hand and was released."[9]

The following spring, the Tigers sent Casey to the Huntington (West Virginia) Boosters of the Class C Middle Atlantic League. Casey remembered his first spring training camp mainly for the weather. "We worked out in a snow bank," he recalled. "I never did see so much snow before."[10]

During camp, he developed a blister on his throwing hand, and the Boosters released him before he ever got into a game. Later in that 1932 season, he signed with his hometown Atlanta Crackers of the Class A Southern Association. The president of the Atlanta club was Wilbert Robinson, who had managed the Brooklyn Dodgers (alternately called Robins in his honor) from 1914 to 1931, winning pennants in 1916 and 1920. Said Hugh, "I worked the 1932 season with them but never won a game. I lost three. Just a kid."[11]

After the season, Robinson took Casey with him to Dover Hall, Georgia, his offseason retreat where he spent his days hunting and fishing. Among Robinson's old friends who spent time with him at Dover Hall were Cap Huston, Jacob Ruppert's former partner in ownership of the New York Yankees; sportswriter W. O. McGeehan of the *New York Herald Tribune*; and Bill Pipp, the father of former Yankees first baseman Wally Pipp.

None of them were teetotalers, so while hunting and fishing occupied their days, storytelling and drinking were the prime night-time activities. According to Dodgers historian Tom Knight, Robinson supposedly spotted the 18-year-old Casey throwing rocks at bottles atop fences on the property. "Throw at them bottles and hit 'em," Robinson told him, "but always make sure they're empty."[12]

"No one to this day," wrote Clarence Greenbaum of the *Brooklyn Eagle*, "knows whether Robinson liked Casey more because the six-footer was a great natural pitcher—the kind Robbie liked—or because Hugh always knew where the fish were biting, was a Deadeye-Dick with a shotgun, and had a way with bird dogs."[13]

Ralph McGill, editor in chief of the *Atlanta Constitution* and a future Pulitzer Prize winner, believed Uncle Robbie had a theory that for a pitcher to be successful, he had to have strong legs to go along with a strong arm.[14] Robinson liked Casey because the youngster had both physical attributes and because, as McGill stated, "[w]hen a quail got up anywhere in the vicinity of Hugh Casey, that quail was as good as dead."[15]

McGill had long been a lone voice in Atlanta journalism in opposing social and educational segregation, and political disfranchisement. He had started his career as a sportswriter and would often write columns pertaining to sports, particularly if there was an Atlanta connection. The day after the conclusion of the 1947 World Series, he wrote of Casey's discovery by Robinson and the glories of Dover Hall:

> This was in the days when Dover Hall was heaven on earth. It was out in the piney woods from Brunswick. An artesian well splashed before the main lodge. There were deer in its pines and quail in its clearings. The buildings, left from an old English plantation of the sea-island days, were hard by the marshes. . . .
>
> Casey served as Robbie's "meat hunter." Whenever the lodge's food supply ran low on quail or deer meat, Robbie would call for Casey. Hugh would take his gun and wander off in the woods, with a dog or so along. By nightfall there would be fresh deer liver and steaks, and for breakfast there would be quail.[16]

For the rest of his life, Casey would remember with great pleasure the days he spent at Dover Hall, and he was forever grateful to Robinson for giving him the opportunity to be there. He told reporter Harold Parrott in the spring of 1940,

> You can say for me that Mr. Robinson is one of the finest men I've ever met. Why, he was like a father to me. He taught me many things about pitching, encouraged me when my arm was sore, and gave me good advice.
>
> Why, I can remember back in 1932, when Robbie and I first got acquainted. It was bird dogs that really brought us together. We both loved 'em. I'd always hunted a lot with dad, and Robbie, of course, worshipped dogs and guns.
>
> I had finished at Tech High in Atlanta in 1931, and after a brief whirl with Detroit, I came back to sign with the Atlanta club. But, of

course, I was underage, and there was some trouble about my contract. I had not made a good record with Atlanta, but they liked my stuff, and Robbie, who was president of the club, came down on the bench to see me. He said, "Why not come over to Dover Hall and spend a week with me after the season is over. I'll show you some real hunting and we can straighten this contract matter out."

Well, I went over to Dover Hall, and what a beautiful place that was! It consisted of about 7,700 acres that before the Civil War had been one of the richest rice plantations in the South. The abolition of slavery ruined the rice industry, of course, and about 20 years ago, Robinson, Colonel Til Huston, [and some Cincinnati businessmen] purchased Dover Hall as a hunting club.

There were plenty of swamp deer, quail, and opossum. There were wild turkeys, and during the duck-hunting season, the gunning was great on a marshy inlet of the sea.

Casey said he stayed a week and then mentioned he was going home.

Robbie said, "Don't you like it here? What's your hurry?" I said, "Gosh Mr. Robinson, I can't stay; I have no money to stay in a place like this." Robinson's answer was, "Boy, you don't need money here. Make yourself at home."

Well, I came for a week and stayed all winter. Uncle Robbie and Ma Robinson [Wilbert's wife Mary] were like a second set of parents to me. It was the greatest time I ever had in my life. Every day, all winter long, Robbie and I were out hunting. . . . And, of course, Robbie and I would talk plenty about baseball, and pitching. He liked me because I was a big fellow, I guess. He liked big, strong chuckers. [17]

Atlanta demoted Casey to the Charlotte Hornets of the Class B Piedmont League for 1933. Although he missed the first month of the season, he won 19 games (19–9). "There was some sort of rhubarb because I had signed while under age," Casey remembered. He had signed the contracts with Atlanta and Charlotte himself, which had made them technically unenforceable because of his age. After some negotiating with Hugh and his father, Atlanta team president Robinson signed him legally. "Back to the Crackers I went," said Casey, "and in 1934 I won eight and lost six." [18]

The next year, he was with the Cubs. The *Sporting News* issue of February 7, 1935, mentioned the Cubs had added three minor-league pitchers to their roster: Clay Bryant, Fabian Kowalik, and Casey, whom they called by his middle name, Thomas. In those years, *Sporting News* printed profiles each winter of minor-league players expected to make their major-league debuts the following season. In February 1935, they wrote the following about Casey:

> If averages alone were considered in the case of Hugh Casey, 22-year-old pitcher purchased by the Cubs from Atlanta late last season, the scout who recommended him would not have much to stand on in his own defense. But Casey was not taken on his record. He was acquired because of native ability that had not fully developed, and which might require another season or two in the minors before it comes into full bloom.
>
> Casey, a strapping right-hander, who owns a fast one, has been pitching professionally for three seasons. He was originally a discovery of the Detroit Tigers, getting his start with Huntington in 1932. However, he was passed up in a few weeks and was signed as a free agent by Atlanta. In 1933, the Southern Association club sent him to Charlotte, where he won 19 and lost nine. This was enough to result in his recall, and for Atlanta to keep him in 1934.[19]

Years later, at spring training in Havana in 1947, Casey recalled his first big-league training camp with the 1935 Cubs: "What I remember about Catalina Island [California] was that there was hot salt water baths right in the clubhouse, and if you came up with a sore arm you could give it treatment right on the spot while you were still in uniform. Now they have sun lamps and all sorts of gadgets."[20]

Casey made the major-league roster and his major-league debut on April 29, 1935, in a free-scoring game against Pittsburgh at Wrigley Field. The Cubs won, 12–11, sparked by a 10-run eighth inning. The game was marred by on-field brawls that led to ejections for Pittsburgh's Cookie Lavagetto and Guy Bush, an ex-Cub, and Chicago's Billy Jurges and Roy Joiner. National League president Ford Frick fined Bush and Jurges $50 each and suspended Bush for five days and Jurges for three. Casey was the third of seven pitchers manager Grimm used, and the most effective, allowing no runs in two-and-a-third innings.

The next day's newspapers credited him with the win, but that was later changed and the win awarded to Fabian Kowalik, who allowed three runs in the one inning he pitched, the eighth. When the Cubs regained the lead by scoring 10 runs in the home half of the inning, Kowalik was deemed the pitcher of record.

Chicago kept Casey for the entire season, but he didn't see much action, appearing in just 13 games, all in relief. "That was the worst year I ever spent," he told sportswriter Harold Parrott in a 1940 interview. "Sometimes I think Charlie Grimm never knew I was with the club. He just ignored me. I pitched only 26 innings [actually 25 and two-thirds] all season, and I knew every blade of grass in every bullpen throughout the league. The only thing that saved that season for me was the share of the World's [*sic*] Series swag that I got."[21]

2

A SENSE THAT GOOD TIMES WERE COMING TO BROOKLYN

Although the Cubs thought enough of Casey to vote him a full share of the 1935 World Series pot, they were undecided whether to keep him on the roster for 1936 or send him back to the minors. The primary arguments for sending him to the minors were his youth and the chance to develop him into a full-time starting pitcher.

During spring training at Catalina Island in California, the Cubs announced they would keep most of the players from the 1935 squad. Nevertheless, they would likely farm out two promising young pitchers—Casey and Clyde Shoun—because the two needed more work honing their skills. Manager Charlie Grimm had said earlier that he would give them opportunities to make the team during spring training. But after the Cubs played a series of exhibition games in Los Angeles against their farm club, the Pacific Coast League Angels, in mid-March, Grimm left Casey behind. Grimm said he thought Casey had a good chance of rejoining the Cubs if he had regular work with Los Angeles and gained experience.

"They never knew I was on the payroll," he would say four years later, his bitterness still apparent. "I pitched well that year in spring training against the Yankees and against the White Sox. I pitched well when they used me in relief later, but whenever the game got close or they had a chance to win Charlie Grimm would take me out."[1]

Casey made an immediate impression on his new club. Pitching against a team of Angels rookies in his first start, he held them to just four hits. Manager Jack Lelivelt was so pleased with what he had seen, he said Casey was in the mix to be his opening-day starter. Meanwhile, Casey settled into his new surroundings. He rented a bungalow with veteran PCL catcher John Bottarini, whom he called the ideal room-mate. Bottarini did all the cooking, Casey said, while he took care of washing the dishes.

After he missed 10 days in the early weeks of the season with a sore arm, Casey returned on April 12, tossing a complete-game, 5–1 victory over the Mission Reds. On May 6, he defeated the San Francisco Seals, 16–0, to register the Angels' first shutout of the season. By early August, however, his arm was bothering him so much, he asked to be put on the voluntarily retired list.

Years later, Casey told J. G. Taylor Spink the sore arm was the real reason Chicago had sent him to the Angels. When Spink asked him about the type of pitches he threw, Casey said sinkers and curves, adding,

> I developed the sinker after I had injured my arm in 1936. I found that I had lost some stuff and said to myself, "Hugh, you gotta pick up something special and extra, or no major leagues." I had been pitching curves and sliders but put the slider away when I found I had developed a sinker. I got the slider back these last few years.[2]

Casey pitched only 106 innings for the 1936 Angels, winning five games and losing eight. Nevertheless, Lelivelt recommended he be paid his full season's salary, but the Cubs would not agree. They put him on their suspended list and placed him with Birmingham of the Southern Association for 1937.

"The Cubs apparently did not think much of me," remembered Casey, "or my chances of making the grade, because in 1937, I was tossed down to Birmingham." He got off to a 6–1 start with manager Riggs Stephenson's Birmingham Barons and at one point was 10–5, before finishing 14–13 for the seventh-place Barons. A better measure of his performance was his league-leading 2.56 earned run average.

On October 25, 1937, the 24-year-old Casey married Kathleen Thomas in Atlanta. Kathleen, born in Atlanta on November 17, 1914, was the daughter of Cona Avory Thomas and Lillie C. Thomas (née Estes). She and Hugh met at Monroe A&M and Technical High School, when she was 14 years old and he was 15, and the two had been going together ever since. Kathleen followed his baseball career while she was in school, and later, while she worked for the Postal Telegraph Company, she would often copy the play-by-play accounts for games he pitched.

In December, the Cubs sent Casey to the Memphis Chicks as part of a deal for Coaker Triplett, the Southern Association's batting champion and Most Valuable Player. At that point, Casey felt his career had stalled. "I was fat and disgusted and rapidly getting more so," he said in a 1940 interview.[3]

Still, owner Colonel Tom Watkins and manager Billy Southworth said they had high hopes for their new acquisition and expected he would be their best pitcher. Casey reversed his won–lost record from the previous year, winning 13 and losing 14 for the fourth-place Chicks. No longer bothered by a sore arm, he threw a league-leading 291 innings and had 16 complete games. He also led Southern Association pitchers with a perfect fielding record.

One of Casey's teammates at Memphis was Cy Block, a Brooklyn native who was in his second season as a professional. Block quickly became the victim of several of Casey's practical jokes.

"The first trip I made with Casey was a dilly," Block remembered 30 years later, continuing,

> It was a week's visit to Atlanta and Chattanooga. The first thing he did was to get a porter to take my bag off the train and ship it to the Memphis club's office. I made the junket with a toothbrush. Then I was sitting on the train and he walked by and snipped my tie in half with scissors.[4]

Block recalled that Casey also set fire to a paper he was reading.

But Seymour "Cy" Block would get the last laugh. Although his baseball career was short—he played a combined 17 games with the Cubs in 1942, 1945, and 1946, and appeared in one game of the 1945 World Series—after leaving baseball, he made millions in the insurance industry.

Charlie Dressen, a former and future major-league skipper, was managing the Nashville Vols of the Southern Association in 1938, and thought he saw major-league potential in Casey. Later that year, when new Dodgers manager Leo Durocher hired Dressen as a coach, Dressen told Leo, "Grab that Casey." Durocher passed the suggestion on to team president Larry MacPhail, who made the deal.[5]

The minor-league draft was held in Chicago on October 4, 1938. Casey was the third of 17 players chosen, behind pitcher Bill Beckmann, selected by the Philadelphia Athletics, and infielder Jack Juelich, taken by the Pittsburgh Pirates. Several of those drafted never made it to the big leagues, and among those that did, Casey, by far, had the most successful career.

"In 1938, with the Chicks, I won 13 and lost 14, and was drafted by the Dodgers," Casey remembered a decade later. "I have been with Brooklyn ever since, a very fortunate man. Because you know what Brooklyn means to a ball player, how the fans here treat a player."[6]

There was a certain "buzz" surrounding the Brooklyn Dodgers team that Hugh Casey joined in the spring of 1939. The Dodgers had been a forlorn franchise for many years. They had not won a pennant since 1920 and had finished no higher than fifth place for the last six seasons under Wilbert Robinson's successors: Max Carey, Casey Stengel, and Burleigh Grimes. (They had finished third in 1932, Carey's first season as manager.)

Larry MacPhail had been making changes to revitalize the debt-ridden franchise since taking over as the team's president in 1938. The Brooklyn Trust Company, which controlled the majority of the team's stock, had recruited MacPhail after Cincinnati Reds owner Powel Crosley no longer wanted his service as vice president and general manager. But before accepting the position, MacPhail prevailed in getting the bank to agree to spend the money needed for the revitalization. He began with the physical plant, spending hundreds of thousands of dollars to refurbish a deteriorating Ebbets Field. Some of it went toward installing lights at the park.

The Dodgers played their first night game on June 15, 1938, against Cincinnati. The fans loved it, although the game is mostly remembered as the one in which Reds pitcher Johnny Vander Meer tossed his second consecutive no-hitter.

In bringing night baseball to Brooklyn, MacPhail broke an agreement among the pre-MacPhail Dodgers, Jacob Ruppert's Yankees, and Horace Stoneham's Giants that had kept nighttime baseball out of New York City. And he was not finished. In December 1938, MacPhail announced he had sold the radio rights to General Mills, maker of the breakfast cereal Wheaties, and the Socony Vacuum Oil Company to broadcast Dodgers games beginning in 1939. In doing so, he terminated another long-standing agreement among the three clubs to ban broadcasts of baseball games in the New York area.

By 1938, the only teams with no radio broadcasts were the three in New York. In 1939, the Yankees and Giants also began broadcasting games. MacPhail hired Walter Lanier "Red" Barber, who had been with him in Cincinnati, as the voice of the Dodgers. The soft-spoken Barber's game accounts, delivered with a Southern drawl and peppered with "down-home" witticisms, first on radio and later on television, added joy to the lives of Brooklyn fans for the next 15 years.

The Dodgers had been without a legitimate home-run threat since the 1932 season, when Hack Wilson had 23 and Lefty O'Doul had 21. Manager Burleigh Grimes's plea for a slugger had gone unanswered prior to MacPhail's assuming the presidency. On March 6, 1938, MacPhail answered that plea when he purchased first baseman Dolph Camilli from the Philadelphia Phillies. Camilli, nearing his 31st birthday, had hit 25 or more home runs in each of the past three seasons with the Phillies, and his 27 home runs in 1937 were only 10 fewer than the entire Brooklyn team had hit. The Dodgers gave up Eddie Morgan, a player with just 66 at-bats in his big-league career, which was now over. The Dodgers also reportedly sent Philadelphia $45,000, a sum thought to be the most they had ever paid for a player. Other estimates ranged as high as $75,000.

The acquisition of Camilli helped put fans in the seats—1938 attendance increased by almost 200,000—and he was a huge success on the field. He hit 24 home runs, batted in 100 runs, and drew a league-leading 119 walks. But the addition of one power hitter clearly was not enough, and Brooklyn finished seventh. As with Ebbets Field, the Dodgers needed a complete renovation, and MacPhail set about to provide it—beginning at the top.

After the season, MacPhail fired Grimes and replaced him with his 32-year-old shortstop, Leo Durocher. Grimes, suspecting he would be fired, suggested to Durocher, the team's captain, that he apply for the job. Leo did, and he got it.

Durocher had just finished his first season in Brooklyn, after having played for the Yankees, the Reds, and most notably the Cardinals. It was MacPhail, when he was with the Reds in 1933, who had traded

Durocher to St. Louis, where Leo became the shortstop and captain on Branch Rickey's Gashouse Gang clubs.

Durocher was a volatile, mercurial man, just like MacPhail, and the two would clash repeatedly in the years to come. He was coarse, brash, a gambler both on the field and off, and a scourge of umpires, but he knew baseball and could motivate men. Those who played with and against him mostly loved or hated him.

Sportswriter Gene Karst, using an eclectic string of adjectives, described Durocher as a "supreme egotist, brash loudmouth, natural ham, narcissistic monologist, hunch player, strategist, has-been strutting clothes horse, manicured, pedicured, perfumed, ruthless, sarcastic, bitter, amiable, flirtatious, charming, dapper."[7]

Dick Bartell, a major leaguer for 18 seasons, and a contemporary of Durocher, quoted one member of the '39 Dodgers as saying, "When Leo was shortstop and captain of the team in 1938, we hated him. We were ready to sock him for the first offside remark. Now we're ready to break our backs for him."[8]

Early in spring training, Durocher, running his first camp, publicly proclaimed his confidence. "Why shouldn't we be confident?" he asked. "We have great spirit. Everybody's in great condition. There are no prima donnas on this club. It's all for one and one for all with us," he said, channeling his inner Alexander Dumas. MacPhail was leery of Leo's optimism. "I'm a little afraid that these boys may get a little too cocky unless they're knocked off in some of these 31 games this spring."[9]

Brooklyn fans, too, were excited about the upcoming season. "The Brooklyn of 1939 was a wonderful place, made up of a myriad of ethnic neighborhoods, many of which had the feel of a small town. Moreover, the people of Brooklyn loved their baseball team—in good times and bad—and in 1939, there was a prevailing sense that good times were coming."[10]

Spring training was scheduled to start on March 1, in Clearwater, Florida. But Durocher, wanting to get a jump on the other clubs, ordered many of his players to report to Hot Springs, Arkansas, on February 15. Hot Springs was a traditional "boiling out" spot for players to shed any weight they had accumulated during the winter. Eddie McCormack, an assistant to Artie McGovern who ran a famous gym in New York, was hired by MacPhail to put them through a strict exercise regimen. Among those ordered to report were third baseman Harry "Cookie" Lavagetto and outfielder Tuck Stainback, both of whom were hampered by leg injuries in 1938, and former Yankees second baseman Tony Lazzeri, signed as a free agent.

Most of the invitees were pitchers, five of whom were new to the club, including Casey. Tommy Holmes of the *Brooklyn Eagle* described Casey as an "outstanding workhorse pitcher for the pennant-winning Atlanta club."[11] (Atlanta did win the Southern Association pennant in 1938, but Casey pitched that year for the fourth-place Memphis Chicks.) Casey was only 25 in 1939, but the *Eagle* already was calling him "heavyset" or "full-faced." These and other euphemisms for being overweight would accompany stories about him in the *Eagle* and other newspapers for the rest of his life.

MacPhail's hiring McCormack drew some laughs and snide remarks from other clubs, but it worked. No Brooklyn pitcher who was with the club in spring training had a sore arm all season, and no player had a sore or pulled muscle in any part of his body.

In addition to Casey, three other newcomers made the Dodgers pitching staff out of spring training. Two had been their league's Most Valuable Player in 1938: Whit Wyatt for the Milwaukee Brewers of the American Association and Red Evans for the New Orleans Pelicans of the Southern Association. The third was Bill Crouch, 21–8 for the Nashville Vols of the Southern Association. Casey, at 25, was by far the youngest. Wyatt and Crouch were 31, and Evans was 32.

Casey and Wyatt, a fellow Georgian, would become good friends, with their careers linked until Casey's death years later. The two made their first appearances as Dodgers in Brooklyn's opening exhibition game against Cincinnati. Wyatt, coming off his outstanding 23–7 season with Milwaukee, seemed the newcomer most likely to succeed. Yet, it was Casey who had been drawing the most attention. "Casey's two-way fastball—sometimes it sinks and sometimes it 'takes off'—has been the talk of the camp," wrote Holmes. "He has only thrown his curve the last couple of days, and hitters call that no. 2 delivery just as good as his hard one."[12]

Casey, although inconsistent throughout the exhibition season, clinched a spot on the roster with four hitless and scoreless innings against the Detroit Tigers 10 days before the regular season opener. Durocher used him for long relief stints in two of the traditional exhibition season wrap-up games against the Yankees. Casey finally made his Dodgers debut in the team's fifth game of the season, on April 23, in Philadelphia. He relieved Wyatt, also making his Brooklyn debut, in the 11th inning of a 3–3 game. He held the Phillies scoreless but, after Brooklyn scored in the top of the 12th, allowed a two-run single to Heinie Mueller that gave Philadelphia the 5–4 win. The Dodgers were now 1–4, with the other two losses going to Casey's roommate, Red Evans.

Durocher used Casey in a few more relief appearances before his first big-league start, on May 30, in the second game of the Memorial Day doubleheader at the Polo Grounds. National League president Ford Frick had recognized this unofficial start of summer by dressing his three umpires—Ziggy Sears, Beans Reardon, and Larry Goetz—in cream-colored pants.

Each team was below .500 in the standings; nevertheless a crowd of 58,296 squeezed into the old horseshoe-shaped ballpark in Harlem, and more than 10,000 were turned away. The Dodgers versus the Giants had long been baseball's most heated rivalry, and their won–lost records and positions in the standings when they met were mostly irrelevant.

Still, it was apparent that under MacPhail and Durocher, the Dodgers were on the rise. Meanwhile, after back-to-back pennants in 1936 and 1937, the Giants had slipped to third in 1938, and would not finish first again until 1951.

The Giants' Harry Gumbert had bested the Dodgers' Vito Tamulis in the opener, and a sweep would allow New York to move ahead of Brooklyn into fifth place. Casey's mound opponent was Carl Hubbell, the National League's best pitcher from 1933 to 1937. Hubbell had fallen off in 1938, winning only 13 games, and had just one victory so far in 1939.

"Leo threw me in to start the second game of a doubleheader against the Giants," Casey remembered several years later. "We had lost the first game, and Carl Hubbell was working the nightcap for [Giants manager Bill] Terry. There were about 60,000 fans in the stands that Memorial Day, and I'd never seen that many people in my life."[13]

The Dodgers got a run in the first and two more in the seventh on back-to-back home runs by left fielder Ernie Koy and catcher Al Todd. The Giants scored their only run in the seventh, on a single by Mel Ott, Zeke Bonura's second double of the game, and an infield out.

The win was the first of Casey's big-league career. When a sore arm caused Wyatt to miss a turn, Durocher called on Casey to fill the slot on June 4. Again it was in the second game of a doubleheader. Although they had 14 hits against him, Casey shut down the Pirates, allowing only one run. Every Pirate in the starting lineup except second baseman Bill Brubaker had at least one hit. On their way to a 14–1 victory, the Dodgers already had an 8–0 lead when Pittsburgh scored. At the plate, Casey had two hits, both doubles against Ken Heintzelman, and scored a run.

Casey's performance against the Pirates had many Brooklyn fans calling him the new Christy Mathewson because of the many times Matty allowed a team numerous hits but few runs. (In 1939, New York's greatest pitcher, the late Christy Mathewson, was someone many local fans had seen pitch.)[14]

Holmes, who covered the game for the *Eagle*, reported that he had seen more than 3,000 games in his career as a sportswriter, but this was the first time he had seen a pitcher allow 14 hits and only one run, and the first time he had seen every member of a team (the Dodgers) get at least one hit and score at least one run.[15] Holmes added that based on Casey's two consecutive complete-game wins, the "burly young Irishman from Georgia" was not a cinch to return to the bullpen when Wyatt returned to action.

3

BROOKLYN'S BEST PITCHER

Casey initially had been a long shot to make the Brooklyn club in the spring of 1939. In addition to his reporting to camp 20 pounds overweight, rookie pitchers Red Evans and Bill Crouch were more highly regarded. So too was Boots Poffenberger, whom the Dodgers had purchased from Detroit just before the season started. But Casey had made the team, and after the two doubleheader starts, he slowly worked his way into the starting rotation. By the time the Dodgers began their second swing through the West, on June 14, at St. Louis, he had become a key member of their pitching staff.

"Hugh has a smooth delivery," said Dodgers coach Charlie Dressen, who managed against Casey in the Southern Association and recommended the Dodgers draft him. "It isn't deceptive or jerky, the kind that would make him tough the first time out and a lot easier after the batters had seen him. His effectiveness is due to his stuff and his use of it."

Dressen predicted that Casey would be even tougher for batters in the second half of the season, "because he will be in better shape and because he is the kind of pitcher who is always learning and improving." Even at age 25, weight was a problem for Casey and always would be. "Casey was 20 pounds over his best weight in the spring," Dressen continued. "He got 14 of it off. Six more and he'll be right." Dressen also praised his pitcher's willingness to follow instructions and pitch to batters the way Durocher and his catchers advised him.[1]

Casey made his third start of the season on June 11, in the opener of a doubleheader against league-leading Cincinnati. It resulted in a hard-luck loss to Bucky Walters, the Reds' right-hander, who was developing into the league's best pitcher and would be voted the National League's Most Valuable Player. Through nine innings, each pitcher had allowed just one run, but 10th-inning doubles by Bill Werber, Ival Goodman, and Frank McCormick gave the Reds a 3–1 win. A bit fewer than 36,000 attended the twin bill, raising the total attendance for the three starts Casey had made to almost 120,000.

Casey was proving to be a successful starter, although Durocher continued to use him in relief when needed. Against St. Louis, on June 16, Casey relieved Luke Hamlin with no outs in the fourth inning. He held the Cardinals scoreless the rest of the way, allowing only three hits. But two of them were singles by the first two batters of the fifth inning: Stu Martin and Jimmy Brown. Casey then retired the heart of the Cardinals' order—Terry Moore, Joe Medwick, and Johnny Mize—without the runners advancing. Brooklyn blasted Bill McGee for four runs and added another against Mort Cooper to win, 8–3. At this point in the season, Casey had allowed only eight earned runs in 43-and-a-third innings, leading *New York Times* sportswriter Roscoe McGowen to call him the "best pitcher on Durocher's staff, barring the injured Whit Wyatt."[2]

Strong efforts on July 1 and July 9 resulted in losses to Harry Gumbert, who was rapidly replacing Carl Hubbell as the ace of the Giants staff. Those starts surrounded a decision won in long relief from the Phillies on Independence Day.

On the morning of July 8, with the Dodgers in third place, the *Brooklyn Eagle* printed brief biographies of the local heroes. Calling Casey a "sort of twentieth-century Huckleberry Finn," they related the story of how "this burly, round-faced, easygoing boy from Atlanta" was the "last pitcher discovered by old Wilbert Robinson." Making use of a good curveball and a fastball that acts as a sinker, Casey had ridden his Memorial Day win over the Giants to a place in Leo Durocher's starting rotation. The *Eagle* described his pitching as "marked by the cool poise and confident resourcefulness of your typical outdoorsman."[3]

"He had control and he had a natural sinker, and that was about it," said Durocher. "His fastball was used only to brush the hitter back, and he had a slider (called a nickel curve in those days), which he used only to show the batter that he could throw something else."[4]

By July 24, although Casey was pitching well, his team was struggling. While Casey's won–lost record was an unexceptional 5–5, he had an impressive 2.65 earned run average; the Dodgers, at 40–41, had slipped to fifth place, 12 games behind Cincinnati. Wyatt was out with a leg injury, and Van Lingle Mungo had broken his ankle the previous day while sliding into second base as a pinch-runner. Expected to miss six weeks, Mungo would not return that season.

There was general gloom surrounding the Dodgers, but a little-noted deal would make this day one of the most memorable for the team. MacPhail claimed 28-year-old outfielder Dixie Walker from the Detroit Tigers. Once regarded as the man who would be Babe Ruth's replacement with the Yankees, injuries had marred Walker's American League career in New York, Chicago, and Detroit. When healthy, he was a consistent .300 hitter, but he clearly was not healthy when he reported to Brooklyn.

"He could barely walk; he looked like a cripple," remembered one Dodgers executive after Walker reported. "We needed a ballplayer who could give us a lift, and we got one who looked as if he needed a blood transfusion."[5]

Walker reported to the Dodgers in Chicago, where they were beginning a 15-game visit to the league's western cities. He entered the clubhouse limping slightly but told his new teammates, "I've never been on a second-division club in my life, fellas. Don't spoil my record now."[6] He made his Brooklyn debut the next day, as a pinch-hitter in the first game of a doubleheader. The game served as an immediate introduction to the aggressive and argumentative style that would forever be associated with Leo Durocher's managerial tenure in Brooklyn.

The Cubs had overcome Brooklyn's 5–0 lead with a six-run rally in the sixth inning. The big blow was Rip Russell's home run to left field, a drive the Dodgers did not believe had cleared the fence. When the umpires refused Durocher's 10-minute appeal to get them to reverse their decision, the Brooklyn manager announced he was playing the game under protest. The protest proved unnecessary, as the Dodgers rallied with three in the ninth to win the game, 8–6. Casey made it a sweep for the Dodgers with a six-hit, 3–1 win in the second game.

Another tempest developed less than a week later, on July 30, when the Dodgers lost a doubleheader at St. Louis, both games by a 5–2 score. Durocher and his players felt they had gotten the short end of the calls from the umpiring crew of Larry Goetz, Bick Campbell, and Dolly Stark.

Goetz had been a National League umpire since 1936, and would continue in the job until 1957. By the time he retired, he had established a reputation as one of the game's finest arbiters. Yet, he had been having problems with Brooklyn since entering the league. "[T]he Dodgers haven't had a peaceful afternoon with umpire Larry Goetz calling them since Goetz has been in the league," wrote columnist Tommy Holmes.[7]

The problem in the first game came when Goetz called Brooklyn's Johnny Hudson out on an attempted steal of home. To the Dodgers, it appeared Cardinals catcher Don Padgett had missed the tag by two feet. Durocher roared out of the dugout to argue the call but, as usual, to no avail.

Feelings of bitterness had been festering between the Dodgers and Cardinals all season, and these two games only increased the hard feelings. In the third inning of the nightcap, St. Louis pitcher Bob Bowman spiked Cookie Lavagetto while sliding into third base. Later in the inning, Pepper Martin, also on a slide into third, kicked Lavagetto in the wrist, knocking the ball loose.

Later in the game, Johnny Mize crashed into Lavagetto. The third-inning antics led to three unearned runs against starter Casey, who went the distance in the loss. Casey showed his disapproval of St. Louis's overly aggressive baserunning by throwing close to several Cardinals batters, including Bowman and Mize. Bowman retaliated by throwing at Dodgers hitters and exacerbated the situation by inviting Casey to meet him under the stands.

With an offday before opening a series in Pittsburgh, the Dodgers were still steaming about the umpires and the Cardinals aggressive behavior the day before. But they had lots of good things to say about Casey's reaction to the near-maiming of Lavagetto by Bowman, Martin, and Mize. The young Georgian, "without saying a word or changing expression on his placid round face," used some tight pitches to let the Cardinals know his team would not be intimidated. "Players like a pitcher who'll help fight a battle, and Casey proved himself the fightingest pitcher the Dodgers have had since Burleigh Grimes," said Holmes. "I've never seen a more artistic job of putting the fear of God in the enemy."[8]

July had been a busy month for Casey, as Durocher continued to use him as a starter and a reliever. He appeared in 10 games, starting six and completing four. His record for the month was 3–4, along with one save.[9] As a result, he was growing popular among the Brooklyn fans and gaining a reputation throughout the league as a first-rate pitcher.

Casey lost his first two starts in August and was at 6–8 before defeating the Giants and Harry Gumbert, 5–1, on August 17. Mel Ott's home run was the only run by the Giants. He evened his record at 8–8 in his next start, an 8–5 win over the Cardinals. It was a gritty performance, reminiscent of the one against Pittsburgh in June. Before being relieved by Vito Tamulis with one out in the ninth inning, the Cardinals had touched Hugh for 15 hits.

The Dodgers had won five straight going into an August 26 doubleheader against the Reds at Ebbets Field. Bucky Walters ended the streak with a 5–2, two-hit victory—his 21st win of the season. Luke Hamlin was the loser, but Hamlin gained lasting fame by throwing the first televised pitch in a major-league game. (On May 17, 1939, the National Broadcasting Company had televised a college game between Princeton and Columbia universities from Columbia's Baker Field.) Cincinnati's leadoff batter was Billy Werber, who grounded out to second baseman Pete Coscarart.

NBC transmitted the telecast via experimental station W2XBS, with Red Barber at the microphone. Between games, Barber conducted on-field interviews with Walters, Whit Wyatt, Dixie Walker, Dolph Camilli, and managers Durocher and Bill McKechnie. Following the interview, Casey earned the Dodgers a split by breezing to a 6–1 win in the nightcap.

The game was broadcast to the Dodgers club offices and press room; the Broadway Theater at 53rd Street and Broadway in Manhattan; and the television building at the New York World's Fair in Flushing Meadows Park, Queens. Sparked by the magnificent fair, being held just a few miles from Ebbets Field, new technologies were rapidly being introduced to the American people. Many of these innovations would be put on hold because of the world war that began in Europe less than a week after this doubleheader. Television in the home was one of those innovations that would have to wait until the war ended.

The reaction to televised baseball from those who saw it was mostly positive. *Sporting News* reported the response was "instantaneous and amazing."[10] But, as always, there were naysayers. "It's difficult to see how this sort of thing can catch the public fancy," said an anonymous critic in the *New York Times*.[11]

Complete-game wins over Boston on September 5 and New York on September 9, Casey's third straight against the Giants, gave him a six-game winning streak and raised his record to 12–8. The streak ended when Cincinnati's Gene Thompson shut out the Dodgers, 3–0, on September 13. A sweep of the Cubs at Wrigley Field on September 17 moved the Dodgers to within a game of third-place Chicago. Casey won the opener, and Hamlin won the nightcap. Chicago had been the only team Hamlin had not defeated that year. The win was Casey's 13th of the season and one of the sweetest, a bit of revenge for his unhappy season with the Cubs in 1935.

Casey finished his first season in Brooklyn with a complete-game win at Boston and a win at home against Philadelphia on the final day of the campaign. Starting on one day's rest, he pitched seven innings before yielding to Carl Doyle. He had won nine of his final 11 decisions to finish with a 15–10 record. The victory, along with the Cubs' previous day's loss to the Cardinals, allowed the Dodgers to finish in third place, a jump of four positions in the standings from 1938, and their highest finish since 1932. Attendance, which had been 482,500 in 1937, rose to 663,100 in 1938, MacPhail's first year, and soared to 955,500 in 1939.

After Casey's win against the Phillies, fans presented him with a shotgun and a traveling bag as a show of appreciation for his fine season. He was one of the few pitchers in the league to defeat each of the seven other National League clubs and one of nine Dodgers pitchers who made no errors during the season.

For their third-place finish, Brooklyn players received $787.67 as their share of the World Series pot.[12] In addition, Casey was one of 12 members of the Dodgers who received bonuses of an undisclosed amount. Club secretary John McDonald made the announcement on November 9, saying the bonuses were awarded for the players' part in helping the team finish in third place.[13]

Although he was happy to have won 15 games, Casey predicted he would win 20 in 1940. Moreover, he made a case for not having done so in 1939:

> Now that I'm set on this club, I think I should win 20 games for Durocher next season. . . . You see, this year it was a long time before I got my chance. The club was going well early in the season, and Wyatt and Hamlin were pitching well, and Evans was getting a lot of starts. I lost a lot of time there that I figure I won't lose next season. I figure now that I'll be a starting pitcher from the opening bell. [14]

Evans lost eight of his nine decisions for Brooklyn. In early September, the Dodgers sold him to the Boston Red Sox as part of the deal that brought Pee Wee Reese to Brooklyn. Evans never again pitched in the major leagues.

Casey's 15 wins were second on the club to Hamlin, although many in the league considered Casey Brooklyn's best pitcher. Hugh was inclined to agree with them. At spring training in 1940, he reminded the press that he did not start a game in 1939 until Memorial Day, six weeks into the season.

"[I]f I'd been given my regular turn, it's fair to suppose I'd have won five more games and hit the 20 mark, isn't it?" He went on to say he thought he had pitched in hard luck even after he won a starting job. "When I was at six won and six lost, Durocher came to me and said, 'Don't get discouraged, kid; with a few breaks you'd stand at 10 and two right now.'" [15]

Casey had won over Durocher by the way he beat the Giants and Carl Hubbell in front of 60,000 people at the Polo Grounds in his first start. Leo had no qualms about using him against the toughest teams. Ten of Casey's 15 wins in 1939 were against Cincinnati, St. Louis, Chicago, and New York. It was not until his final start of the season that he got to face the cellar-dwelling Phillies. He had been Brooklyn's best pitcher in the second half of the season, generating high hopes that he would be a standout in Brooklyn for years to come.

After the season, *Sporting News* published their major-league rookie All-Star team, a group led by Ted Williams of the Red Sox and Charlie Keller of the Yankees. They listed three pitchers: Gene Thompson of Cincinnati (13–5), Atley Donald of the Yankees (13–3), and Mort Cooper of the Cardinals (12–6). And for those Dodgers fans who wondered why Casey had been omitted, the reason was simple: Because he had been on the roster all season with the Cubs in 1935, *Sporting News* no longer considered him a rookie.

Despite his success, MacPhail continued to be worried about Casey's weight. He had reported in the spring at 205 and was 215 when the season ended. MacPhail believed that had he been lighter, he would have done even better. Columnist Dick Farrington of *Sporting News* revealed MacPhail's purported plan of monetary incentives to keep Hugh in shape: "He'll be given a nominal contract prior to February 15, and if he reports at camp weighing 205 pounds, the pay will be $7,000; if he weighs 200, $8,000; 195, $9,000, and 190, $11,500."[16]

Meanwhile, Casey spent many mornings during the offseason traveling to Manhattan to work out at Artie McGovern's gym at Madison Avenue and 42nd Street. At the end of November, he had his weight down to 207. "I could get down further," he claimed, "but Artie says it would be bad for me. He says I should go into spring training with a little beef to spare, and that if I went down to 190, as I promised MacPhail, I'd be weak as a cat. . . . Artie said he'd go over and see MacPhail, and kill all those ideas of getting down to 190."[17]

At a time when most players had jobs or ran small businesses in the offseason, Casey was no exception, selling Chryslers for Brooklyn auto dealer Henry Caplan. He was also a member and the star of the company's bowling team. In a match against a rival auto dealer, Nadler Motors, Casey anchored Caplan's four-man team with a 630 series—208, 206, and 216—in leading his team to a 16-pin victory. Casey again led Caplan Motors to victory over Nadler in a rematch on January 9, 1940. Although he had the highest one-game score, 188, it was a bit below his November performance.[18]

He told Harold Parrott he already had sold five cars and would have sold more had it not been for the recently ended Chrysler strike. "I'm really getting someplace with this salesmanship," he said. "I go every place with the boss, listening to him appraise used cars, and now I know myself what a jalopy is worth. And I know what goes on under the hood of a new car, too."[19] "I can judge the value of used cars and know all the selling points of the latest models. No more hunting for me in the offseason—unless it's hunting sales prospects!"[20]

4

A LEGITIMATE PENNANT CONTENDER

Hugh and Kathleen were now living in Brooklyn, where Hugh had made himself a visible part of the community. Along with selling cars for Caplan Motors and being the star bowler for the company team, he was taking part in local civic events. On January 9, 1940, he and star quarterback Sid Luckman of the Chicago Bears were among the sports celebrities who helped the Williamsburg Young Men's Hebrew Association celebrate its 30th anniversary. A few days later, Casey was at Brooklyn's Broadway Arena to watch a series of elimination bouts in New York's Golden Gloves boxing tournament. And the day after that he was at Brooklyn's Paramount Theater, where he threw up the first ball in an amateur basketball game. Still, he found time in January to put aside his workouts, auto sales, and involvement in community affairs for a two-week fishing trip to Georgia.

Buoyed by Brooklyn's surprising third-place finish, Leo Durocher was already looking ahead to better things in 1940. The Dodgers had been unable to make any significant trades at the 1939 Winter Meetings, but neither had any of the other National League clubs. Manager Durocher figured that was a plus for the Dodgers. "I'll tell you why," he said. "We have the youngest ball team in the league. It's bound to improve more than any other contending club, as time passes. The others, with the exception of the Cardinals, need replacements, while, just as we are, I think we'll be better than we were last year."[1]

Encouraging news came for Durocher and the Dodgers shortly after New Year's. Whit Wyatt reported that offseason surgery at Johns Hopkins Hospital in Baltimore had cured the left knee problem that had bothered him in 1939. Wyatt said he was anxious to get to spring training and positive about the Dodgers' chances in the pennant race, "if the outfield can get going like our infield." He called Casey, his fellow Georgian, and the Phillies' Kirby Higbe two of the game's most promising pitchers, ranking them ahead of the Reds' Gene Thompson. "Casey has lots of stuff and is always red hot to beat the Giants—and does it. He should be better this season," Wyatt related.[2]

Casey's record against the Giants in 1939 was 4–2, and as many a Dodgers player before and after discovered, there was no better way to become popular in Brooklyn than to do well against the Giants.

On February 13, Casey signed his 1940 contract, which called for a base salary of $7,500, an increase of $4,000 from the previous year. But Dodgers management continued to worry about his tendency to gain weight. MacPhail had written into his 1940 contract a list of items he was not to consume during the season. Some of the writers covering the team at spring training doubted he could comply with those prohibitions. One wrote that Casey was a "switch-eater, and works from either side of the dinner plate."[3]

Another doubter was Durocher. "Leo bet me $100 I couldn't make my diet fit the contract," said a smiling Casey. "Why, that's just more money in my pocket. . . . And despite the stories you read, my weight hasn't even been mentioned. No, I won't lose money if I go over 200; but how can I possibly be going over 200 on MacPhail's menu anyway?" Beginning his second year in Brooklyn, he thought he would soon reach a salary of $10,000, "if I have a good year, as I know I can. I think I could have grabbed off a fatter contract if I'd been tough," he said about his negotiations with MacPhail.[4]

Harold Parrott wrote in the *Eagle* that the "Dodgers chubby pitcher" stated he would get a bonus if he maintained a weight of less than 200 pounds. "I did write it into the contract," Casey said, "more or less as my own idea to prove that I'm going to hustle the limit this year, that I would not touch a glass of beer until October 1."[5]

On the first day of workouts, in Clearwater, Durocher was unconvinced that Casey's current weight was 192 and challenged him to get on the scale. Hugh refused at first but finally got on. The dial kept climbing until it stopped at 207. Only catcher Babe Phelps, at 215, weighed more. Durocher, who had bet Casey he would not come to camp weighing less than 200 pounds, collected his money from Hugh.

Artie McGovern was in Clearwater working with the Dodgers to get them in shape for the coming season. (McGovern and his assistant, Eddie McCormack, were giving special attention to both Casey and Phelps.) In mid-March, the *Brooklyn Eagle* published a letter McGovern had written detailing each player's progress. He wrote, "Hugh Casey is 100 percent better physically this year than he was last season. He had a couple of months work in New York with me before we went to Florida, and he is now within a few pounds of his best pitching weight. He has shed 17 pounds since he started training." McGovern also issued positive reports on Whit Wyatt and Luke Hamlin, and predicted the trio of Casey, Wyatt, and Hamlin would combine for 60 victories in 1940.[6]

Clearly, much was expected from Casey this year. A stronger Whit Wyatt, his injured knee healed, seemed headed for a big year. Yet, the talk at Clearwater was about the "round-faced" Casey being the team's ace. "Huge Hugh Is Likely to Hit 20-Game Mark" was the subheading of an early March story in the *Eagle*.

"Casey is physically sound," wrote Tommy Holmes, "has really good stuff—a sinking fastball and a low-breaking curve, plus the nerve of a second-story worker." But seemingly no Casey story was complete without a reference to his bulk. Holmes ended his piece by calling Hugh "a young fellow with an astounding appetite and a tendency to take on weight."[7]

"He keeps his curveball low and his fastball is a sinker," noted the *Eagle*. "Phlegmatic by nature, his work is marked by poise and resourcefulness."[8] Although Casey was barely more than a rookie, Durocher believed the 26-year-old right-hander understood the art of pitching and had great confidence in him. "He's the one man on my staff who has full permission to go out there and pitch his own game," Durocher said at training camp. "He has a head on him—and he has heart. You won't see him flinch in a jam."[9]

Back in camp that spring was 21-year-old Pete Reiser, whose spectacular hitting in 1939 had been the sensation of the Grapefruit League. In 11 trips to the plate in three games, he collected three walks, four singles, and four home runs.

Reiser originally had been signed out of high school by Branch Rickey's Cardinals in 1937. But Commissioner Kenesaw Landis found that the Cardinals were in violation of the rules by controlling more than one team in a minor league. Accordingly, in March 1938, Landis released 74 players—including Reiser—from their Cardinals contracts.

Rickey suspected Reiser was a special talent and engaged in a little chicanery in an attempt to keep him with St. Louis. He worked out an agreement with Larry MacPhail, his former associate, in which the Dodgers would sign Reiser, keep him in the minors for a few years, and then trade him back to the Cardinals.

But Reiser's play at Clearwater in 1939 so impressed Durocher that he told the New York press Pete would be in his Opening Day lineup. When Rickey read that he called MacPhail and accused him of breaking his word. MacPhail telegrammed Durocher with orders to stop playing Reiser and send him to the minor leagues.

Reiser played the 1939 season with the Class A Elmira (New York) Pioneers of the Eastern League. His season was cut short when he was forced to undergo an operation to remove bone chips from his right elbow. He played in just 38 games, batting .301.

The talk of this year's camp was another 21-year-old, shortstop Harold "Pee Wee" Reese. Reese and Reiser quickly became best friends, and before long the newspapers began calling the two budding stars the "Gold Dust Twins." It was truly the beginning of better days for baseball in Brooklyn.

The Dodgers had acquired Reese in July 1939, from the Boston Red Sox Louisville farm team, for $35,000 and players to be named.[10] Louisville had tried to sign Reese in 1938, but he turned them down because at that time Louisville had a working agreement with Brooklyn and Reese was not enamored of the "daffy" image associated with the Dodgers.

"That's the last place in the world I'd want to go," he said. "All you ever read about is guys getting hit in the head with fly balls . . . I don't want to go there."[11]

He had been one of several players the Red Sox kept when they purchased the Louisville club and was expected to one day replace player-manager Joe Cronin as Boston's shortstop. Upon learning of the trade, Reese said he had changed his mind about going to Brooklyn. "Brooklyn's in the major league [sic], isn't it?" he asked.[12]

As stipulated in the sale, Reese finished the season with Louisville. He batted .279 and stole a remarkable 35 bases in 36 attempts. Reese's manager at Louisville, Donie Bush, called him the "best-fielding shortstop I've seen in my 31 years in the game."[13]

Reese would spend his entire 16-year Hall of Fame career with the Dodgers. Later promoted to team captain, he would become one of the most beloved men to play in Brooklyn. Like Dixie Walker, his fellow Southerner and soon-to-be lifelong friend, Reese confessed that his acquisition by the Dodgers was the biggest break of his professional career.

The youngster made an immediate impression in his first appearance on the field in a Dodgers uniform. The manner in which he handled two ground balls and rifled the throws to first base did much to convince Durocher, like Cronin, a shortstop-manager, that he would mostly be a bench manager that year.

"I don't need to see anymore," he told Dodgers scout Ted McGrew. "That kid can play shortstop for anybody's ball club for my money." McGrew, who had seen much of Reese at Louisville in 1939, said, "If you think you're seeing something now, wait until he gets in shape and you see him in a game on the bases."[14]

The next day, the big news at Dodgers camp was 20-game winner Luke Hamlin ending his holdout. That left Dolph Camilli, Dixie Walker, Cookie Lavagetto, and Pete Coscarart unsigned. But Durocher still had Reese on his mind.

Leo now seemed reluctant to surrender his shortstop position to the rookie. He said he planned to start the season at shortstop and would work Reese in slowly. "If he plays 50 games this year I'll be satisfied," Durocher said. "I expect to play a hundred. Still, McGrew tells me that Pee Wee will take my job, so maybe he'll play more games than I."[15] Durocher also had MacPhail to deal with. In 1939, MacPhail would complain loudly whenever Leo missed a game.

Casey had a so-so spring, including an afternoon at Clearwater when he gave up three home runs over the short right-field fence to left-handed slugger Johnny Mize. Still, when the Dodgers broke camp and traveled through the South on their way home, Casey proved to be one of the team's most popular players. He was not only a native of Georgia, but also was familiar to Southern fans from his years in the Piedmont League and the Southern Association.

Sportswriter Grantland Rice wrote an article that appeared just be-fore Opening Day, in which he predicted who would be the stars of 1940. "Casey ranks as one of the best of the younger pitchers in either league," he wrote, while also predicting Reese would be among the major league's best rookies. "Reese makes me think of Durocher when Durocher was a kid," Rice added. [16]

Leo expected a healthy Wyatt to join Casey and Hamlin in giving him three first-rate right-handed starters. Based on Wyatt's strong per-formance in the spring, Durocher chose him to pitch the opener at Boston.

In the days of the 154-game schedule, the season started in mid-April, as opposed to the modern-day start at the beginning of April; however, the extra two weeks was no guarantee the weather would not be wintry on Opening Day, which it was in 1940. A crowd of only 3,517 turned out to see Wyatt shut out the Bees, 5–0. In 1936, the National League team in Boston had changed its name from Braves to Bees. In 1941, they changed it back to Braves.

The second game of the series was rained out, followed by a travel day, on which the Dodgers left Boston for New York. While still on the train, Durocher named Casey to pitch Brooklyn's second game, the home opener against the Giants. Casey was sitting nearby, puffing on a cigar, and the "round-faced young Irishman from Georgia" took the announcement in stride. Pitching the home opener, especially when the Giants were furnishing the opposition, was something that would stir the blood of even a seasoned veteran—but Casey seemed unemotional. Touted throughout the spring as a potential 20-game winner, he thought he would do just fine during the season.

"I've never been in better shape," he said. "I haven't had a glass of beer for so long I've forgotten what it tastes like. I'm down to about 192 pounds. . . . That hasn't affected my strength. Right now I feel strong enough to pitch all day." [17]

Casey had an equally, if not more, important reason why he ex-pected to do even better during the campaign—his increased knowl-edge of the hitters. He explained that he was often instructed on the way to pitch to certain hitters. Yet, he typically found that the sugges-tions did not work for him. When he switched to throwing those hitters different pitches, ones of his own choosing, he had greater success. "I had my system pretty well organized by the time the [last] season ended. If you remember, I won nine of my last 11," he reminded every-one.[18]

The weather remained damp and dreary for the home opener; nevertheless, 24,741 onlookers were at Ebbets Field to see Casey shut out the Giants, 12–0. Brooklyn's lead was only 3–0 when Giants starter Hal Schumacher left after six innings. But the Dodgers pounded Cliff Melton for three runs in the seventh and six more in the eighth. Casey contributed to his cause by laying down three perfectly executed sacrifice bunts.

Four days later, Brooklyn's winning streak reached three when new-comer Tex Carleton beat Boston, 8–3, at Ebbets Field. Reese made his big-league debut in the game, starting at shortstop after Durocher benched himself with a sore arm. In Casey's second start, he became the team's first two-game winner, defeating Philadelphia, 3–1, on April 25. Freddie Fitzsimmons won the next day, 6–0, and for the first time in their 50-year history, the Dodgers had won their first six games.

Two wins at the Polo Grounds extended the streak to eight. The wins had come against Boston, Philadelphia, and New York, all weak teams; nonetheless, Brooklyn fans were convinced they had a legitimate pennant contender. The next day the team headed west, where they knew they would find their strongest opposition—in Cincinnati and St. Louis.

Carleton, a 33-year-old right-hander MacPhail had purchased from Milwaukee of the American Association in January, got the road trip off to a spectacular start. He not only extended the winning streak to nine games, tying the major-league record, but also he did it with a 3–0 no-hitter.[19] It was the second no-hitter of the season after none had been thrown in 1939. (Bob Feller of Cleveland had thrown one against the Chicago White Sox on Opening Day.)

No Dodgers pitcher had thrown a no-hit shutout since Nap Rucker against Boston on September 5, 1908. Dazzy Vance had thrown a no-hitter against Philadelphia on September 13, 1925, but the Phillies had scored an unearned run.

Dixie Walker, picked up in mid-1939, had gained immediate popularity in Brooklyn with his timely hitting and excellent defense. Playing center field, he caught Ival Goodman's sinking liner for the game's final out. It was as tough a play as he had ever made, Walker said. "Not that the chance was so hard," he explained, "but so much was at stake. I had goose pimples."[20]

Casey was scheduled to pitch the next day, when Brooklyn attempted to set a new record—10 straight wins from the start of the season. "I don't hope to do that well, Tex, but don't think they won't have a fit," he said to Carleton. But the Reds did not "have a fit" the next day. Bucky Walters won his third of the season, as the Reds thrashed the Dodgers, 9–2, to end the streak. For Walters, a 27-game winner and the National League's Most Valuable Player in 1939, it was his eighth consecutive win against Brooklyn.

By retiring the first nine batters, Casey had extended the Reds' hitless streak to 12 innings, but Cincinnati pounded him for eight runs in the fourth. He allowed six hits in the inning, including a grand slam by Ernie Lombardi and a double and home run by Bill Werber. He also hit a batter. Yet, Durocher kept Casey on the mound for the entire inning.

Following a rainout in Cincinnati and two rainouts in Pittsburgh, Brooklyn won two games in St. Louis, with Casey picking up a save in the first game. Two days later, on May 7, he absorbed an even worse loss than he had against the Reds, losing to the Cardinals, 18–2. St. Louis had 20 hits, including seven home runs—Johnny Mize and Eddie Lake each had two—a pair of triples, and four doubles against Casey and Max Macon. The Cardinals established the modern National League record for total bases, with 49, and the seven home runs tied the league record. In Casey's seven innings, he allowed 13 earned runs, 15 hits, and 5 home runs. The Dodgers were now 11–2, and Casey had both losses.

As with the game in Cincinnati, some wondered why Durocher was allowing Casey to stay out there and absorb so much punishment. But, said Casey, it was at his own request. "Let me keep pitching," he asked Durocher, after giving up five runs in the third inning. "I need the work."[21] Durocher confirmed that he allowed Casey to stay in the game at the pitcher's request. "He hadn't had much work, and as long as the game was gone, I let him continue."[22] (Casey had pitched only four innings in 10 days.)

In his brief time in the league, Casey had established two principles: He hated to lose, and he had no problem throwing at hitters. Both traits came into play in this game, as he forced several Cardinals batters to hit the dirt to avoid his pitches. Three—Johnny Mize, Don Padgett, and Enos Slaughter—did not get out of the way in time and were hit. Earlier that afternoon, Mize and Padgett had homered off Casey, and Slaughter had tripled.

5

BEANBALLS, SPIKINGS, AND RHUBARBS

The final stop on this first western swing was Chicago. To get there, the Dodgers made the first mass flight in baseball history. The team boarded the plane at St. Louis's Lambert Field at about 6:00 p.m. and arrived at Chicago's Municipal Airport after 9:00 p.m. After the Chicago series, they would fly home to Brooklyn. Whether this would become their regular mode of travel in the west was uncertain.

"We'll fly from Chicago to Brooklyn for our Friday game with the Giants, and then we'll see," said Durocher. "MacPhail wants the club to fly. I'm willing, and, I imagine, most of the players will be after these two flights. But I want all of them to be satisfied, and flying won't be a good idea if it's going to lead to dissension."[1]

Half the team members had never flown before, but most enjoyed the flight. Babe Phelps had been the most hesitant, but he too made the trip, reluctantly, to say the least. "I smoked a pack of cigarettes in the cab from the hotel to the airport, and if I'd had a pint I'd have broken training," Phelps said. "I still think the Wright brothers were crazy."[2]

To no one's surprise, Phelps was on a train when the Dodgers flew home from Chicago. Using two planes, they landed at Floyd Bennett Field in Brooklyn at 12:40 a.m. on May 10. With a 12–2 record, the team was in first place, and 10,000 appreciative fans were there to greet them, including borough president John Cashmore. With pennant fever mounting in Brooklyn, Cashmore said he looked forward to throwing out the first ball at the World Series.

Chicago began its first series at Ebbets Field on May 19, and the first two games featured hard, borderline illegal slides. In the first game, the Cubs' Dominic Dallessandro spiked Brooklyn second baseman Pete Coscarart so severely he was expected to miss a week. Durocher "got even" when his slide into Augie Galan, an outfielder playing second base, spiked Galan in three spots. Galan had made a hard slide of his own in the first inning, bruising his left little toe. Combined with the spiking by Durocher, it was enough to keep him out for the rest of the series.

The overly aggressive baserunning continued in the second game. Al Todd, the Cubs' burly catcher, dumped Dodgers shortstop Pee Wee Reese on a slide into second, preventing a potential double play. Brooklyn's revenge came when Ernie Koy spiked Cubs shortstop Billy Rogell on a play where Koy was thrown out trying to stretch a single into a double. Earlier in the inning, Dodgers outfielder Roy Cullenbine had also spiked Rogell.

The Cubs won the more important battle by taking both games. Casey's loss in the second game was his third straight defeat and the fourth consecutive time he had failed to pitch a complete game.

"It puzzles me," said Durocher. "I gave him plenty of work, and he wasn't effective. Then I rested him for a week, and he didn't win. I don't know what to do with him now."[3] The next day, Durocher decided to temporarily remove Casey from the rotation and use him strictly in relief.

Preseason prognosticators had expected an improved Brooklyn team, and the Dodgers were living up to those expectations. On the first day of June, they had a 21–10 record and were in second place, two games behind the defending National League champion Cincinnati Reds.

What was surprising was how well the team had done without the help of their big three. Whit Wyatt (4–3), Luke Hamlin (2–3), and Casey (2–3) had a combined record of eight wins and nine losses. Meanwhile, some of their other pitchers, of whom little was expected, were a combined 13–1, led by Freddie Fitzsimmons (4–0), Tex Carleton (2–0), and Vito Tamulis (2–0).

The Dodgers had been in first place until Memorial Day, when a sellout crowd at Ebbets Field watched in disappointment, as the Giants swept them in a doubleheader. Cincinnati's sweep at Chicago that afternoon propelled them ahead of the Dodgers into first place.

Durocher gave Casey his first start in two weeks on June 3, in Chicago, and Hugh responded with a five-hit, 3–2 victory. Four days later, in Cincinnati, Casey was back in the bullpen. He relieved Tot Pressnell in the sixth inning and shut out the Reds on two hits in the final five-and-a-third innings, as Brooklyn notched an 11-inning, 4–2 win. Bucky Walters, who went all the way, was the loser, his first loss after opening the season with nine consecutive wins.

Casey threw a perfect fifth inning at Pittsburgh on June 10, but he left the game with a sore shoulder. His trouble had started in the 11th inning of the game against the Reds.

"There seems to be a lump just back of the shoulder," he said. "I can raise my arm without trouble, and I can throw easily. But when I start to bear down and really throw hard it just stops me, that's all." Casey added that when he began pitching in the 11th inning, his arm would not get loose. "It hurt every time I threw, and the harder I threw the more it hurt," he elaborated.[4] Why he did not remove himself from the game or why Durocher did not notice his discomfort on the mound and remove him went unquestioned by the press.

The Dodgers sent Casey to Johns Hopkins to have the arm examined by Dr. George Bennett, who specialized in such injuries. He became the sixth Dodger to visit Dr. Bennett within the last year. He joined Durocher; pitchers Wyatt, Van Mungo, and Max Macon; and catcher Herman Franks. Casey returned to the team two days later, reporting that Dr. Bennett had found nothing wrong with his arm but did suggest a week of rest.

The team returned from its western jaunt in first place, percentage points ahead of Cincinnati. Durocher had been rotating his outfielders throughout the season but remained unsatisfied with their meager power production. Larry MacPhail felt the same and was trying to put together a trade for Max West, the Boston Bees' slugging outfielder.

That deal fell through, but on June 12, MacPhail acquired outfielder Joe Medwick from the Cardinals. The 28-year-old Medwick had led the National League three times in runs batted in, total bases, and doubles, and had never hit below .300. He was the league's Most Valuable Player in 1937, the year he won the Triple Crown.[5]

Medwick had tailed off ever so slightly the past few seasons, but he remained among the game's top sluggers. He was, however, the Cardinals' highest-paid player, a red flag for the parsimonious Branch Rickey. In addition, Rickey was earning a reputation for getting rid of stars a year too early rather than a year too late.

Moreover, Medwick had experienced run-ins with several of his Cardinals teammates, most notably Terry Moore, and they were happy to see him leave. Nevertheless, he did not come cheap. Along with outfielder Ernie Koy, minor-league infielder-outfielder Bert Haas, and little-used pitchers Carl Doyle and Sam Nahem, MacPhail sent $125,000 to the Cardinals. Rickey also threw in pitcher Curt Davis, a 36-year-old right-hander. Davis had won 22 games in 1939, his best season, but he was 0–4 so far in 1940, and had been bothered by a sore arm.

"We've got a chance to win now," said Durocher, Medwick's former roommate with St. Louis and probably his closest friend. "I know Medwick," said Leo. "I ought to. I roomed with him for six years. For us he'll hustle three times as much and be twice as good a hitter as he was in St. Louis."[6]

Medwick and Davis were with the Cardinals in Buffalo when they heard the news. They packed their bags and took a plane to New York, arriving several hours before they were expected by the Dodgers, who assumed they would be coming by train.

The trade for Joe Medwick convinced Dodgers fans that team president MacPhail was going all out to bring a championship to Brooklyn. And they responded accordingly. Police had to be called out and streets blocked off to control the crowds at the Dodgers ticket office at 215 Montague Street in downtown Brooklyn. There was a run on tickets for the upcoming two series, one against Cincinnati and one against St. Louis.

After splitting four games with the Reds, which allowed them to stay in first place, percentage points ahead of Cincinnati, the Dodgers welcomed the Cardinals for a three-game series. St. Louis had finished second under manager Ray Blades in 1939, but they had started slowly this season. On June 7, after their record dropped to 14–24, owner Sam Breadon fired Blades. He replaced him with Billy Southworth, who had been managing the Rochester Red Wings, the Cardinals farm team in the International League. A victory in the series opener was the fifth-straight win for St Louis under their new manager. Medwick, in his first game against his old club, had gone hitless in four at-bats against Clyde Shoun.

In the second game—on June 18—Dixie Walker led off the first inning with a single off Cardinals pitcher Bob Bowman. Cookie Lavagetto followed with a double, and Joe Vosmik singled. Next up was Medwick, his former teammate, who Durocher had installed as his cleanup hitter. Bowman had no love for Medwick, whom he had accused of "lackadaisical play in the outfield."[7] His first pitch was a fastball that struck Medwick on the left side of his head. Medwick fell to the ground and lay spread-eagled in the batters box, temporarily unconscious.

He was carried off the field on a stretcher and examined by team physician Dr. Henry Classen. Although Dr. Classen saw no sign of a hemorrhage on the brain, which suggested there was no skull fracture, he ordered that Medwick be sent to Caledonian Hospital. While he was in the dressing room waiting for the ambulance, Medwick said, "It's funny. That makes two bad days in a row. Yesterday I couldn't get a base hit, and today this thing happens."[8] MacPhail, trying to assure himself that Medwick was all right, asked him to repeat what he had just said, which Joe was able to do.

At Caledonian, x-rays were taken, and staff doctor Daniel McAteer and Dr. Jeff Browder, a brain specialist called in by Dodgers management, examined Medwick further. They confirmed there was no fracture of the skull. Dr. McAteer said that Medwick was resting comfortably and at the moment his condition was not serious.

Immediately after the beaning, several Dodgers, led by Durocher, started out of the dugout after Bowman. Everyone on the Dodgers side was certain he had hit Medwick deliberately. The umpires quickly intervened and protected Bowman from being attacked. No one was more upset than MacPhail, who was physically restrained from going after the Cardinals pitcher by Babe Phelps and coach Charlie Dressen. Southworth immediately removed Bowman from the game, at which point several stadium policemen escorted him off the field.

Meanwhile, MacPhail crossed over to the Cardinals dugout and castigated Southworth and everyone on the bench for what had happened. Close to 100 New York City policemen soon appeared, clearly there to protect the St. Louis players from any irate Brooklyn fans. Fortunately, there were no such incidents. The Cardinals eventually won the game,

7–5, in 11 innings. Casey, making his first appearance following his arm problems, was the losing pitcher in relief.

A history of mutual antagonism existed between Bowman and Durocher, and also between Bowman and Casey. The two pitchers had opposed each other in a 1939 game, where each had accused the other of throwing beanballs. Both were likely right in their accusations. Casey would do anything to win, said Whit Wyatt years later about his former teammate and friend. "He didn't care if he hit you right between the eyes; it wouldn't faze him a bit," Wyatt declared.[9]

MacPhail's request that the police arrest Bowman and charge him with attempted murder was ignored; however, the day after the beaning, Brooklyn district attorney William O'Dwyer began an investigation into the possibility that Bowman's pitch had made Medwick the victim of a criminal assault. O'Dwyer, who later served as mayor of New York City and U.S. ambassador to Mexico, said he had been prompted to act by published reports that there was ill feeling among the players involved and that threats had already been made. O'Dwyer dispatched his aide, Burton Turkus, to Caledonian Hospital to take a statement from Medwick. (As a prosecutor for the Brooklyn district attorney's office, Turkus sent seven members of the crime organization Murder Incorporated to the electric chair in the 1940s.)

Medwick told Turkus that on the morning of the game, he and his wife were passengers in an elevator in Manhattan's Hotel New Yorker. Also on the elevator were Bowman, Cardinals pitcher Mort Cooper and his wife, Durocher and his wife, and three or four other people he did not know.

Medwick said he recalled Durocher and Bowman "ribbing" one another about that afternoon's game and the merits of their respective teams. He said he paid little attention to the conversation and knew of no threats by Bowman or any other Cardinals player to do him injury.

But J. G. Taylor Spink reported in *Sporting News* that Bowman heard Durocher say he was bruised up from the day before and did not plan to play that afternoon. "Of course, you ain't going to play," Bowman supposedly said. "You know I'm going to pitch." Durocher answered that he expected his team to drive Bowman from the game before he even batted.[10]

Turkus requested that Durocher and Dressen appear at the district attorney's office for questioning. He said he would not question any of

the St. Louis players at that time but would do so later if the investigation so required.

O'Dwyer said his entry into the Medwick case was a matter of official duty. "I'm going to investigate first of all to determine if a crime has
been committed," he said, continuing,

> I'm going into the matter with an open mind because ordinarily
> there would not be a second word about a baseball player being
> struck by a pitched ball. But in view of the reports that there was bad
> feeling between the players involved and some alleged threats, I
> believe that the entire case should be sifted in a thorough inquiry.
> My concern is to establish whether a crime was committed and if
> there is any evidence to support the charges published. I feel I would
> be remiss in my duty if I didn't look into this matter. [11]

Spink wrote it would be an extremely difficult legal task to establish the
intent to assault as required by criminal law. That Medwick said he
knew of no threat to do him injury made the task even more difficult
and more or less left the authorities without a complaining witness.

National League president Ford Frick also looked into the case. He
held a preliminary investigation in his office, attended by Southworth,
Bowman, and most of the Cardinals players. Only MacPhail, Durocher,
and secretary John McDonald were there to represent the Dodgers.
"Even if I had a decision to announce right now," Frick said after the
hearing, "I would withhold it until after the investigation started by
District Attorney O'Dwyer has been closed." [12]

Both Frick and MacPhail voiced their resentment of O'Dwyer's investigation, saying it was a matter baseball could handle on its own.
When O'Dwyer found no evidence of criminality, he dropped the investigation.

On the positive side, Southworth and several of his players visited
Medwick at the hospital, but only Southworth was allowed into the
room. He apologized on behalf of his club. MacPhail also made peace
by visiting the Cardinals clubhouse and wishing them luck, which elicited a cheer from the players gathered.

Bowman's roommate, pitcher Max Lanier, said Bowman had no reason to throw at Medwick and he was distraught about the injury. Lanier
blamed Charlie Dressen, Dodgers third base coach and a notorious sign
stealer. It was his theory that Dressen had told Medwick that Bowman's

next pitch would be a curveball. "Bowman was wrapping his curveball, and then he wrapped a fastball the same way, and it faked Dressen," Lanier said. "Medwick stepped right into it, thinking it was going to be the curve. I think that's what happened. And Joe got hit hard."[13]

Lanier's explanation was consistent with what Bowman was saying. "Medwick was looking for a curveball, expecting the ball to break, as he made no attempt to get out of the way," Bowman claimed, while continuing to deny the beaning was deliberate. Cardinals owner Sam Breadon also came to the defense of his pitcher. Breadon cited the May 7 game between the Dodgers and Cardinals at Sportsman's Park, in which Casey hit Padgett, Mize, and Slaughter. "We did not accuse the Dodgers of using beanball tactics that afternoon," said Breadon.[14]

Enos Slaughter also placed the blame on Dressen. "Don Padgett, who was catching for us that day, noticed that Dressen was whistling every time Bowman threw a curve," he said. "With Medwick coming up to bat, Padgett went to the mound and told Bowman to hold the glove the way he did when he was throwing curves but to fire a fastball in high and tight." According to Slaughter, when Medwick heard Dressen whistle, he leaned in, expecting the curve, and was unprepared to duck out of the way of the fastball.[15]

Despite Lanier and Slaughter's explanations, Dodgers players did not believe for a moment Bowman's beaning of Medwick was accidental. Having lost four straight, they saw this incident as the possible spark they needed to get back on track. Generally, Brooklyn's pitchers were not averse to throwing at opposing batters, yet the *Eagle*'s Tommy Holmes thought they were not doing enough of it to dissuade opposing pitchers from throwing at their hitters.

"Outside of Hugh Casey, who'll take no guff from anyone," Holmes wrote, "the Dodgers haven't had a really good knockdown specialist, and they've wound up with the worst of the decision in a long succession of feuds as a result."[16]

The heated rivalry that would persist both on and off the field between St. Louis and Brooklyn throughout the 1940s was just getting started. At the Hotel New Yorker, the morning after the Medwick beaning, Durocher stopped at the table where Southworth and several of his players were having breakfast. The two men exchanged angry words, but it went no further. That night, Cardinals catcher Mickey Owen slid hard into Pete Coscarart at second base on a force play.

As Owen was leaving the scene, Durocher yelled something at him from shortstop, and the two men began fighting. Owen, who threw the first blow, was ejected, but Durocher was allowed to remain in the game. Frick fined Owen $50 and suspended him for four days. The Dodgers won the game, 8–3, ending their losing streak and the Cardinals' and Southworth's six-game winning streaks.

6

CASEY FUELS A FEUD WITH THE CUBS

Casey, whose last start was June 3, expected to return to the rotation for the June 25 game against Chicago at Ebbets Field. Instead, Durocher went with Luke Hamlin, but he called on Casey in the eighth inning with the Cubs leading, 3–2. Hugh pitched four scoreless innings, despite allowing seven baserunners and being in trouble in almost every inning.

Newt Kimball, who replaced him with one out in the 12th, was hammered for five runs in the 13th, as the Cubs won, 8–3. It was Brooklyn's seventh loss (plus one tie) in their last nine games of this homestand, causing growing discontent among the fans. They were especially hard on Medwick. Joe had failed in several clutch situations during his first two weeks with the club, and he was starting to hear boos from patrons in left field. As with most fans, they did not consider his recent near-brush with death sufficient reason for his failure to hit with runners in scoring position.

Casey picked up an easy win on July 3, with one inning of relief against the Giants. Two days later, in Boston, he again allowed numerous baserunners (six hits and eight walks, five of which were intentional)—but no runs. This time he spread those baserunners throughout nine-and-a-third innings, the equivalent of a complete-game shutout. The game was tied, 2–2, when he relieved Hamlin in the 10th inning. The score was still the same when he departed in the 19th frame. The Dodgers eventually won the 20-inning marathon, 6–2.

The game set a major-league record for elapsed time, lasting five hours and 19 minutes, four minutes longer than the two teams had played in 23 innings the previous year.

Kimball, who relieved Vito Tamulis, who relieved Casey, pitched to four batters and walked two of them but was awarded the win, an excellent example of why won–lost records can be deceiving. Boston reliever Joe Sullivan, who had also entered the game in the 10th inning, surrendered all four Brooklyn runs in the 10th, although only one run was earned.

Tot Pressnell's 2–0, three-hitter on July 6 raised the Dodgers winning streak to seven. The streak ended the next day with two tough defeats by Boston, 1–0 and 2–1.

The double loss and Cincinnati's win moved the Reds ahead of Brooklyn into first place. Whit Wyatt, who lost the opener to Manny Salvo, his second 1–0 defeat of the season, was so upset by the loss that he was reportedly in tears after the game.

During the All-Star break, the Dodgers, while on their way to Cincinnati, where they would begin a crucial road trip, played three consecutive exhibition games. It would be a costly exhibition series for Casey. On July 10, against the Johnstown Johnnies, Brooklyn's Class D team in the Pennsylvania State Association, acting manager Charlie Dressen inserted Casey in right field to give Dixie Walker a breather. In the fourth inning, in Casey's first at-bat, he faced Vincent Shupe, an 18-year-old left-hander. Shupe was primarily a first baseman who did not pitch in any regular-season games in 1940.

His first pitch hit the right-handed-batting Casey above the left temple with full force. Although he was knocked down, Casey struggled to his feet and wanted to stay in the game. A doctor from the stands examined him and said he was okay, but Dressen sent him back to the hotel, accompanied by Hamlin and trainer Charley Wilson.

Shortly after the trio returned to the hotel, Casey began complaining of a painful headache and dizziness, and started to stagger. Hamlin and Wilson got him into bed, where he slipped into unconsciousness and was rushed to Johnstown's Mercy Hospital. Casey stayed in the hospital only one day, but the doctor recommended he not play for a week. A few days later, he rejoined the club in Pittsburgh, wearing a bandage on his head. Although his doctors had instructed him to take it easy, Durocher had him warming up in the Brooklyn bullpen.

Back in June, the day after Bowman had beaned Medwick, Joe had told J. G. Taylor Spink that it was "just one of those things"; however, he believed it prudent that the National League adopt a rule similar to that of the American League regarding beanballs. The AL rule made it the umpire's duty to warn a pitcher if he threw too close to a batter's head. If he threw a second similar pitch, he would be ejected from the game. If he were to repeat the practice in a subsequent game, he would be automatically suspended for 10 days without salary, and for a third game, he would be automatically suspended for 30 days without pay.[1]

Medwick's beaning had again raised the question of batters using head gear to protect them from potentially serious injuries. The Spalding Company had even offered to make a specially designed helmet, with earflaps, but their proposal was mostly ignored.

"Apparently the only objection to the innovation," theorized the *Brooklyn Eagle*, "is that the fans might get the idea that the home-run clouters were sissies."[2]

MacPhail was Durocher's boss, but the helmet issue was one of the many things on which they disagreed. Larry was in favor of batters wearing helmets, but Leo's reaction was similar to that of most players. "I've been getting by without a skullpiece for 15 years, and I don't need one now," he said.[3]

At the All-Star Game in St. Louis, the *St. Louis Star-Times* asked several National League managers their opinion on helmets. The response was almost universally negative.

Bill McKechnie of the Reds: "I'm noncommittal, but no player of mine will have to wear one against his will."

Casey Stengel of the Bees: "Not such a good idea."

Doc Prothro of the Phillies: "It would be hard to force players to wear a helmet."

Leo Durocher of the Dodgers: "That thing would be nothing but a target for pitchers to throw at."

Frankie Frisch of the Pirates: "No player on my team will ever be seen in one."

Billy Southworth of the Cardinals: "Helmets were tried in the International League and proved unsuccessful. I'm afraid the same thing would hold true in the majors."

Outfielder Terry Moore of the Cardinals was the only player to agree to have his picture taken wearing a helmet. "They might be all right if they get a good one," he said, "but I'll never wear one."[4]

When regular-season play resumed after the All-Star Game, the 1940 National League pennant race continued to be marred by bean-ball wars and overly aggressive slides. Shortly before the break, on June 23, Reds pitcher Bucky Walters had beaned Chicago's Billy Jurges. Jurges had to be carried off on a stretcher and missed three weeks of play. The Dodgers, led by their pugnacious and confrontational manager, were in the thick of many of the battles.

"Brooklyn had a tough-as-nails pitching staff that year, anchored by Casey and Whit Wyatt, neither of whom were shy about throwing at hitters," wrote author Jonathan Weeks. "Casey had led the league in beanings the year before with 11. In all, the Dodgers ended up plunking 31 batters in 1940—third highest in the majors."[5]

Jack Kavanagh, an usher at Ebbets Field that season, remembered, "Both at home and away the Dodgers were embattled. At Ebbets Field they were viewed as playing aggressive baseball. On the road they were vilified as dirty players with head-hunting pitchers and a manager without a conscience."[6]

In addition to the increasing acrimony with the Cardinals, they had developed a running feud with the Chicago Cubs. The enmity between the Dodgers and Cubs likely traced back to before the start of the 1939 season. Gabby Hartnett, then-manager of the defending National League champions, had predicted that Brooklyn would finish last. A few days later, Durocher, the newly appointed manager, was asked about Hartnett's prediction during a coast-to-coast radio interview.

"His team might finish last," Leo responded, "but if we win, I wouldn't take myself out of the lineup after losing three World Series games."[7] Durocher was referring to Hartnett using Ken O'Dea behind the plate in the fourth game of the Yankees sweep of the Cubs in the 1938 Series.

The feud between the Dodgers and Cubs was renewed on July 19, when Casey hit opposing pitcher Claude Passeau in a game at Wrigley Field. The Dodgers had not forgotten that during an earlier visit to Wrigley, on June 1, their rookie shortstop, Pee Wee Reese, had been hit in the head by a pitch from Jake Mooty. Reese spent 18 days in the Illinois Masonic Hospital and missed three weeks of play; however, the more likely explanation for Casey hitting Passeau was his frustration with his poor performance that day.

Durocher had brought him in during the eighth inning with the Dodgers trailing, 8–3. He had not pitched since being beaned in Johnstown, so this stint was mostly to give him some live action. The lack of work showed, as he was obviously rusty. The first batter he faced, Jimmy Gleeson, doubled, and the second, Bill Nicholson, hit a home run. A single, a walk, and a wild pitch scored another run, and Casey was in a foul mood when his fellow Southerner, Passeau, stepped in. At 6-foot-3 and weighing about 200 pounds, Passeau was a big man whose reputation as a "terrible-tempered Mississippian" was well earned.

When Casey's first pitch was close to Passeau's head, Passeau responded with a threatening gesture and had to be held back by umpire Ziggy Sears. Passeau next tried a bunt up the first-base line, hoping Casey would field it and he would take the opportunity to run over him, but the ball went foul. Casey responded with another pitch high and tight, and then a fastball, which hit Passeau between the shoulder blades.

Passeau flung his bat at Casey, causing Casey to take steps toward him as both benches emptied. Brooklyn's Joe Gallagher left the Brooklyn dugout and tackled Passeau before Casey could get there.

According to the Brooklyn *Eagle*, "Passeau had a stranglehold on Gallagher, Leo Durocher had a stranglehold on Passeau, and George Uhle, a Cubs coach, had a stranglehold on Durocher."[8] It took the umpires, ushers, and members of the Chicago police to end the brawl. Once order was restored, Sears ejected both Gallagher and Passeau, but not Casey. National League president Ford Frick fined Passeau $75, for throwing his bat at Casey, and Joe Gallagher $50, for "mixing in something that wasn't his business."[9]

Brooklyn had no particular rivalry with Cincinnati, but that did not prevent a brawl from breaking out between the two clubs on July 23, at Ebbets Field. It started when Reds infielder Lonny Frey slid into second base in an attempt to break up a double play. Brooklyn's second baseman, Pete Coscarart, evidently felt Frey's spikes were too high and took a swing at him, which led to the inevitable free-for-all. The Dodgers came out on top in the fighting, but the Reds swept the doubleheader to move seven games ahead of Brooklyn.

Chicago gained some revenge for the Casey–Passeau incident when they took three of four at Brooklyn in early August. The first game of the series was particularly painful, as the Reds lost a doubleheader in Boston that day. Instead of gaining ground on the league-leader, the Dodgers dropped six full games behind.

Cubs players were still talking about Casey hitting Passeau, but they were not sure who to blame. Some said they heard Durocher tell Casey to put Bobby Mattick, the Cubs' number-eight hitter, on base and then add, "You know how to take care of the next guy." [10] The next guy was, of course, Passeau, and "taking care of him" can mean different things to different people. For the Cubs, there was no doubt it was Durocher's way of telling Casey to hit Passeau.

A win in the second game of the Sunday, August 4, doubleheader prevented the Cubs from leaving town with a four-game sweep. Casey was Brooklyn's starter that game, and, fittingly, his opponent was Passeau. Making his first start since June 3, Casey was handled easily by the Cubs. He gave up four runs on five hits in the first inning and was replaced by Vito Tamulis in the second. Despite the hole Casey had dug for them, the Dodgers eventually won in 11 innings, 7–6.

Clearly, Casey was not the pitcher he had been in 1939. He demonstrated this again on August 14, when he appeared in relief in both ends of a doubleheader against Philadelphia. His combined record for the two hotly contested games was 4 innings pitched, 2 runs, 4 hits, and 4 walks. Not terrible, but well below what was expected of him, and the four walks stood as the most disturbing aspect of his performance.

"That's the first time in my life I remember being wild," he said. "I had great stuff but just couldn't do anything with it. A week ago Sunday, when I started against the Cubs, I didn't have a thing. I had everything today, but you can see what happened." He suggested that his problems might have stemmed from a lack of work, but Durocher dismissed that idea. "I've tried everything," a visibly frustrated Durocher said, "but that Casey is beyond me." [11]

Casey's wildness reached its zenith in the second game of an August 20 doubleheader in St. Louis. Clyde Shoun had shut out the Dodgers in the first game, and the teams were tied, 3–3, when Casey relieved Tex Carleton in the seventh. He retired the Cardinals in order and got Johnny Hopp, the first batter in the eighth. Johnny Mize then singled, and Enos Slaughter walked. After getting the second out, Casey walked

Don Padgett to load the bases. Then he walked Stu Martin, whose free pass scored Mize with the eventual winning run. The two losses set off a five-game losing streak—three in St. Louis and two in Chicago.

On August 15, Brooklyn, with fading pennant hopes, received a severe setback. Pee Wee Reese broke a heel bone on a slide into second base in a home game against Philadelphia, ending his season. Although he played in just 84 games, he batted .272 and stole 15 bases, fifth highest in the league. Defensively, the rookie shortstop had more than lived up to expectations.

Later in the month, Cookie Lavagetto was stricken with appendicitis, and he too was lost for the rest of season. Durocher used Pete Reiser to replace Lavagetto at third base. Reiser had been sent back to Elmira to start the 1940 season, but the Dodgers soon realized he had nothing left to prove there. He was batting .378 when they promoted him to their top farm team in Montreal. From there he arrived in Brooklyn and appeared in his first game on July 23. After an 0-for-9 start, he batted .293 in 58 games and was one of Durocher's most-used bench players.

If Casey was a disappointment in 1940, Fred Fitzsimmons was a pleasant surprise. Durocher used the 38-year-old right-hander sparingly, giving him just 18 starts and two relief opportunities during the course of the season. But within those parameters he had been Brooklyn's most successful pitcher. Fitzsimmons finished with a 16–2 record, a 2.81 earned run average, and a league-best .889 winning percentage.

One of his starts was on September 2, in the first game of the Labor Day doubleheader at Boston. It was his worst outing of the year, as neither he nor Bees starter Dick Errickson survived the first inning. After the Dodgers scored four runs in the top of the frame, the Bees matched that total in the home half.

Casey came in to get the final out of the inning and then pitched the next nine and two-thirds innings. The 10 innings pitched was the longest relief stint of his career. During that time he allowed just three runs, but one was unearned, when a two-out 11th-inning error by Pete Coscarart allowed Gene Moore to score the winning run. Rookie Al Javery, who relieved Errickson with one on in the Dodgers' first, went 10 and two-thirds innings to pick up the win.

A doubleheader sweep at the Polo Grounds on September 8, combined with a Cincinnati loss at Chicago, moved the still-hopeful Dodgers just six-and-a-half games behind the Reds. Curt Davis defeated Carl Hubbell in the opener, and Casey, in relief of Hamlin, won the night-cap, 4–2.

Hugh, who had pitched a 14–3 complete-game victory at Philadelphia two days earlier, pitched five-and-a-third innings of scoreless relief in this game. As the Dodgers left the field after the final out, they gathered around Casey, shaking his hand and slapping him on his back. Feeling they were back in the race, the team's mood was joyous and confident, and Durocher's favorite battle cry, "Let's rack 'em up," was heard loud and often in their clubhouse.[12]

The team fell back during the next few days, losing three in a row, until Casey gained his 10th and 11th victories as the winning pitcher in both games of a doubleheader on September 12, against Pittsburgh. He blanked the Pirates, 7–0, in the first game, yielding just three hits. The final score is not indicative of the closeness of the game. Through seven innings, the Dodgers had scored only once against Pittsburgh's Ken Heintzelman, before exploding for six runs in the eighth inning.

Durocher then used Casey to relieve Hamlin in game two, and he pitched another two and two-thirds scoreless innings to pick up the win. No one in the Ebbets Field press box could recall the last time a Dodgers pitcher had won two games in one day.

The Dodgers also won the next three against Pittsburgh but were still eight games behind the Reds. Any hope for a miracle finish ended when they followed the five-game winning streak with a five-game losing streak.

7

BUILDING A CHAMPION

Since coming to Brooklyn, Red Barber had been telling his radio audience there was never a dull day at Ebbets Field, and he was usually right. The biggest riot, or rhubarb, as Barber called them, of the 1940 season occurred in the 10th inning of a game against Cincinnati on September 16. With the score tied, 3–3, Curt Davis, who had gone all the way for Brooklyn, was facing Frank McCormick. Mike McCormick was at second base, Ival Goodman was at first, and one man was out.

McCormick hit a ground ball to shortstop Johnny Hudson, who flipped the ball to second baseman Pete Coscarart to force Goodman. Coscarart then set to throw to first, to complete what would have been an inning-ending double play. But as he made the transfer from his glove to his throwing hand, he dropped the ball.

First-base umpire Bill Stewart ruled Goodman out, claiming Coscarart had held the ball long enough. Reds manager Bill McKechnie appealed the call to third-base umpire George Magerkurth, who reversed Stewart's call. The reversal enraged Leo Durocher, causing him to stage one of his classic temper tantrums, directed at Magerkurth. The arbiter listened patiently for several minutes before ejecting the Brooklyn manager from the game. When play resumed, Cincinnati catcher Bill Baker lined to left field, deep enough to score Mike McCormick with what proved to be the winning run.

Durocher later would be suspended for inciting the riot that began after the game, when hundreds of irate fans stormed the field. One, a 21-year-old parolee named Frank Germano, threw the much larger

Magerkurth to the ground, sat on top of him, and started beating him. Stewart tried to rescue his partner, but another "fan" kicked him in the head.

The official end to Brooklyn's pennant hopes came against St. Louis on September 18, at Ebbets Field. Johnny Mize, with four singles and six runs batted in, led the Cardinals to a 14–7 victory. The Dodgers had led, 4–0, after one inning, but rookie starter Ed Head could not hold the lead. Casey relieved Head in the Cardinals' five-run fifth and allowed three runs without retiring a batter, and was the eventual losing pitcher.

Brooklyn had to settle for second place, the first time they had finished that high since 1924. They clinched the runner-up spot with a 5–4 win over the Giants on September 24. It was an odd game in that the Dodgers scored their five runs against starter Bill Lohrman in the home fifth, and the Giants scored their four off starter Whit Wyatt in the eighth. Wyatt left with no one out, and Casey saved the game with two scoreless innings. The home-plate umpire was Al Barlick, a 25-year-old recently brought up from the International League to replace the injured Bill Klem.

The next day's game, the final one scheduled between the two clubs, was rained out. Of the 21 contests played that season, the Dodgers had won 16 and the Giants five. It was the most wins ever by the Dodgers against the New Yorkers, and had they played and won that final game, it would have been the first time in the Giants' long and glorious history that they had lost 17 games to one team in a season.

Dodgers management, both on and off the field, had been disappointed with Hugh Casey's 1940 season. Casey had finished with an 11–8 record and an earned run average of 3.62 in 154 innings, a decline in every category from his 1939 record of 15–10, with a 2.93 ERA in 227-and-a-third innings. His 25 starts and 15 complete games in '39—second in both departments to Luke Hamlin—had dipped to 10 starts and five complete games. Six Brooklyn pitchers had more games started, and four had more complete games.

Casey had missed out on a win against the Phillies on May 13, which usually would have been awarded to him. He started and left after five innings with a 4–3 lead. Vito Tamulis relieved him and pitched four scoreless innings in a game Brooklyn won, 6–3. In the judgment of the official scorer, Tamulis, who allowed just two hits, had been the more efficient pitcher.

Casey had given up his auto salesman job in Brooklyn, and he and Kathleen spent the winter in Jacksonville, Florida, although Hugh did manage to do some quail hunting with his pal Whit Wyatt in Buchanan, Georgia. He signed his 1941 contract at the end of January but was four days late reporting to spring training, which was being held in Havana, Cuba. The club fined him $100—$25 for each day—which he paid without complaint.

His weight, always a contentious subject, appeared to be just about what it had been at the end of the 1940 season. Although he pitched well in spring training, Ed Hughes, a columnist for the *Brooklyn Eagle*, wondered whether Casey would return to his 1939 form. Hughes wrote,

> Casey is a young man, possessing certain pitching talents. However, last year the gentleman could do no better than 11 wins and eight beatings. It is no special secret that Casey should have done better than that. The trouble was the Irishman simply didn't attend to his knitting. . . . If he got away with it then, he may do likewise this season. So you've got to sling him in the problem class until he can really be called dependable.[1]

Tommy Holmes was more optimistic about Casey than his colleague at the *Eagle*. In analyzing the "big, round-faced fellow from Georgia," Holmes wondered if the no-beer-drinking clause Larry MacPhail had inserted into Casey's 1940 contract had contributed to his poor performance.

Casey's habit of having a few beers after each game had not resonated with MacPhail, who wanted his player to avoid gaining too much weight. Casey had stayed on the wagon all season, but during the spring there were no such restrictions, and at 210 pounds he was looking like the Casey of 1939, and would start the season in Leo Durocher's rotation. "[H]is sidearm fastball is sinking again, and his curve is breaking off sharp," Holmes declared.[2]

Tom Meany wrote from Havana that the team had an excellent chance to dethrone the Reds as National League champions in 1941. Much depended, he thought, on the return to form of Luke Hamlin and Casey. He was especially high on Casey. Under a subtitle prophetically titled "Casey Has Everything, But an Item Called Luck," Meany said, "Hugh has all the stuff to make him a winner—good pitching equipment, control, competitive spirit, and finesse."[3]

MacPhail considered both Casey and Hamlin flops during the 1940 season, but he was hopeful they would bounce back. He believed he had two solid pitchers in Whit Wyatt and Kirby Higbe but knew that would not be enough.

MacPhail had brought Higbe to Brooklyn in November, trading pitchers Vito Tamulis and Bill Crouch, catcher Mickey Livingston, and $100,000 to the Philadelphia Phillies for the 25-year-old right-hander. In addition to leading the National League in strikeouts, the hard-throwing Higbe had won 14 games for the last-place Phillies. "Durocher and I feel that he [Wyatt] and Higbe are 20-game pitchers," Mac-Phail said. "If we were as sure about Hugh Casey and Hamlin we'd be very happy."[4]

A few weeks after the Higbe trade, MacPhail landed his coveted catcher, acquiring Mickey Owen from St. Louis to replace Babe Phelps. To get Owen, the Dodgers sent catcher Gus Mancuso, minor-league pitcher John Pintar, and $65,000 to St. Louis.

In early April, as the Dodgers played their way north, MacPhail was in Waco, Texas, talking about other potential trades. Regarding the rumored trade for Cubs second baseman Billy Herman, MacPhail said he never made an offer to Jimmie Wilson, who had replaced Gabby Hartnett as Chicago's manager. "We talked about it," he admitted, "but the fact is that Wilson hasn't made up his mind as to just what he needs."

MacPhail also revealed that before securing Owen, he had talked to Bill Terry, who said the Giants were willing to trade catcher Harry Danning for Babe Phelps, Dixie Walker, and a pitcher. "When he named Hugh Casey as the pitcher," MacPhail recalled, "that stopped everything."[5]

If the fans back in Brooklyn needed any more encouragement that this would be their year, it was the daily reports on Pete Reiser coming out of Havana that spring. Reiser had played shortstop, third base, and right field after coming up in July 1940. Now Durocher was playing him in center field, where he continued to impress, and often amaze, anyone who saw him. MacPhail was sure he had found the man to lead Brooklyn to a pennant in 1941.

"I don't go in for predictions," MacPhail told the reporters in camp. "But if a young fellow with no. 27 on his back [Reiser's number] comes through as I think he will, we've got a first-place club. Reiser is the boy I mean," said MacPhail, "and he very well may be the best hitter on the club. He can hit, is fast, and can throw well."[6]

The Dodgers had moved up from third in the National League in 1939, to second in 1940. They were poised to make a run for the pennant in 1941, but to do so, according to Pat McDonough of the *New York World-Telegram*, they would need a return to 1939 form from six specific players, including Casey. The others were Joe Medwick, Cookie Lavagetto, Pete Coscarart, Curt Davis, and Luke Hamlin.

McDonough blamed Casey's falloff on his recurring arm problems but reported he had been in the best of health during the spring. He thought the 27-year-old Casey surely had his best years ahead of him.[7]

Time, the popular weekly news magazine, was among the prognosticators that believed the Dodgers had an "excellent chance to win the National League pennant." In their preseason issue, they described Brooklyn as 50 percent better than last year's second-place club and warned there was no laughing off the Dodgers this year. To emphasize their potential, *Time* cited an old rival, famous for his disparaging remarks regarding the Dodgers, stating, "Even Bill Terry, manager of the Brooklyn-hating New York Giants, admitted last week that the Dodgers are the team to beat in the National League."[8]

Terry's assessment seemed dismissive of the Cincinnati Reds, the league's two-time defending champions. But Reds first baseman Frank McCormick, the National League's Most Valuable Player in 1940, told reporter John Lardner he expected his team to win again in 1941. When Lardner said MacPhail had predicted a Brooklyn pennant in '41, McCormick was skeptical. "How does he figure that? I can't see it," he said.

He agreed that newly acquired pitcher Kirby Higbe would help but did not consider newly acquired catcher Mickey Owen much of an improvement over Phelps. As for Brooklyn's best pitcher and best hitter in 1940, McCormick was unimpressed with both men, saying, "Fred Fitzsimmons, he won't win any 16 games next year like he did this year. Dixie Walker, their best hitter, is no kind of hitter at all for my dough. No power. Lots of his hits are leg hits and bloopers, and swinging bunts. For me, a hitter should bat in those runs."[9]

The Dodgers opened the 1941 season with three games at Ebbets Field against the Giants. Because fan anticipation was so high, the three successive victories by Terry's club against Wyatt, Higbe, and Davis were humiliating. Impatient Brooklynites began calling their beloved Dodgers "Larry MacPhailures."

The team that had won its first nine games in 1940 did not register its first win of 1941 until its fourth game, 11–6, in Boston's home opener. The Casey Stengel–managed Bees made six errors, providing Brooklyn with six unearned runs.

Casey started for the Dodgers, but he was wild and allowed four runs before leaving with two outs in the fourth inning. "I was wild in Boston in my first start, something that rarely happens to me," he said later.[10]

New York had won their first five games when they hosted the Dodgers on April 20. The crowd of 56,314 was, at that time, the biggest ever for a single game at the Polo Grounds. The score was 9–9, when Casey, Brooklyn's fourth pitcher, came on in the bottom of the eighth. He pitched two scoreless innings, earning the win when the Dodgers pushed across a run in the ninth.

When Casey beat the Giants a second time, 7–4, on April 22, he became the first Dodgers pitcher to win two games that season. In throwing his first complete game, he pitched much better than the score would indicate. All four Giants runs were unearned, thanks to two errors by left fielder Joe Medwick and one by Casey himself.

Pete Reiser had gotten off to a terrific start. He was batting .355 when he was hit in the face by a pitch from Phillies moundsman Ike Pearson in the third inning of an April 23 game at Ebbets Field. There was no indication of intent on Pearson's part; nevertheless, the ball had hit Reiser squarely on the right cheekbone. "You could plainly see the imprint of three stitches where it hit him," said Dolph Camilli.[11]

Reiser collapsed but regained consciousness as he was being carried off the field on a stretcher. Sadly, this was to be a scenario repeated several more times in Pete's hard-luck career.

As with Medwick the year before, medical personnel rushed Reiser to Caledonian Hospital, where doctors determined the cheekbone was badly bruised but not fractured. Reiser and all the Dodgers were wearing the helmet liner ordered by MacPhail and designed by Dr. Walter Dandy. MacPhail's innovation was in response to the numerous beanball wars of 1940, which had hospitalized Medwick, Billy Jurges, and others. The liner had been designed to protect the temple, but Pearson's pitch had been a few inches lower. "Anyone hit in the temple with a ball thrown as hard as that would be lucky to keep on living unless he wore protection," MacPhail said. [12]

Success against the Giants in his first two seasons had earned Casey a reputation as a Giant killer. He enhanced that reputation on April 27, when he defeated the New Yorkers for the third time in eight days. His 7–5 victory was not nearly as effective as his previous start against them, but three innings of scoreless relief by Lee Grissom assured him of the victory. Brooklyn's starters had been pitching so well that Higbe, Hamlin, Davis, Wyatt, and Casey himself had gone the distance in each of the previous six games.

After Hamlin beat the Reds, 13–2, on April 29—the Dodgers' 12th win in 13 games—Walker lauded the team's pitching. "I can hear the Reds whisperin' to each other," he said in the clubhouse, "and they're sayin', Wyatt yesterday, Hamlin today, Higbe tomorrow, and either Davis or Casey the next day. . . . Dawgonned if I've ever been on a club that had four or five starters working that way in the spring." [13]

When Casey picked up a win against Cincinnati on April 30, he became the first four-game winner in the majors. The Dodgers had trailed the Reds, 3–0, but tied the score on home runs by Walker and Medwick. Casey replaced Lee Grissom in the ninth inning with one out and two Reds on base. He got Frank McCormick and Billy Werber to fly out. In the home ninth, his roommate, Pee Wee Reese, doubled to drive in pinch-runner Reiser with the winning run. The victory was Brooklyn's ninth straight, matching the nine-game winning streak to start the 1940 season.

Reiser's appearance was his first since being hit by Pearson a week earlier. Originally expected to be out for two weeks, he had returned in one. Durocher would use him as a pinch-hitter the next day and return him to the lineup the following day.

To get MacPhail to come to Brooklyn in 1938, the Brooklyn Trust Company had promised to provide the financial resources he needed to revitalize the franchise. They had held to that promise, providing the money to greatly spruce up Ebbets Field and allow MacPhail to make the deals that had brought Camilli, Higbe, and Owen to Brooklyn.

On May 6, he added another major piece to the Brooklyn lineup. He sent $65,000, along with second baseman Johnny Hudson and outfielder Charlie Gilbert, both of whom were at Montreal, to the Chicago Cubs for second baseman Billy Herman. Herman was batting just .194, but he was only 31 years old, had been an All-Star for the past seven seasons, and had a .309 lifetime batting average.

In July 1945, MacPhail, then running the Yankees, sold Hank Borowy, the team's best pitcher, to the Cubs for $97,500. Many years later, a plausible explanation surfaced for the sale of Borowy. It was, the theory went, MacPhail's repayment to Chicago general manager Jim Gallagher for the 1941 deal that brought Herman to Brooklyn.

The Cubs, in New York to play the Giants, were staying at the Commodore Hotel in Manhattan. When Gallagher notified Herman he was leaving the last-place Cubs to join the pennant-contending Dodgers, he said a quick good-bye to his now-ex-teammates and crossed the East River to Brooklyn. He arrived at Ebbets Field at 12:30 p.m. and made his Dodgers debut by going 4-for-4 in a 7–3 win over the Pirates. The victory was Wyatt's fifth in a row since losing to the Giants on Opening Day.

Later in the season, the Dodgers would add two more veterans from the Cubs: pitcher Larry French on August 20, and infielder-outfielder Augie Galan on August 26. Neither man would contribute much to this season but would do more in the future.

In late May, *Time* magazine ran an article demonstrating how Brooklyn's sensational play had reached beyond the everyday fan and into the world of classical music:

> Radio listeners last week heard a piece of music inspired by a baseball team. Composer Robert Russell Bennett, who in his youth was a semipro ballplayer, played a new *Symphony in D* for the Dodgers on his WOR-Mutual program, Russell Bennett's Notebook. To the Dodgers and their music-loving president Larry MacPhail, the symphony was a great comfort. Although they were still out in front in the National League, they had just lost a game in Pittsburgh, which ended a seven-game winning streak.
>
> Composer Bennett began his symphony with conventional jubilant trumpetings. That was "The Dodgers Win." "The Dodgers Lose" was a dirge, almost Oriental in its luxurious grief. The scherzo of the symphony opened with plaintive bassoon bleats: President MacPhail

offering Cleveland the Brooklyn Bridge and Prospect Park in trade for Pitcher Bob Feller. Thudding minor chords were Cleveland's repeated "No." The symphony ended with "Red" Barber himself, the Dodgers' own radio announcer, rattling off an account of a ninth-inning rally against the Giants, a home run, and victory. *Symphony in D* for the Dodgers had much of the Dodgers' elusive, faunlike charm, and rated a place with such sporting music as Constant Lambert's "Prizefight," Arthur Honegger's "Rugby and Skating Rink," [and] the ballets *Card Game* (Igor Stravinsky) and *Checkmate* (Arthur Bliss).[14]

8

CASEY THE WORKHORSE

The Dodgers opened their first 1941 western swing on May 13, in Cincinnati. Casey went the distance without allowing a walk in beating Bucky Walters and the Reds, 4–3. The win raised his record to 5–0, and elevated the record of the first-place Dodgers to 21–6. The young Cardinals were close behind, at 18–6, but when Wyatt defeated the Reds the next day—his seventh-consecutive win—the defending champions had fallen 10 and a half games behind.

Casey's unbeaten streak ended with a thud on May 19, in Chicago. After a scoreless first, the Cubs exploded for nine runs in the second against Hugh and Mace Brown, on their way to a 14–1 victory. Six of the runs, five of which were earned, were charged to Casey, who exited after yielding a grand slam to his frequent antagonist, Claude Passeau.

Durocher used his knowledge of the roster rules to protest the game, and also the previous day's loss. The Cubs had been unclear in establishing the status of outfielder Charlie Gilbert, whom they had received from Brooklyn in the Billy Herman trade a week earlier. Leo claimed Gilbert was officially on the Cubs roster, making them one player over the 25-man limit.

Ford Frick denied the protest, but he did rule that the Cubs had committed a rules infraction and fined them $500. The ruling came as no surprise to the *Brooklyn Eagle*'s Tommy Holmes. He had predicted the Dodgers would lose the protest because, "(1) Frick isn't given to drastic decisions such as would be involved if two games were thrown out, and (2) Ebbets Field rarely wins any kind of an argument with either the National League office or Commissioner Landis."[1]

Durocher echoed Holmes's Brooklyn-against-the-world mindset. "Why are the rules in the book if they aren't meant to be followed?" he asked. "Every time our club turns around we have somebody cracking down on us, and it's my job to do all I can to have the ballgames thrown out of the records when they're beating us with 26 men."[2]

Late in his career, Casey told J. G. Taylor Spink of *Sporting News* how that May 19 game in Chicago had turned him from a starting pitcher into a reliever:

> I was tossed into it by a home run. A home run with the bases loaded by that renowned slugger, Claude Passeau. Just think of that . . . I opened that season as a starting pitcher and took six in a row. I then lost a game and was chased to the bullpen by Leo Durocher. I have been out there ever since. I was going after no. 7 against Passeau and the Cubs at Wrigley Field. The bases got loaded in the second inning and—*boom* went the old ballgame.[3]

(Casey was 5–0 at the time, not 6–0, and he was going for win number six, not number seven.)

He added, "I was allowed to start only one more contest that season. Leo told me I was much more valuable as a relief pitcher. That's how a man's career is affected by small things. Or is a homer with the bases loaded by a pitcher no small thing?"

Casey's memory is faulty here. His next five appearances were all starts, although by the second half of the season, Durocher was using him almost exclusively out of the bullpen. He did not become a full-time reliever until the 1942 season.

The Dodgers had lost five straight when he took his regular turn as the starter in St. Louis on May 22. The Cardinals, led by home runs by Johnny Mize and Don Padgett, battered him for seven runs in four innings on their way to a 7–6 win. Having defeated Brooklyn the day before, the Cardinals now led the Dodgers by a game and a half. After the season, Casey wondered about his lack of success against St. Louis. "I don't know why," he said. "I beat them my first year, but I haven't won from them in the last two seasons."[4]

Durocher was his usually blustery self after the game. "Sure, we lost six in a row," he told sportswriters, "but I guess we're entitled to lose a few. It's nothing. The hawks have us, that's all. We'll come out of it. We still have the best team in the National League," he said. "Don't tell me you think that's a great Cardinal team we blew two games to. We'll take care of them later."[5]

In his next start, Casey threw his first shutout of the season, defeating the Phillies, 6–0. The victory was the fourth in a row for Brooklyn, which had followed their six-game losing streak with a nine-game winning streak. On Memorial Day, a crowd of 59,487 at the Polo Grounds saw them sweep a doubleheader from the Giants, highlighted by Whit Wyatt's shutout in the opener and a five-run ninth-inning rally in the nightcap.

Consecutive win number eight came a day later, when Casey defeated Carl Hubbell to raise his record to 7–2 overall and 4–0 against New York. By the end of May, the Dodgers had already compiled winning streaks of seven, eight, and nine games.

When the Reds opened a three-game series at Ebbets Field during the first week of June, they trailed the Dodgers by 11 and a half games. With a chance to drop the two-time defending National League champions out of the race, the Dodgers got swept instead. Walters and Paul Derringer won the first two, but the Dodgers appeared to have salvaged the third game. They had a 5–0 lead after six innings, and Casey, who had not allowed a hit in the first five, looked to be in complete control. But he weakened in the seventh, as the Reds rallied against him and three relievers to win, 9–7.

As a part of the Brooklyn community, Casey was one of many Dodgers who appeared regularly at social and civic events in the borough. That evening, following his breakdown that afternoon, Casey was one of a large group of Dodgers who appeared at a Holy Name Society gathering at Our Lady of Refuge Roman Catholic Church in Brooklyn.

It was becoming increasingly apparent the race for the National League pennant would be between Brooklyn and St. Louis. On June 13, when the Dodgers began a four-game series at Sportsman's Park, they had fallen two games behind the Cardinals. It was only June, but there was much to be gained, or lost, for Brooklyn in these four games. Winning all four would put them two games ahead of St. Louis, while taking three of four would gain them a tie.

But the best the Dodgers could do was split the four games, allowing St. Louis to retain its two-game lead. Luke Hamlin and Kirby Higbe won for Brooklyn, while the two losses were the first shutouts they had suffered that season. Young left-handers threw both shutouts. Max Lanier, 25, beat Wyatt, 1–0, and Ernie White, a 24-year-old rookie, topped Casey, 3–0. Hugh lasted only into the third inning, when his wildness contributed to the Cardinals scoring their three runs.

At this point in the season, the race for third place was between Cincinnati and New York. Both had been easy pickings for Casey, whose eighth win came on June 20, at Crosley Field. The complete-game, three-hit, 6–2 victory was his third win against the Reds. (He had beaten the Giants four times.)

He made it four wins against the Reds two days later in the first game of a doubleheader. An all-time Crosley Field record crowd of 35,792 witnessed the games. Playing in 90-degree heat, accompanied by high humidity, Brooklyn won both games by a single run. The Dodgers' sweep appeared to put to rest any hopes the Reds had for a third-straight pennant.

Wyatt and Derringer were the starters in the opener, which was scoreless until Wyatt put the Dodgers ahead with a home run in the 11th. But between innings, Wyatt had accidentally washed down a salt tablet with mouthwash, making him too ill to continue. Durocher called on Casey to get the final three outs. He got the first two, with the aid of a sensational throw by Reiser to cut down Lonnie Frey, who was trying to stretch a double into a triple. With two outs and no one on, the Reds had three consecutive hits to tie the score.

It remained tied until the Dodgers pushed across an unearned run in the 16th inning to win, 2–1. Reiser, who had used his great speed to score the winning run, came through with another great throw in the Reds' 16th, nailing Billy Werber, who was attempting to stretch a single into a double.[6]

By holding Cincinnati scoreless from the 12th inning through the 16th, Casey earned the win to raise his record to 9–3. A hard-luck Derringer pitched the entire 16 innings for the Reds.

Higbe went the distance to win the second game, 3–2. In winning his ninth game, Higbe joined teammates Casey (9) and Wyatt (10) as the only National League pitchers with nine or more wins.

Casey lost his next two decisions within a space of three days, going only three innings against Boston on June 29, and losing in relief against Philadelphia on July 1. He had survived the heat in Cincinnati but succumbed to it in the loss to the Phillies at Brooklyn. He pitched five-and-a-third innings of relief, and despite throwing up on the mound in the ninth inning, Durocher kept him in the game. He then sent him out for the 10th, with the score tied, 4–4, whereupon a heat-exhausted Casey surrendered two runs, giving Philadelphia the win.

As befitting a team with a three-game lead at the All-Star break, the Dodgers had the most members of the National League squad, with six for the July 8 game. Three were starters, pitcher Whit Wyatt, catcher Mickey Owen, and center fielder Pete Reiser, while Billy Herman, Cookie Lavagetto, and Joe Medwick entered the game later. Still, that was not enough for the citizens of Brooklyn, who could not understand manager Bill McKechnie bypassing Casey, Higbe, and Dixie Walker.

During the break, Bill Terry, who before the season had called the Dodgers the "team to beat," predicted they would hold onto their lead and win the pennant. "If that strong-arm trio of mound aces, Whitlow Wyatt, Kirby Higbe, and Hugh Casey, continue at top form, it appears the Dodgers will march in easily."[7]

With no games to cover during the break, Tommy Holmes devoted a column to the synergy among Brooklyn's three aces from the old Confederacy: Casey and Wyatt from Georgia and Higbe from South Carolina. "There is no jealousy among them," he wrote, "and Casey and Higbe readily acknowledge Wyatt is the ace of the staff."

"Whit is by far the best pitcher in the league," said Higbe. "He has everything, knows what to do with it, and makes a minimum of mistakes." Such an admission was unusual from the normally boastful Higbe. "I'm a little surprised at myself for saying that," he confessed. "You see, until a month or two ago, I thought I was the greatest pitcher in the league." As Casey nodded in agreement with Higbe's assessment of Wyatt, Higbe continued.

"Whit can really pitch," he said. "Every time anything happens to Wyatt it hurts Casey. Hughey [sic] can't forgive himself because Wyatt didn't win that [June 22] game in Cincinnati." Higbe remembered Casey bawling out loud when he returned to the bench after the Reds tied the score. "Why not?" asked Casey. "I felt worse about that game than any I've lost. It was criminal that Wyatt didn't get the credit."[8]

The Dodgers were home to host the western clubs when the season's second half began. They took two of three from Cincinnati and, after losing the opener of a five-game series against Chicago to Claude Passeau, won the next four.

Brooklyn had a three-and-a-half-game lead over the Cardinals, and pennant fever was increasing daily. More than 33,000 fans were at Ebbets Field on July 15, to see Curt Davis and Luke Hamlin sweep the Cubs. That evening, Casey and a bunch of his mates participated in an exhibition bowling match at the Roxy Bowling Center, a new alley at 50th Street and Seventh Avenue in Manhattan, on the site of the old French Casino supper club. Casey's team, captained by Freddie Fitzsimmons and including Pee Wee Reese, defeated Cookie Lavagetto's team, which included catchers Herman Franks and Tony Giuliani, 1,556 to 1,440, in a three-game total-pins match. Casey, an accomplished bowler, had the best individual game, bowling 218 in his second round. [9]

Following two losses to Pittsburgh, the Dodgers lost one of the several games they believed they had let slip away. On July 22, in Cincinnati, Hamlin took a 4–0 lead into the ninth but never got an out. Frey led off with a double and scored on Frank McCormick's single. After he walked Billy Werber and had two balls on Dick West, Durocher replaced Hamlin with Casey, who completed the walk to load the bases. The next batter was the weak-hitting Chuck Aleno, who managed a checked-swing, pinch-hit triple that cleared the bases and tied the score.

Bucky Walters, who had pitched the entire game, was the next batter. Walters was a former infielder and one of the best hitting-pitchers in the game, so Bill McKechnie allowed him to bat. He lined out to center fielder Reiser, but Lloyd Waner, running for Aleno, scored the winning run.

In describing the Aleno triple, columnist John Kieran of the *New York Times* wrote, "His bat was practically knocked out of his hands and the ball bounced back over Dolph Camilli's head for a fluke triple." [10] It was a heart-breaking loss for Casey and the team. Combined with the Cardinals win over the Giants, it left Brooklyn and St. Louis tied at 57–31.

On July 27, at Pittsburgh, Casey was knocked out in the fifth inning and saddled with his fourth-consecutive loss. The pitching staff was tiring and struggling, so on July 30, MacPhail claimed fiery veteran Johnny Allen from the St. Louis Browns. The 36-year-old right-hander had won 119 games (119–58) in 10 American League seasons with New York, Cleveland, and St. Louis.

Allen made his first National League start on August 1, in Chicago. He went six and two-thirds innings to pick up the win, aided by an excellent relief effort from Casey. The Cubs had closed to 5–4 in the home eighth against Tom Drake, also making his Dodgers debut. Casey relieved with one out and the tying run on second base. He struck out Lou Stringer and Bobby Sturgeon, and then retired the side in order in the ninth to preserve the win for Allen.

Casey, who had not won a game since June 22, lost his fifth straight, 2–0, in the second game of an August 12 home doubleheader against New York. He pitched well—the two runs he allowed were unearned—but Cliff Melton, who allowed just three hits, pitched better. It was Casey's first loss to the Giants after beating them four times early in the season.

Durocher was using Casey in a dual role, as a starter and reliever, much more than any of his other pitchers. Eighteen of his 45 appearances in 1941 were starts, fourth highest on the club, while his 25 games finished were far and away the most on the club and the fourth highest in the league. It was as a reliever against Pittsburgh, on August 18, that he broke his five-game losing streak. He relieved Fitzsimmons in the ninth inning and allowed an unearned run that allowed the Pirates to tie the score at 5–5. Casey earned the win when Reiser led off the bottom of the ninth with a home run.

In the third game of a four-game series the Dodgers swept, Casey preserved Tom Drake's first and only major-league victory with one inning of scoreless relief. And, on August 22, he made yet another appearance, saving Newt Kimball's 8–5 victory over Chicago. "Casey is the Dodger workhorse," wrote Roscoe McGowen. "In a week he has hurled 13 and one-third innings of relief in six games, permitting only two earned runs."[11]

St. Louis trailed Brooklyn by a game and a half when the Cardinals made their final trip to Ebbets Field for doubleheaders on Sunday, August 24, and Tuesday, August 26. (The second doubleheader was necessitated by a rainout on Monday.) More than 31,000 fans attended the first doubleheader, and a far-above-capacity 39,000-plus attended the second. Such a huge crowd on a weekday afternoon was an indication of how this Brooklyn club and the pennant race had captivated the fans.

"We could have sold 200,000 tickets for this doubleheader," Mac-Phail claimed. "Only the facilities to accommodate such a crowd are lacking."[12] "By 10:00 a.m., three and a half hours before game time, 50,000 fans had been turned away. Extra policemen were called to form a cordon around the park. Mobs, stampeding out of nearby subways, were urged to go back home unless they had reserved seats."[13]

National League president Ford Frick recognized the importance of the games by assigning four umpires rather than the customary three.

The Cardinals were minus their two best outfielders for this series: Enos Slaughter and Terry Moore. Slaughter, the team leader in home runs and runs batted in, had broken his collarbone when he collided with Moore chasing a fly ball on August 10, and was out for more than four weeks. Center fielder Moore was beaned 10 days later by Art Johnson of Boston, and he too missed several weeks. Max Lanier, who in 1952 was briefly a teammate of the young Willie Mays, called Moore the "greatest outfielder I ever played with."[14]

During his career, Moore was recognized as the league's best defensive center fielder; nevertheless, Lanier's ranking him above Mays was no doubt influenced by loyalty to an old teammate.

The Cardinals suffered a number of significant injuries to key players that year. "In addition to Slaughter and Moore, catcher Walker Cooper missed several weeks with a broken collarbone; brother Mort was out from mid-June to mid-August, with bone spurs on his right elbow; and Mize's broken finger and sore shoulder contributed to his home-run total dropping from 43 in 1940 to 16 in 1941."[15]

Despite losing Moore and Slaughter, Cardinals president Branch Rickey waited until mid-September to bring up their best prospect, outfielder Stan Musial, from the International League's Rochester Red Wings. "Why didn't he bring Musial up earlier? That's what all the players wanted to know," remembered Johnny Mize. "We might have gone ahead and won the pennant."[16]

The teams split both twin bills, with Sunday's second game being the most dramatic. The Dodgers won that one, 3–2, when Whit Wyatt singled home the winning run in the bottom of the ninth. Reese led off the inning with a bunt single against Howie Pollet, a 20-year-old left-hander. Pollet, who had a record of 20–3 with Houston of the Texas

League, after going 20–7 for the Buffs in 1940, was making his second major-league start.

Mickey Owen sacrificed Reese to second. Durocher allowed Wyatt to bat for himself. With darkness setting in and the clock reading 7:25 p.m., Wyatt ripped Pollet's first pitch back through the middle, bringing Reese home with the winning run. After these four crucial games, Brooklyn (79–44) remained a game and a half ahead of St. Louis (77–45).

The night of the Tuesday doubleheader, Casey showed off his bowling skills again when he teamed with Andy Varipapa, America's foremost bowler, to win an exhibition match over Pete Reiser and Jimmy Wasdell. The two-game match was held at the Kenmore Bowling Center at Flatbush and Church avenues in Brooklyn. The winners totaled 764 (410 for Varipapa and 354 for Casey), while the losers had 604.[17]

9

NATIONAL LEAGUE CHAMPIONS

Brooklyn's two-week reign in first place ended on August 30, when they lost a doubleheader to the Giants. Higbe and Casey were the starters and losers. Meanwhile, Lon Warneke tossed a no-hitter at Cincinnati to move the Cardinals into first place by .002 percentage points. Knocking Brooklyn out of first place was no doubt sweet for Bill Terry, his team, and those Giants fans who remembered the Dodgers ending the Giants' pennant hopes seven years earlier.

On September 1, in the first game of the Labor Day doubleheader at Ebbets Field, the Dodgers fell behind Boston, 4–0, before rallying to win, 6–5, in 15 innings. (The second game was called after six innings with the score tied at 2–2.)

Casey picked up win number 11 in the opener, tossing four innings of scoreless relief. In addition, he led off the bottom of the 15th with a walk, and Pete Coscarart, who ran for Casey, scored the winning run on Dolph Camilli's bases loaded, two-out single. For Camilli, whose 29th home run of the season had sent the game into extra innings, his game-winning single was his fifth hit of the afternoon.

The following Sunday, Casey defeated the Giants, 4–3, with two innings of scoreless relief in the second game of a Brooklyn sweep. This too was an extra-inning game won by the Dodgers in their final at-bat. And again Casey played a key role in the run scoring. He followed Mickey Owen's 10th-inning leadoff single with a sacrifice bunt, moving Owen to second. Pete Reiser's single brought Owen home with the game-winner. The win was Casey's fifth of the season against the Giants and raised his overall record to 12–9.

St. Louis had faltered this last week, and Brooklyn's sweep of the Giants had moved them three games ahead of the Cardinals as they embarked on their final western trip. They would play 17 games on the road, in six different cities, before ending the season with two games at Ebbets Field against Philadelphia. Meanwhile, the Cardinals would play most of their remaining games at home, before finishing with six on the road.

The first stop for the Dodgers was Chicago, where they lost both ends of a doubleheader to the Cubs. The Cardinals defeated the Phillies twice that day to cut the lead to one game. On September 11, the Dodgers arrived in St. Louis for the final three games between the two contenders.

The local press was calling it the "Little World Series," reclaiming the title they had used for the crucial series played at Sportsman's Park between the St. Louis Browns and the Yankees in 1922. Baby Doll Jacobson, the star center fielder of that Browns team, visited the Cardinals dressing room to wish them luck.[1]

The third game, on Saturday, drew Sportsman's Park's largest non-Sunday crowd since 1927. Cardinals fans were as devoted to their team as Brooklyn fans were to theirs. Likewise the bickering with the umpires and the abuse heaped on the visitors—it was the same in both parks.

The Dodgers won the first game, 6–4, on Dixie Walker's two-run single in the 11th inning. It was a sloppily played game, with each team committing four errors. Freddie Fitzsimmons pitched the first 10 innings to earn the win, and Casey protected the lead by setting down the Cardinals in order in the 11th.

St. Louis won the next day, 4–3, behind Howie Pollet and Max Lanier, setting up the rubber game on Saturday. Unless the two teams ended the season deadlocked, this would be their final meeting. Opposing pitchers Wyatt and Mort Cooper were at their best, as each held the opposition to just three hits.

The Dodgers scored the game's only run on back-to-back eighth-inning doubles by Walker and Billy Herman. Walker always claimed he stole catcher Gus Mancuso's sign and signaled Herman that the next pitch would be a curveball. "Billy's eyes bugged out so far that I was sure the Cardinals would catch on and switch," he said.[2] Herman hit the pitch safely into right-center to win the game. And "Walker, running as if a horde of red demons were on his heels, galloped across with the all-important run."[3]

Wyatt retired the last six St. Louis batters, including a strikeout of pinch-hitter Enos Slaughter on three fastballs to end the game and give him his 20th win. Slaughter's appearance was his first action since his injury a month earlier.

Speaking of this game, years later, Wyatt said, "I think that was the best game I ever pitched in my life."[4] That winter, Walker told *Sporting News* editor J. G. Taylor Spink, "I have been in baseball for some years, but that series of three games with the Cardinals was the most thrilling of my life." He called Wyatt's 1–0 win over Cooper "one of the greatest games in the history of the major leagues."[5]

Leaving St. Louis with a two-game lead, the Dodgers traveled to Cincinnati, where they took two of three contests. Casey was involved in all three decisions, winning the first two games and losing the third. Each win was the result of two innings of relief. The second game went 17 innings, the longest of the season for the Dodgers.

The game was scoreless through the first 16 innings. Paul Derringer had gone all the way for Cincinnati, while Johnny Allen had pitched the first 15 innings for Brooklyn before giving way to Casey. The Dodgers finally broke through when Reiser led off the 17th inning with a 400-foot home run. They added four more runs against Derringer and two relievers, which was more than enough to offset the run Casey allowed in the home half of the inning.

Casey's second victory in two days was his sixth of the season against the Reds and his 14th overall. The Dodgers' lead was now one and a half games; meanwhile, back in Brooklyn, the club announced they would begin accepting mail-order applications for World Series tickets. In his third-straight decision out of the bullpen, Casey was charged with the 4–3 loss when he allowed the Reds to score the winning run in the 11th inning.

Umpire George Magerkurth had a history of trouble with the Dodgers, especially Durocher. It surfaced again in Brooklyn's getaway game at Pittsburgh on September 18. The game was one of the wildest in a season of wild games. The Pirates led, 4–0, until the Dodgers erupted with two out in the eighth for five runs against Johnny Lanning and Rip Sewell.

The comeback took Freddie Fitzsimmons off the hook, preserving his 13-game win streak against the Pirates. With a one-run lead, Durocher called on Luke Hamlin to nail down the win. But after Vince DiMaggio singled to open the inning, Durocher replaced Hamlin with Casey. Hugh got the next two batters, with DiMaggio moving to third.

As Casey prepared to pitch to Al Lopez, home-plate umpire Magerkurth called a questionable balk on him, allowing DiMaggio to trot home with the tying run. Durocher came out but was unsuccessful in arguing the call. After getting two strikes on Lopez, a fuming Casey threw three consecutive pitches dangerously close to Lopez's head.

After the third throw, as Magerkurth headed to the mound to warn Casey, Durocher ran toward Magerkurth, whereupon he was ejected. After a fourth ball to Lopez put him on first base, Alf Anderson tripled to score him with what proved to be the winning run.

When word of what had happened reached him in the clubhouse, an already enraged Durocher exploded. "Alf Anderson," he shouted. "For Christ's sake, Alf Anderson. Who the fuck is Alf Anderson?"[6]

"There was an aftermath to the dispute . . . under the stands after the game," wrote Tommy Holmes.[7] It involved Magerkurth, Durocher, and Brooklyn players Camilli, Wyatt, Coscarart, Joe Medwick, and Herman Franks. Umpire Bill Stewart intervened, preventing any fisticuffs. Ford Frick called Durocher to his Manhattan office the next day, severely reprimanded him, and fined him $150. Each of the five players was accused of using "vile and profane" language against Magerkurth and fined $25 apiece. Magerkurth did not umpire another Dodgers game in 1941. He was replaced by Beans Reardon for the remainder of the regular season and Larry Goetz in the World Series.

Although the newspapers believed Casey was showing his displeasure by throwing at Lopez, author Richard Goldstein believed his target was Magerkurth. "He fired three straight fastballs aimed not at the catcher's mitt, but at Magerkurth's head," Goldstein said.[8]

The Dodgers got back on the winning track in Philadelphia by sweeping a doubleheader. The two wins, combined with a Cardinals loss to the Cubs, increased Brooklyn's lead to two games. Wyatt, with Casey in relief, and Higbe each picked up their 21st win of the year. Higbe won his 22nd at Boston, on September 24, as Casey picked up his seventh save with three scoreless innings. He finished the season at 14–11, with an earned run average of 3.89 in 162 innings.

Sportswriter George Kirksey called Casey the league's most valuable relief hurler. "In one stretch," he wrote, "Casey pitched in six out of eight games with the pennant riding on almost every pitch."[9] According to Red Barber, writing 35 years later, after the deciding game in Boston, Durocher said, "We couldn't have won it without Casey."[10]

Wyatt, needing no help, matched Higbe's total a day later when he shut out the Bees, 6–0, to clinch the pennant. The Dodgers and Cardinals had spent the entire spring, summer, and fall trading places at the top of the standings. Brooklyn was in first place 99 days of the season and St. Louis 82 days. Rud Rennie of the *New York Herald Tribune* called it the "longest and closest pennant struggle in the history of baseball, with neither team ever more than four games out of first place."[11]

"We Win," read the headline in the *Brooklyn Daily Eagle*. Another local newspaper, the *Brooklyn Citizen*, had erected a board near Brooklyn's Borough Hall for fans to follow the game. Thousands gathered to watch, but their presence served to disrupt traffic in the surrounding blocks. People throughout the borough, both indoors and out, followed Red Barber's transcription of the game on radio."[12]

According to *Time* magazine,

> Last Thursday, at 5:08 p.m., bedlam broke loose in Brooklyn. Staid citizens dashed out of their homes and shops, yelling, "We're in, we're in!" Housewives stood on their stoops, beating dishpans; kids tooted tin horns; barkeeps opened their taps, "set 'em up on the house." For 21 long years, Brooklynites had waited for this moment. Their beloved Dodgers had just clinched the National League pennant in Boston. Many another baseball town has gone wild over a pennant victory. But Brooklyn's faithful fans—victims of an inferiority complex provoked by the pompous, pennant-heavy New York Giants and Yankees across the river—burst into a demonstration last week that looked like New Orleans' Mardi Gras, New Year's Eve in Times Square, and the 1918 Armistice.[13]

With the season-long tension finally lifted, the Dodgers celebrated with champagne in the clubhouse and continued celebrating on the train ride back to New York. Amid the festivities, Casey told Tommy Holmes he regretted that Wilbert Robinson had not lived to see this. "There's one thing wrong," Casey said. "I wish old Robbie were here with us tonight. God, how he'd have loved it."[14]

The train was bound for Grand Central Station, but MacPhail, who was not with the club in Boston, wanted to share in the glory. He had gotten word to the conductor to tell Durocher to have the train make a stop at the 125th Street Station, at East 125th Street and Park Avenue in Upper Manhattan. He would board the train there and accompany his champions to Grand Central.

But the train sped right by 125th Street, never slowing and leaving a furious MacPhail ready to fire Durocher. Later that night he did fire his pennant-winning manager but rehired him the next day. "He fired me 60 times if he fired me once," Leo would later say.[15] "There is a thin line between genius and insanity," Durocher once said of MacPhail. "In Larry's case it's sometimes so thin you can see him drifting back and forth."[16]

Durocher claimed he never got MacPhail's message. And even if he had, he likely would not have stopped anyway. Durocher had overheard some of his players saying they would get off the train at the uptown stop to avoid the anticipated mob scene at Grand Central, and he did not want the long-suffering Brooklyn fans snubbed in that manner. "I don't care if they tear your clothes off," he recalled saying years later. "We belong to those fans. They've been waiting 21 years for this chance to celebrate, and we've gotta go through with it. There'll be no stop."[17]

In the opinion of *Time*,

> Durocher's decision was an appropriate one, a recognition that Dodger fans had supported the team in record numbers. Attendance at Ebbets Field reached a new high in 1941—more than 1.2 million people. Four days later, after the last game of the regular season, more than a million people marched down Flatbush Avenue behind their heroes in a gigantic victory parade.[18]

The Baseball Writers' Association of America recognized the outstanding seasons by many Brooklyn players. Foremost among them was Dolph Camilli, who they selected as the league's Most Valuable Player.

"I don't think you could ever get a first baseman better than Camilli," said Whit Wyatt. "He was a great hitter and the best fielding first baseman I ever saw."[19]

Reiser was the runner-up, while Wyatt finished third, marking the first time in either league three men from the same team had taken the top three spots. The writers also recognized Kirby Higbe, who finished seventh, Dixie Walker 10th, and Billy Herman 11th.

Playing his first full season, Reiser led the National League in batting, runs scored, total bases, slugging average, and triples, and he tied Johnny Mize for the lead in doubles.

"Any manager in the National League would give up his best man to obtain Pete Reiser," wrote Arthur Patterson in the *New York Herald-Tribune*, continuing,

> On every bench they're talking about him. Rival players watch him take his cuts during batting practice, announce when he's going to make a throw to the plate or third base during outfield drill. They just whistle their amazement when he scoots down the first-base line on an infield dribbler or a well-placed bunt. [20]

Historian Bill James has called the 1941 Dodgers "that close to being a perfect team," citing a lineup that featured future Hall of Famers Leo Durocher as manager, Joe Medwick in left field, Pee Wee Reese at shortstop, and Billy Herman at second base. Other key regulars included near-Hall of Famer Dixie Walker in right field; the league's Most Valuable Player, Dolph Camilli, at first base; the MVP runner-up, Pete Reiser, in center field; and quality players Cookie Lavagetto at third base and Mickey Owen behind the plate. "In the history of baseball, that is probably as close as any team has ever come to putting out a lineup of eight legitimate stars," James declared. [21] On the mound, Whit Wyatt and Kirby Higbe were 20-game winners, and Hugh Casey was one of the early outstanding relief pitchers.

Twenty-one years had passed since Brooklyn had played in the World Series, a 1920 loss to the Cleveland Indians. They also had lost to the Boston Red Sox in 1916. [22] By contrast, the American League champions, the New York Yankees, had played in 11 World Series beginning in 1921, winning eight, including four straight from 1936 to 1939. After losing the 1940 pennant to the Detroit Tigers, Joe McCarthy's Yankees had run away with the 1941 race, finishing 17 games ahead of the runner-up Red Sox.

Offensively, the Yankees topped the American League in home runs, led by an outfield composed of three of the league's top four home-run leaders: Charlie Keller (33), Tommy Henrich (31), and Joe DiMaggio (30). Red Ruffing, Lefty Gomez, Marius Russo, and Spud Chandler made up a formidable quartet of starters, and bullpen ace Johnny Murphy was the American League's best relief pitcher.

Defensively, the Yankees were strong up the middle, with Bill Dickey behind the plate, DiMaggio in center, and a double-play combination of Joe Gordon at second base and rookie Phil Rizzuto at shortstop. They had the most double plays in either league (196), while the Dodgers had the fewest (125). Following Brooklyn's first pre-Series workout at Yankee Stadium, Casey made an observation about the playing field that he hoped would help him. "It's a slow infield, and a ball must be walloped pretty hard to get through," he said. "After an hour or so up in the Bronx I see why the Yankees made 194 [sic] double plays this season."[23]

Casey had plenty of familial support for the World Series. A caravan of his relatives made the trip north to see Hugh pitch. The group included his widowed father Buck, his brother Frank, his sister Rebie, his sister Nellie, Nellie's husband, and their son.

Because he had spent the previous winter in Jacksonville, Florida, hunting, fishing, and playing golf, Casey had not seen his father since February, when he made a brief stopover in Atlanta. One afternoon, he took the entire group to Manhattan for a day of sightseeing.[24]

The Dodgers were mostly a veteran club, not easily awed by the Bronx Bombers. When Dixie Walker was asked if he thought the Dodgers could beat the Yankees, he replied, "I do, definitely. I'd hate to have us come this far and not think we're going to win. We all do."[25] Walker's bravado aside, oddsmakers had installed the Yankees as 2-to-1 favorites.

In their pre–World Series issue, *Time* explained why the Yanks were such heavy favorites:

> The smooth-running Yankee machine may hit on all cylinders after four weeks of coasting, while the high-strung Dodgers, after a neck-and-neck race with the St. Louis Cardinals since the first week of the season—a race during which the Dodgers were in and out of the lead 10 times—may be on the verge of collapse.[26]

The night before the Series opener, Connie Mack, who as manager of the Philadelphia Athletics had battled the Yankees for almost 40 years, had some advice for Pee Wee Reese and Pete Reiser.

"If you give 'em one break, they'll beat your ears off."[27] These would be prescient words.

10

A DRAMATIC WORLD SERIES ENDS A MEMORABLE SEASON

The Yankees had run away with the American League pennant, clinching the flag on September 4, and raising some concerns about the scheduled start of the World Series. Game One was scheduled for Yankee Stadium on October 1, which coincided with Yom Kippur, Judaism's holiest day. With the largest number of Jews in the nation, the New York City Council unanimously passed a resolution, optimistically introduced by the council's Brooklyn members in mid-September, urging the start of the Series be postponed for one day.

The Dodgers led by two games with 12 games left to play on September 16, the day of the resolution, creating a strong possibility that two New York City teams would be playing in the Series. Telegrams urging the delay were sent to National League president Ford Frick, American League president Will Harridge, and baseball commissioner Kenesaw Landis, with Landis having the final say.

The resolution argued that New York had several million people of the Jewish faith and that "for 21 long years the people of the borough of Brooklyn have waited for the day when the Brooklyn Dodgers would engage in a World Series, and it is now apparent that their hopes and expectations are about to be realized."[1]

Commissioner Landis ignored the appeal and a record crowd of 68,540 (which likely included many Jews) attended the Series opener. Joe McCarthy chose Red Ruffing as his opening-game pitcher. The 36-year-old right-hander was a veteran of the Fall Classic, with seven starts and a 5–1 record. The only Dodgers pitchers with World Series experience were Johnny Allen, Larry French, and Fred Fitzsimmons. But Leo Durocher, always a hunch player, surprised everyone by starting 37-year-old Curt Davis, a pitcher with no World Series experience.

A Joe Gordon home run in the second inning and a run-scoring double by Bill Dickey in the fourth had the Yankees up, 2–0, after four. They added what would prove to be the winning run in the sixth on a one-out walk to Charlie Keller and singles by Dickey and Gordon. Casey relieved Davis and retired Rizzuto and Ruffing on fly balls. Jimmy Wasdell batted for Hugh in the seventh, and Johnny Allen pitched the final two innings. The Dodgers had single runs in the fifth and seventh but lost, 3–2.

Brooklyn tied the Series the next day, winning by the same 3–2 score after falling behind, 2–0. Whit Wyatt went the distance, defeating Spud Chandler. The venue then shifted to Ebbets Field, which was set to host its first World Series in 21 years. Game Three, postponed for a day by rain, matched 27-year-old left-hander Marius Russo for New York against the 40-year-old Fitzsimmons, another surprise choice by Durocher. Fitzsimmons had appeared in only 13 games during the season, with a 6–1 record.

The first two games had been tense and low scoring, and this contest was more of the same, and then some. Through seven innings, neither Fitzsimmons nor Russo had allowed a run, but the Yankees' last out of the seventh would have a crucial effect on the outcome. Russo's line drive had struck Fitzsimmons on his left knee and caromed on the fly to shortstop Pee Wee Reese. Fitzsimmons, his kneecap broken, had to be helped off the field and was unable to continue. Durocher had Casey warm up in the bullpen and brought him in to pitch the eighth inning.

"I don't think the Yankees would have touched him the rest of the way if he'd been able to stay in there," Dolph Camilli said of Fitzsimmons.[2] Durocher agreed. "We would have won, 1 to 0, if Fitz could have stayed in there," he said after the game.[3]

Casey retired the leadoff batter, Johnny Sturm, but then yielded consecutive singles to Red Rolfe, Tommy Henrich, Joe DiMaggio, and Keller. That was all for Casey. Larry French, his replacement, induced Dickey to hit into an inning-ending double play. But the Yankees had scored two runs against Casey, all they needed to make him the losing pitcher. With a run in the eighth, the Dodgers fell one run short.

Harold Parrott of the *Brooklyn Eagle* excoriated Casey for his performance—not the physical part, but for two unforgivable mental errors. The first was on Henrich's single, a ball pulled to the right side that first baseman Camilli could not reach but second baseman Pete Coscarart could. Coscarart started to throw to first, expecting Casey to be covering the bag, but Casey had broken from the mound late and was not there. This would have particularly pained Fitzsimmons, Parrott wrote, because the veteran had always pushed Casey to hustle.

The second mental miscue came with Rolfe on second, Henrich on first, and DiMaggio at bat with a 3–2 count. Durocher had signaled for a pickoff play on Rolfe. Coscarart ducked in behind the runner, and it appeared Rolfe would be an easy out if Casey threw him the ball. But Casey missed the sign; he pitched to DiMaggio, whose single scored Rolfe with the game's first run.[4]

Casey always believed that was the key play of the inning. Six years later, with the possibility of another Dodgers–Yankees World Series looming, he told Bill Roeder of the *New York World-Telegram* the following:

> The hit that meant the game for the Yankees was a single by Joe DiMaggio. Coscarart was standing on second base and the ball went to his left, where he should have been. But that was my fault too, because I didn't work out any signs with Coscarart the way I always did with [Billy] Herman. (Herman had left the game in the fifth inning after hurting his side while swinging.) It was a three-and-two pitch, and I think Billy would have been where the ball was hit.[5]

Casey seemed to have forgotten that Durocher had signaled for a pickoff play, and he missed it.

Roscoe McGowen described Casey as "[sitting] in front of his locker staring into space and seemingly unconscious of the movement about him." When reporters asked Durocher if Casey could have covered first on Henrich's hit, he answered, "I have no comment on that."[6]

But he did have a lot to say about the missed pickoff of Rolfe, even during the offseason:

> I say to Casey after that game, "You got the signal for the pickoff?" and Hugh says to me, "Yes."

Then, I say, "Why didn't you pick the man off?" and Casey just shrugs.

So I said to him, "Casey, that's just like you coming in here telling me there was $1,000 laying out on second base today but you walk in here without picking it up!"[7]

MacPhail also was critical of Casey, but for a different reason. He was unhappy with the lax way he had warmed up in the bullpen. "I sat beside Ted McGrew" (Brooklyn's chief scout)," MacPhail said, "and when we watched Casey just lobbing the ball up in the bullpen we both relaxed, feeling sure Fitzsimmons would be back. We both almost fell out of our seats when we saw Casey called in."[8]

And as Casey sat stone-faced and miserable in front of his locker after the game, he no doubt felt that nothing in the Series could go as wrong as things had on that day. Sadly, he was wrong. And his name would be forever linked with what happened in Game Four, not Game Three.

Trailing two games to one, the Dodgers fell behind quickly in Game Four. The Yankees scored a run in the first and two more in the fourth against Kirby Higbe. Brooklyn fought back against Atley Donald with two runs in the fourth on Jimmy Wasdell's pinch-hit double and two more in the fifth on Pete Reiser's home run with Dixie Walker aboard.

The Yankees had loaded the bases against Johnny Allen with two out in the top of the fifth when Durocher replaced Allen with Casey. Having properly warmed up, Hugh dispatched Gordon on a fly ball and preserved the 4–3 lead into the ninth. He got the first two batters, Sturm and Rolfe, on ground balls. Casey now needed only to retire Tommy Henrich to end the game and tie the Series.

Henrich worked the count full, at which point he swung and missed at Casey's delivery, a pitch with a sharp downward break. Home-plate umpire Larry Goetz raised his right hand, indicating strike three, sending the crowd into a frenzy of joy.

The Dodgers came out of their dugout to celebrate, while the Ebbets Field police began moving into position to keep the exultant spectators off the field. But that joy was short-lived, as the crowd realized the ball had gotten away from catcher Mickey Owen and rolled back to the screen, as Henrich hustled down safely to first.

Years later, Phil Rizzuto described what happened from his perspective on the Yankees bench:

When Henrich swung and missed, we all got up and started toward the runway that led out of the dugout. Some of us were already into it. I know I was. Then we heard all that yelling, and we jumped back. There was Tommy running down to first base. Owen was chasing the ball over by his own dugout. By the time he got to it, Tommy was on first and there wasn't any play.[9]

After the game Henrich said,

It was a bad pitch—I mean a ball—but it had me fooled, completely. I'll admit that. I thought it was the best curve Casey broke off all afternoon. I started to swing, tried to stop, but "broke" my wrists and couldn't. It was a strike then. A strikeout, too. But I'll take a strikeout like that once a day if I have to. I don't know where the ball was going, but I'm not left-handed for nothing. I just started to run. You know what else happened. Yeah, I do feel a bit sorry for Owen, at that.[10]

Henrich later added, "I saw that little white jackrabbit bouncing, and I said, 'Let's go.' It rolled all the way to the fence. I could have walked down to first."[11]

The fans settled down, and Dodgers players, who had been ready to mob Casey, returned to their positions on the field or in the dugout. It seemed a temporary setback. There were still two outs, and the potential tying run was 270 feet away. Nevertheless, many in the crowd had a sense of foreboding, conjuring up their own versions of Connie Mack's pre-Series warning of what awaits if you give the Yankees a break. Mack proved prophetic, as the Yankees took full advantage of the situation. DiMaggio jumped on the first pitch, ripping a single to left that moved Henrich to second. "I didn't want Casey throwing me any of that garbage," he later said.[12]

Casey again came within one strike of victory when he got ahead of Keller, 0–2. In normal circumstances, Casey would waste a pitch or two, hoping to get Keller to swing at a bad one. But he was clearly floundering, and the next pitch was in the strike zone. Keller smashed it off the right-field screen for a double, scoring Henrich and DiMaggio to put the Yankees ahead, 5–4.

In a 1943 interview with Shirley Povich of the *Washington Post*, Casey praised Keller and credited him with winning the game:

I had two strikes on him and no balls, and it was the perfect spot for me to throw one high inside and brush him away from the plate. Our bench kept yelling "knock him down!" and Keller heard 'em. He acted as if he thought I was going to do just that on the next pitch.

He was cautious up there, and I figured I'd fool him with a curveball on the outside corner. That's what I threw, and Keller banged it against the screen in right-center for a triple. He's just a great hitter. [13]

(Casey misremembered here. Keller's hit was a double, not a triple.)

As the crowd watched in stunned silence, Casey walked Dickey and allowed a double to Gordon that scored two more runs. Durocher never left the bench. He had Curt Davis warming up but left Casey out there as if it were a spring-training game and Casey needed the work—or, as managers sometimes did during the season, allow a pitcher to get shelled as some sort of punishment.

But this was neither of those situations. Durocher would go on to a Hall of Fame career as a manager, but he clearly mishandled the ninth inning of Game Four of the 1941 World Series. Later that winter, he said it was the only time in his life he couldn't think, although he was more measured regarding his "brain freeze" in his autobiography.

It wasn't the pitch to Henrich that did it, anyway. There was still only a man on first with two out. It was what happened afterwards. And right there I do think it is possible for a manager to second-guess himself. Considering Casey's actions within a very short period of time—pitching too quickly in Cincinnati, throwing those beanballs at Magerkurth in Pittsburgh, and freezing twice within a matter of minutes the previous day—I should have called time and gone to the mound to remind him that he still needed only one out to end the ballgame. To slow him down, in other words, until I was absolutely sure that he was in full control of himself. [14]

Durocher surely was not taking any blame after the game. He had kept reporters out of the clubhouse for 30 minutes, and if he lost his composure during that time, he had regained it when he answered their questions. "Today was just one of those things," he said. "You can't blame anyone for it. It just happened." Then, with his characteristic false bravado, he said, "But let me tell you this—this Yankee club hasn't shown anything to be called great. They couldn't hold the gloves for some of those other Yankee outfits."[15] Leo may have had in mind the 1928 Yankees, led by Babe Ruth and Lou Gehrig, for whom he played in his rookie year.

Durocher's failure to remove Casey remained a mystery to Owen, who blamed himself equally for what had happened—or, more precisely, for what had not happened. Years later, he said he still could not understand why no one went out to talk to Casey. "It was like a punch on the chin," Owen said. "You're stunned. You don't react. I should have gone out to the mound and stalled around a little. It was more my fault than Leo's."[16]

The likelihood of the Dodgers coming back to tie or win the game after suffering such a shocking reversal of fortune seemed infinitesimal. Johnny Murphy, who had retired them in order in the eighth, easily set down Reese, Walker, and Reiser in the ninth to secure the win. Casey became the first pitcher to lose World Series games on consecutive days.[17]

In the view of the *New York Herald Tribune*, Owen had entered the list of the classic "goats," along with Fred Merkle and Fred Snodgrass.[18] "I don't mind being the goat, Harold," Owen told Harold Parrott in the Brooklyn dressing room, "but the tough part is that it costs these other fellows money. I'm square with myself. I knew I gave it everything I had, although I can't tell you for the life of me how that ball got away in the ninth."[19] Yet, unlike his lambasting of Casey the day before, Mac-Phail was supportive of Owen.

After the game, "my father went immediately to the clubhouse, where the gloom and sense of doom was thick," wrote MacPhail's son Lee, a future president of the American League, who was at the game. "He searched for Owen to console him, and when he finally found him in the shower, he ignored the stream of water and walked in himself to throw an arm around Mickey. He then tried to rally his players, telling them that they could still win."[20]

But the loss had put them in a terrible hole. Instead of the World Series being even, the Yankees now held a commanding lead, three games to one. Wyatt, Brooklyn's lone winner, went the distance in Game Five but lost to Ernie Bonham, 3–1. The Series was over, ending what had been a magnificent baseball season, highlighted by DiMaggio's record 56-game hitting streak, Ted Williams batting .406, and an exciting wire-to-wire National League pennant race between Brooklyn and St. Louis.

The postgame comments in the Yankees locker room ranged from the philosophical, by Joe Gordon and Joe McCarthy, to the acerbic, by Joe DiMaggio.

"Never take anything for granted in baseball, boys. The game sometimes isn't over until they have the last out in the ninth twice," said Gordon.

"Sure it was a break," McCarthy admitted. "But it could have happened in the third inning, the seventh, or any time. Those things happen in a ball game. They've happened before and will happen again. But it wasn't so much the break we got as what followed, which won the ballgame," he added.

"I don't know what they're so peeved about," DiMaggio commented. "Didn't they always say, 'Everything happens in Brooklyn?'"[21]

If any of the Yanks felt a bit of sympathy for Owen, they kept it well hidden. While they had lauded Fitzsimmons's gallant efforts of the day before, they seemed to take pleasure in Owen's misfortune.

"As long as there had to be one (a goat), I'm glad it was him," said DiMaggio.

"The right guy got it," chimed in Atley Donald, who would have been the losing pitcher. "He tried to cut down Phil Rizzuto earlier in the Series. He's played dirty ball and is only getting what he deserves."[22]

DiMaggio went even further in expressing his dislike for Owen and the joy he obviously took in the catcher's misfortune. American League pitchers seldom brushed back the Yankees' lordly center fielder, but the Dodgers had been pitching him tight—too tight, he thought—and he suspected Owen had been calling for such pitches.

Owen also had a habit of jumping in front of the plate to direct the infielders to play farther in or out at the same time hitters were setting themselves in the batter's box. "That guy was so busy telling the other Dodgers where to play," DiMaggio declared, "he forgot to tell any of 'em to back him up behind the plate. That's where he needed a man."[23]

The Dodgers were as ungracious in defeat as the Yankees were in victory. "Great Yankees. Huh?" MacPhail said sarcastically in the Dodgers locker room. "Why, they haven't beaten us a game yet. Lousy luck that's what it is. We would have won all four games if we had some of their luck."

A day earlier, Kirby Higbe had also attributed the Yankees Series lead to Lady Luck. "I'd have licked them easy if I'd had my control," he said. "They're lucky—not sluggers. I've pitched to better hitters in semipro ball."

Jimmy Wasdell thought the Yankees "must have a lucky angel flying for them," while Cookie Lavagetto believed that with any luck, Brooklyn would have swept the Series. "We should be on our way home now. They didn't have a right to one game," claimed Lavagetto. "Those lucky Yankees caught lightning in a bottle," he said, echoing MacPhail. "It could never happen again. Is that the great team everyone talks about?"[24]

Yankees "luck" seemed to be the only way the Dodgers could explain their loss. "The Lord must be on their side," Dixie Walker had said after Game Four.[25] Walker called them the luckiest team ever. "Every break in the book went to them," he lamented. "Why, even in that big ninth-inning rally, that ball that Keller hit fiddled around on top of that concrete wall and let DiMaggio go home with the second, or winning, run. Not that it would have meant anything as things turned out, you understand," he added, "but it just shows you. That ball stayed up there on the fence like somebody was holding it."[26]

In his 1948 book *The Dodgers and Me*, Durocher also invoked the luck factor, tying it directly to Casey. "To help us with our bad luck," he wrote, "Hugh Casey was not himself. He pitched as if he were still peeved about the Magerkurth incident in Pittsburgh. And luck again, the whole Series revolved around Hughie."[27]

Casey was perhaps the only Dodger trying to look on the bright side. "We got breaks on errors and mistakes the other fellows made during our September drive to the pennant," he said. "And once we got the breaks we took advantage of them, as the Yanks did yesterday." Casey also revealed he and Owen had gotten some hostile fan mail since the incident. He said he had one letter written jointly by three kids between the ages of 10 and 12 that referred specifically to his failure to cover first base in Game Three. "They asked me if I thought Medwick could come in from left field to cover first for me Saturday, as that was what I seemed to expect." He said the boys had offered to take him out for a beer and then "put arsenic in it."[28]

11

THE PITCH THAT GOT AWAY

With the end of the World Series came the rehashing of Hugh Casey's pitch to Tommy Henrich that had gotten away from catcher Mickey Owen. Rumors that the pitch had been a spitball followed Casey for the rest of his life. Just about everyone involved in the game had an opinion, including Pete Coscarart, who had viewed the pitch from his position at second base. "I think Casey threw a spitter. I really think so," Coscarart said. "Mickey put down his sign for a curveball, but that thing broke too much for a curveball. I really think it was a spitter. He used to throw one once in a while."[1]

Casey mostly denied it. Late in his career, when he was a member of the Yankees, J. G. Taylor Spink asked him about the rumor's persistence. "I give you my word it was not a spitball," Casey answered. "It was a crazy sinker. Sometimes that pitch looks like a spitter. I don't pitch spitters. Who knows where they will go? But I have been suspected," he admitted.[2] Yet, Casey said the opposite to sportswriter Tommy Holmes. "Years later," wrote Holmes, "Casey admitted his third strike to Henrich had been a spitball, which may explain why Owen didn't handle it."[3]

"Right now, with the World Series so fresh in our minds, many things stand out bold and clear in our memories," wrote the *New York Herald Tribune*'s Richards Vidmer, continuing,

> The line drive that shattered Fred Fitzsimmons's knee. . . . Joe Gordon's opening homer. . . . Whit Wyatt's splendid pitching efforts. . . . The thunder of Charlie Keller's bat with men on the bases. . . . The

brilliance of Red Rolfe in spite of ill health. . . . Phil Rizzuto's pivot
on the double play that ended the first game. . . . Flash Gordon's
spectacular fielding. . . . But in the years ahead these will be forgotten when the World Series of 1941 is recalled, and the thing that will
remain fresh in the minds of those who saw it will be the pitch that
Mickey Owen let get away from him as that fourth game should have
ended.[4]

Vidmer is correct. Although more than 75 years have passed, the "pitch
that Mickey Owen let get away from him" remains one of the most-
discussed plays in World Series history.

"I really can't tell you how it happened, fellas, because I don't
know," Owen had told the crowd of reporters in the locker room after
the game. "It was a good pitch, maybe the best curveball Casey threw
all afternoon. It squirted out of my glove somehow. Why, I don't know.
I *do* know that I'm a better catcher than that!"[5] (Owen had recently
finished a regular-season streak of 511 consecutive chances without an
error. The streak ran from September 22, 1940, to August 29, 1941, and
was the National League record at the time.)

Owen always maintained the pitch was a curveball on which he
crossed himself up. He said Casey threw two curveballs, "a big one, and
the quick, hard one." When the first two big curves he threw hung, they
switched to the quick, hard one and had been using that one exclusively. "I got into a rut catching it," he said, "and didn't dream he'd go for
the big curve . . . on the 3–2 pitch."[6]

While not taking the blame for the pitch, Casey did blame himself
for what happened afterward. "I shouldn't have cracked up after Mickey's muff," Casey said in the Dodgers' glum locker room. "If he's the
goat, then it's my fault."[7]

It is important to note Casey's use of the word *muff*, a baseball
synonym for an error. For that is how it was officially scored—an error
to the catcher—not a passed ball and not a wild pitch by Casey. The
1930 rule, which was still in effect in 1941, read as follows: "An error,
but not a passed ball, shall be charged to the catcher if he drops or
misses a third strike, allowing the batsman to reach first base. Credit the
pitcher with a strikeout."[8]

Shortly after the World Series, Owen was back on his farm near
Springfield, Missouri, enduring yet another interview about the fateful
play. "That Sunday night I had to pose for lots of pictures, and they

wanted me to look sad," he said. "But I didn't feel as bad as I tried to appear. What bothered me most was the fact that I had played the longest stretch of consecutive games without an error of any National League catcher—then I had to muff the biggest one of the Series."

He said he had received stacks of telegrams and dozens of phone calls telling him to keep his chin up, including one from actor Boris Karloff, a longtime Dodgers fan. Owen also dismissed the idea that he had sold his herd of goats because they would have reminded him that some thought him the goat of the Series.[9]

In 1989, baseball historian Norman Macht interviewed Owen after he had caught three innings in an Old-Timers' Game in Pittsburgh. "I caught Casey all season," said Owen, who was then a deputy sheriff in Springfield. "They did a lot of sign stealing in those days, but Casey wasn't about to let anybody get his. If he thought you were calling his pitches, he'd just throw at you."

Owen described the system he had with Casey:

> He had two good fastballs and two good curves. One fastball he gripped across the seams; the other was with the seams, and he would give it an extra snap and it moved differently. One of the curveballs was a hard, quick curve—not a slider—and the other was a big roundhouse curve that broke more. If I gave him the fastball sign, he could throw either one. If I signed for the curve, I didn't know which one he would throw, and I just had to be ready. . . . All season long we used that system. I never knew which fastball or curve was coming and the batter didn't, either, and we never had any problem.

Owen said Casey would never throw a changeup because he thought it was a pitch even poor batters could hit.[10]

Owen said that when Casey came into the game that afternoon, the "first curveball sign I gave, he tried to roll off his big overhand curve and it didn't break, just hung outside." That happened a few times, said Owen, and "from that point on, when I gave him the curve sign, he threw the quick one, not as sharp breaking but fast, and they couldn't touch it." He said when he gave the curve sign on the pitch to Henrich, he was looking for the quick one, but Casey threw the big one. Said Owen, "I was late getting my glove down there, and it went right by me. My fault."

Owen had taken the brunt of the criticism, but veteran New York sportswriter Dan Daniel thought that Casey was clearly the goat of the World Series. "And I think Hugh himself will admit the justice of that designation, as it was he who blew the fourth game after Owen's lapse, and it was Casey who blew the third contest after Fitz's retirement."[11]

"I can lose 'em every way in the book and a few others, too. Balk 'em away, throw 'em away," a dejected Casey had lamented.[12]

Throughout the years, a narrative has developed that the alleged curveball Casey threw to Henrich was, in fact, a spitball. Casey always denied the allegation, as did Owen. Leo Durocher claimed that despite revisionist history, Casey's pitch to Henrich was not a spitball. Casey made a great pitch, he said, but Owen reached for the ball instead of shifting his feet, and the ball rolled off his glove.

"Hugh Casey didn't even know how to throw a spitball," Durocher said. "Why should he? Casey had a natural sinker—that's why he was a relief pitcher. A good spitball acts exactly the same way. It breaks down and away. Common sense tells you that a man wouldn't bother to develop a pitch that acts the same as a pitch he's already throwing."[13] Whit Wyatt concurred with his former manager, saying, "I really don't think it was a spitter. I think it was Casey's curveball," he told author Paul Green in 1986.[14]

Two of the Dodgers playing behind Casey that afternoon also had differing opinions on the pitch. Billy Herman agreed with Durocher and Wyatt that it was not Casey's fault. "I think Owen might have 'nonchalanted' the ball, putting his glove out for it instead of shifting his whole body to make the catch," Herman said. "Owen had a habit of doing that, and maybe that's what happened there."[15]

Speaking a dozen years later, Pete Reiser said from his vantage point in center field he could only guess as to which pitch Casey threw to Henrich. He said he never asked Casey or Owen, and as far as he knew no one else on the team had asked them.

Reiser said,

I thought about it a thousand times. The only thing I can figure is that Casey either crossed up Owen or threw a spitball. The pitch was low and inside, and whatever it was it had more on it than Casey usually threw. He didn't have a real good curve, but this thing broke a mile. I could see it fooled Owen by the way he acted. He was good on low balls, and he generally handled them smooth. With this one, he went down like somebody kicked him. Even from center field, I could see he wasn't making a normal motion.[16]

We will never know which pitch Casey threw that afternoon, but H. I. Phillips, of the *New York Sun*, summarized the game with a takeoff on Ernest Lawrence Thayer's famous 1888 poem *Casey at the Bat*.

Casey in the Box
The outlook was tremendous for the Brooklyn nine that day.
The score stood 4–3 with fleeting moments left to play;
And so when Casey mowed two down and faced the final out
The Flatbush roars of victory were echoed all about.

There was ease in Casey's manner as he heard the umps "Strike two";
There was pride in Casey's bearing as he sent his third strike through;
(The game was in the bag now as most any one could see—
'Twas just a formal routine to proclaim the next "Strike three!")

And now the leather-covered sphere came whizzing through the air;
It was a perfect strikeout, plainly seen from everywhere . . .
But—no!—the catcher muffed the ball and changed the final score—
It seems a final strikeout doesn't mean the game is o'er;

Oh, somewhere in this favored land the sun is shining bright—
The bands are playing somewhere and somewhere hearts are light;
And somewhere men are laughing and somewhere children shout—
But there is no joy in Flatbush where that third strike was NOT OUT.[17]

Because baseball's most famous poem was and is *Casey at the Bat*, the Casey name was a natural inspiration for poets. The efforts amused Kathleen Casey. "All the other ballplayers get letters and telegrams," she laughed, "but Hugh, for some reason, always gets poems. Sportswriters, lawyers, senators, kids, housewives—many folks—have written poems about Hugh and sent them to us. But then, I like it, and I hope they'll keep writing poems about him for many years."[18]

A full share of the World Series pot for the losing Dodgers was $4,829.40. That was a significant addition to each player's salary, but Casey felt he deserved a little extra. He said he planned to have a talk with Larry MacPhail before leaving New York to discuss a bonus Mac-Phail had promised him if he had a good year. His main argument would be the numerous newspaper clippings quoting Durocher as saying the Dodgers could not have won the pennant without him. If he did not get the bonus, Casey said, he would retire and take a job as superintendent of a fleet of filling stations in Atlanta.

Of course, no one believed him, and Casey later denied he had threatened to quit. "Those New York writers got me all wrong," he said. "MacPhail was plenty sore. I walked into his office to get my bonus check, and he was fuming. He said he had seen the story, and he didn't like it. He tore up the check right in front of me. So it looks like I've lost my bonus."[19]

After a few weeks, MacPhail, having calmed down, asked Casey to drive up from Florida to visit him in Atlanta, where MacPhail was attending the minor-league meetings. During a dinner that included quail Casey had shot, MacPhail relented, and Casey got his bonus.

"So, you see," Casey quipped, "I know Larry will treat me right. And that story that came out of New York is all wrong. The writers just connected my quitting and the bonus—two things which had nothing to do with each other. They misunderstood me."[20]

Casey also recalled the bonus he had gotten in 1940, relating, "That spring, Larry inserted a clause in my contract that stated I would get a bonus of $2,500, provided I refrained from drinking during the playing season." But by mid-August, he had won only four games and was upset with his performance. Casey continued, "So one night I went back to the apartment, poured a drink or two, and relaxed. I drank a little during the rest of the season, and maybe it loosened me up." Whatever the reason, he won seven of his last nine. "After I'd won several games, MacPhail came down to the dugout. He asked me if I had been drinking. I told him he knew the answer to that one as well as I did." To Casey's surprise, MacPhail paid the bonus anyway.

Nine days after the World Series, Casey drove to Cedartown, Georgia, where hometown hero Whit Wyatt was being honored. He took part in the parade and addressed the crowd that had gathered for a barbeque at Cedartown's Peek Forest Park. He called Wyatt the "most valuable man on the Dodger club and the top pitcher in the major leagues."[21]

Casey had a testimonial dinner of his own, held in his hometown of Buckhead. The local Elks club honored their native son and presented him with the kind of gift he appreciated most—a costly new shotgun. Wyatt and a bevy of current and former big-leaguers from Georgia attended. Among them were Cecil Travis of the Washington Senators; Luke Appling of the Chicago White Sox; Jim Bagby Jr. of the Cleveland Indians; Johnny Rucker of the New York Giants; and Pittsburgh's Alf Anderson, whose triple had beaten Casey in the memorable September 18 "balk game."

Casey's father Buck and wife Kathleen were also present at the dinner. So too were three men who had coached him as a youngster: Rache Bell, the coach for his youth team, the Northside Terrors; Red Barron, his coach at Monroe A&M and Technical High School; and Tubby Walton, who coached him when he played as a semiprofessional. Sprinkled throughout the audience were several men who had been his teammates on those teams.

During the evening, several people had made humorous remarks about Casey taking Mickey Owen hunting and using the shotgun on him. But Casey took offense at those attempts at humor. When it was his turn to speak, he thanked everyone and expressed his thanks "for the appreciation shown me." But then he admonished the crowd for their remarks about Owen.

In the weeks after the incident there was almost universal acceptance that the fault was Owen's. Accounts by revisionist historians, who would blame Casey by suggesting he threw a spitball, were still in the future.

"You folks and everybody else have got Mickey Owen wrong," he said. Pointing to the ballplayers surrounding him, he added,

> These boys here . . . can all tell you how easy it is to make mistakes. We know what it means to have guys on the club who get out there and hustle. Mickey is that kind. He's always in there hustling, and there isn't a single man on our club who blamed him for missing that third strike. [Owen would bounce back in 1942, and finish fourth in the voting for the Most Valuable Player Award.]
>
> We all make mistakes. I made one the day before and lost a game. He made one that day and lost a game. That's all there is to it, and it hurts me personally to have people make wisecracks about what I ought to do to Owen. [22]

(As previously mentioned, Casey later admitted to sportswriter Tommy Holmes that the pitch was a spitter, giving him an even greater reason to be upset at the criticism of Owen.)

Casey also discussed his two mental errors in Game Three. Regarding his failure to cover first base on Henrich's single, he said,

> After Rolfe singled to right, I pitched carefully to Henrich. Tom caught my curve and sent it to the right side of the diamond. Instinctively, I broke for first base, but when I saw the ball head for the hole between Camilli and Coscarart, I pulled up. Then Coscarart came up with an amazing stop. I started for first again, but he didn't throw—it was too late. I just wasn't expecting Pete to come up with that ball. It looked too much like a hit.

Regarding the blown pickoff play, Hugh stated,

> Now, about picking Rolfe off second. I was working on DiMaggio then—had him three and two. I didn't see Coscarart edging over. I haven't thrown to second in years. The catcher on our club doesn't give a pickoff signal—we have to watch out for ourselves. I looked at Pee Wee and he was playing straight, so I didn't bother.

Casey's recollection of this play was both mistaken and self-serving. Durocher had signaled for a pickoff play, and Casey had missed the sign.

Hugh and Kathleen had stayed at the home of Kathleen's parents while they were in Georgia but would leave soon thereafter to spend the winter in Neptune Beach, Florida, east of Jacksonville. Kathleen said they planned to rent a furnished house on the beach and were thinking about building a house on the beach someday. The couple planned to do a lot of fishing and hunting during the winter.

"But we'll have one date a week," Kathleen said. "Hugh and I will come into town and eat, and maybe I can get him to do a little dancing." She too was fond of the outdoors, as evidenced by Casey's Christmas gifts to her the year before—a pair of boots and a gun. While she appreciated a good shotgun, like the one Hugh received at the dinner, she preferred fishing to hunting. She said she was "always afraid of stepping on snakes when hunting."[23]

Later that winter, Casey admitted he had flirted with the idea of quitting baseball to go into business. "I've had several business offers," he said, "one from a rubber manufacturer and another from a southern oil company." But everything changed with the Japanese attack on Pearl Harbor on December 7. The U.S. entry into the war, which led to the rationing of tires and cars, and the closing of filling stations at night, convinced him that staying in baseball was the wiser choice. He had earned about $15,000 in 1941, including his World Series cut, and he expected to do even better in 1942.

12

A MEMORABLE NIGHT WITH ERNEST HEMINGWAY

When the United States entered the war in December 1941, the ramifications were quickly felt throughout the nation, including in baseball. On February 3, 1942, the owners held a special meeting, at which they decided to increase the number of night games from seven to 14 for each major-league club that played night games, with Washington allowed 21. In addition, because of the reintroduction of daylight saving time, a 12:50 a.m. curfew was set, an hour later than the previous curfew of 11:50 p.m.

That same week, on the day Leo Durocher signed to manage the Dodgers in 1942, he learned he had lost third baseman Cookie Lavagetto, who joined the Navy Air Corps.

Several of the game's biggest stars, including Cleveland's Bob Feller, Detroit's Hank Greenberg, and Washington's Cecil Travis, were already in the military. Teams with key players older than 30 years of age were less likely to be hurt by the military draft than younger teams. The Dodgers, with many of their best players in the over-30 category—Dixie Walker, Dolph Camilli, Billy Herman, and pitchers Fred Fitzsimmons and Whit Wyatt—figured to fare better than their chief rivals, the young Cardinals. The 28-year-old Casey, who was married, but childless, said he expected to be drafted before the start of the 1942 season. "I'll be glad to go if they want me," he said.[1]

Casey's draft status was 3-A (men with dependents, not engaged in work essential to national defense, available and fit for general military service), but that changed suddenly when Kathleen filed for divorce. On February 12, 1942, the *Washington Post* reported that Kathleen's lawyer, John R. Strother, had initiated the divorce action in Fulton County, Georgia, Superior Court. Among her allegations was that her husband had been constantly nagging her about separating until they finally did so on January 19. She also charged he had told her he did not love her.[2] The divorce would likely have shifted Casey's draft status to 1-A (available and fit for general military service) and make him likely for an early call. Although Hugh and Kathleen's marriage was marked by frequent breakups and reconciliations, there is no evidence the divorce was ever finalized.

In addition to his marital problems, Hugh's winter at Neptune Beach had been trying for another reason, a familiar one. He had gone there to lose weight, and although he missed his goal, his regimen apparently worked, and he later claimed to be down to 205 pounds, 15 pounds lighter than when he arrived.

Shortly after New Year's, the *Brooklyn Eagle* reported the Dodgers had sent copies of a nine-day reducing diet to several players. This included Casey; Joe Medwick; and newcomers Arky Vaughan, Don Padgett, and Johnny Rizzo. According to the *Eagle*, the players were told they would not be admitted to spring training unless they showed results. Padgett, acquired from the Cardinals, would serve in the military from 1942 to 1945. Rizzo, purchased from the Phillies, played in 78 games for the 1942 Dodgers, his last big-league season.

Casey attributed his weight loss primarily to diet. "I'm living on practically nothing but grapefruit juice and sunshine," he said. "By the time spring practice starts, I hope to scale no more than 195."[3]

Larry MacPhail, always seeking to improve his club, made a significant offseason addition in Vaughan, the National League's best shortstop for the past decade. In return, he sent Pittsburgh four veteran players who did not figure in the Dodgers' plans for 1942: pitcher Luke Hamlin, catcher Babe Phelps, second baseman Pete Coscarart, and outfielder-first baseman Jimmy Wasdell.

While the Dodgers planned to keep Pee Wee Reese at shortstop and use Vaughan at third base, they also had a backup plan. The 30-year-old Vaughan, who was married with children, would be the shortstop if the 22-year-old Reese went into the military. (During spring training at

Daytona Beach, Reese's draft status changed when he married his girl-friend, 19-year-old Dottie Walton.)

A few weeks after the issuance of the reducing diet, the *Eagle*'s Tommy Holmes reported neither Rizzo, whom he had never thought of as overweight, nor Padgett, whom he called "too large for a man and too small for a horse," had been heard from.[4]

On February 1, Casey attended the Baseball Writers' Association of America dinner at New York's Hotel Commodore, at East 42nd Street and Lexington Avenue. He came to New York to attend the dinner and also to demonstrate to MacPhail that he had stuck to his diet and lost some weight.

The crowds for spring training games in Havana had been disappointing in 1941, and were more so in 1942. The war had sharply curtailed tourism, and the city lacked the gayety and excitement that helped define the Cuban capital. Nevertheless, Durocher was happy to have the team return. He had been pleased with the facilities, the playing field at Tropical Stadium (La Tropical), and the warm weather.

Not all the players were as happy as Durocher to be returning to Havana. On February 18, when the Dodgers left Miami to fly to Havana, Kirby Higbe was one of several notable absences. "I just don't like the place," Higbe said. "Besides the food being terrible, the water is bad."[5] Also missing were holdouts Dixie Walker and Whit Wyatt.

Eventually, everyone arrived and, wrote Tommy Holmes, enjoyed a "simple and luxurious life" in Havana. On days when no game was scheduled, players practiced until 1:00 p.m., ate lunch in the clubhouse, and "were on their own for the rest of the day."[6] Some played golf at the Havana Country Club, while others returned to the hotel to play cards. Most evenings were spent enjoying soft drinks while watching a floor show in one of the hotel's nightclubs.

There was one added attraction for the Dodgers that spring. Ernest Hemingway, the most renowned American author, was living in Havana at the time while he reviewed the script for the film version of *For Whom the Bell Tolls*, published in 1940. Hemingway was a big baseball fan and enjoyed spending time with the Dodgers players. Several of them, including Casey, were gun enthusiasts, as was Hemingway. Billy Herman remembered the night when he, Casey, Larry French, and Augie Galan went to Finca Vigia, Hemingway's hilltop home, after an afternoon of shooting.

"He had a big, beautiful home," Herman told baseball historian Donald Honig, elaborating,

> He took us into a huge dining room–living room combination, with all terrazzo floors. . . . He came back with an enormous silver tray, with all the bottles, the mixers, the glasses, the ice—the whole works. . . . He gave us each an autographed copy of *For Whom the Bell Tolls*, his book about the Spanish Civil War. . . . We talked a lot about the war [i.e., World War II]. . . .
>
> Then out of a clear blue sky Hemingway looked over at Casey, sort of sizing him up. "You know, Hugh," he said, "you and I are about the same size. We'd make a good match. . . . Come on. I've got some boxing gloves. Let's just spar."
>
> As Hugh was pulling his gloves on, Hemingway suddenly hauled off and belted him. . . . He knocked Casey into that bookstand and there goes the tray with all the booze and glasses smashing over the terrazzo floor. . . . Hemingway didn't bother to pick up the tray or anything, and they were moving back and forth across the broken glass, and you could hear it cracking and crunching on that terrazzo floor whenever they stepped on it. . . . Then Casey belted him across some furniture, and there was another crash as Hemingway took a lamp and table down with him. . . .
>
> Hemingway's wife, journalist Martha Gellhorn, came into the room twice during the fight but was unable to get the two combatants to end it.
>
> Hemingway was getting sore. He'd no sooner get up than Hugh would put him down again. Finally he got up this one time, made a feint with his left hand, and kicked Casey in the balls. That's when we figured it had gone far enough.
>
> The fighters separated, but it was now late, and the players had to be back at the hotel by midnight. As they were leaving, Hemingway grabbed Casey and said, "You stay here. Spend the night. Tonight we're both drunk. But tomorrow morning we'll wake up, we'll both be sober. Then you and me will have a duel. We'll use swords, pistols, whatever you want. You pick it."

Herman thought Hemingway was sore that Casey had bested him. "He wanted to kill Casey," he said, but the players left, ending the incident.[7]

The morning after his brawl with Hemingway, Casey described to broadcaster Red Barber his version of the fight for public consumption:

Hemingway got us into his house, and right off he got out a set of boxing gloves. He insisted I put on the gloves and spar with him. I didn't want to box with him. After all, when I was a little younger I'd done some fighting.

But he wouldn't let me alone. Finally, I put on the gloves, and he said we'd just fool around. Before I knew it he was belting me as hard as he could. I told him to cut it out. He hit me harder than ever. So I just knocked him down . . . and that ended the boxing for the night.[8]

After a few weeks, the players were anxious to leave Cuba, where they felt isolated from the rest of the baseball world, and get back to their training camp at Daytona Beach. But while waiting to board the boat that would take them home, there was an incident that almost prevented their return.

Shortly after a group of players, including Casey, started a poker game, a man with a gun confronted them. The players did not take it seriously until Augie Galan realized the man was a police officer and was about to arrest them for gambling. Galan said he was through playing, but Johnny Rizzo urged they play one more hand. Casey just stared straight ahead, in disbelief anyone in Havana could be arrested for gambling. But the plainclothes officer did arrest Rizzo and Casey, angering Hugh further when he attempted to handcuff him. The two were placed in a locked room, and a police car was summoned. The players, realizing this was a serious situation, telephoned Colonel Jaime Marine, the Cuban minister who had been looking after them. Colonel Marine hurried to the pier and successfully resolved the situation.[9]

In January 1942, a month after the attack on Pearl Harbor, Commissioner Landis had written to President Roosevelt asking for guidance on how, or if, baseball should operate in 1942. Roosevelt answered on January 15, with his famous "green light" letter, saying it would benefit the country to keep baseball going. So, for the first time in 24 years, the baseball season opened with the United States at war.

The president had tried to rally the American people, predicting the country would win the war within two or three years. But the news remained grim, especially in the Pacific, where the Japanese had captured the island of Bataan and were continuing their relentless assault on the island of Corregidor.

Back home, baseball carried on. The Dodgers, behind Curt Davis, won their opener and took two-of-three from the Giants, now managed by Mel Ott. Casey appeared in two of the games, pitching a combined three scoreless innings and picking up a save. He made his first start of the season two days later, against the 0–4 Phillies. He pitched well enough to win, allowing only two runs on solo home runs by Nick Etten and Ron Northey. But his teammates mustered just four hits against Rube Melton in Philadelphia's 2–1 victory.

It was not until the ninth game of the season that Whit Wyatt, the team's ace, had sufficiently recovered from his cold and was able to make a start, dueling Boston's Jim Tobin for nine scoreless innings. Durocher replaced Wyatt with Casey, who kept the Braves hitless and scoreless for three more innings and picked up his first win when Brooklyn scored four runs against Tobin in the 12th. Casey came back the next day to save a 9–5 win for Newt Kimball by retiring Boston's final seven batters. The win, Brooklyn's fifth straight, raised their record to 8–2.

Newspapers in New York were now using the word *fireman* regularly when discussing Casey. "Whenever the Dodgers are in pitching trouble," declared the *Brooklyn Eagle*, "manager Leo Durocher knows the answer. He puts in a hurry call for Hugh Casey. The Brooklyn 'fireman' started one game and relieved in four since the start of the season." The paper noted that Casey had yet to allow a run in his four relief appearances. [10]

The Dodgers opened their first western trip in Cincinnati on April 28. Camilli's first-inning home run gave them a 2–0 lead. In the bottom of the first, Wyatt had grabbed his arm in pain while pitching to Bert Haas but assured Durocher he was okay. Leo allowed Wyatt to continue, and two batters later he allowed a bases-loaded double to Frank McCormick that put the Reds in front, 3–2.

Wyatt finished the inning, but Durocher had Lew Riggs bat for him in the top of the second. Riggs doubled to drive in two runs and later scored, putting Brooklyn ahead, 5–3. Casey replaced Wyatt in the home second and shut out the Reds for the next eight innings in Brooklyn's 7–3 victory. He allowed just five hits, but each one led off an inning. He also walked a leadoff batter in one inning. Yet, despite Cincinnati's leadoff batter getting on against Casey in six of the eight innings, he kept each of them from scoring. "What a man," Wyatt said about his friend. "Old Hughey just isn't at home unless he's pitching with some-body on base."[11]

Because the Dodgers and Cardinals were expected to stage another season-long battle for the pennant, a special sense of anticipation at-tended their first series of the season. The May 3 doubleheader at Sportsman's Park saw the Cardinals win both games. Reminiscent of the Brooklyn–St. Louis battles of 1941, umpires ejected three men in each game. In the first game, umpire Ziggy Sears ejected managers Durocher and Billy Southworth, and pitcher Fred Fitzsimmons. In the second game, umpire Tom Dunn ejected Camilli, Wyatt, and rookie Dodgers pitcher Chet Kehn.

Casey picked up three saves in May, including the game of May 8. That evening, the Giants made their first appearance at Ebbets Field for a twilight game to benefit the Navy Relief Fund. He pitched the final two-and-a-third innings of a 7–6 victory, preserving Wyatt's first win of the season.

More than 42,000 tickets were sold, although many fans bought tickets with no plans to attend. The actual crowd was listed at 34,000, the park's official capacity. Everyone had to pay their way into the park, including Mayor La Guardia, borough president John Cashmore, many top-ranking navy officials, the ballplayers, the umpires, league officials, and even the ushers.

Almost $60,000 was raised for the Navy Relief Fund. The idea had been MacPhail's, and he was both emotional and ecstatic at the way Brooklynites had responded. "Do y'know that we've got 8,000 tickets all paid for that I dumped back in the box?" he asked. "Tickets that people bought just to contribute and then turned back to us."[12]

Players from all cities were now aiding the war effort, helping with blood drives and in any way they could. On May 11, an offday, Casey did his part for the War Bond Drive. He spoke to and signed auto-graphs for workers at Brooklyn's Robins Dry Dock and Repair Compa-ny.

Casey got saves six and seven as the Dodgers were winning four of five in Chicago, during the first week of June. After sweeping a double-header against the Cubs on June 7, the Dodgers, at 37–14, were 23 games above .500 and seven games ahead of the second-place Cardi-nals.

Late in the spring, a minor eruption among Brooklyn fans followed the publication of an article called "Bull Pen," written by veteran sportswriter Frank Graham. Writing in the *Saturday Evening Post*, Graham recalled some of baseball's great relief pitchers and performances.

"How can any story about relief pitchers ignore Dodger Hugh Casey?" asked Harold Parrott in his *Eagle* column. Among those Graham had mentioned were Grover Alexander, Wilcy Moore, Fred Marberry, and Johnny Murphy. But there was no mention of Casey. "Casey's always ready," Parrott wrote. "He was in in both ballgames of Sunday's doubleheader in Chicago. . . . He'll probably be 'heated up' tonight if things go wrong in St. Louis." [13]

Parrott acknowledged that while the Yankees' Murphy was currently the game's most famous reliever, Casey was its most active. "He was in four of those five games in Chicago," agreed Durocher. "What does a guy have to do to get a bit of credit around here!" [14]

St. Louis had cut Brooklyn's lead to four and a half games when they opened a five-game series at Ebbets Field on June 18. They left trailing by seven and a half games after the Dodgers won four of the five, including a 10–4 victory on June 20. Joe Medwick, the National League's leading hitter (.350), had four hits to stretch his consecutive hit streak to 23 games.

Casey, who relieved starter Curt Davis in the third inning, allowed just two hits in winning his third game of the season. The Cardinals' only win of the series came on Mort Cooper's 11–0 shutout. It was Cooper's second shutout against Brooklyn. On May 20, he had outdueled Wyatt, 1–0, at Ebbets Field in the first meeting between the archrivals.

The May 20 game had been a turning point for the Cardinals, who were 17–15 at the time. They had played sloppily in the early going and "lacked the proper mental attitude," according to manager Southworth. "I'm cracking down on everybody, myself included," Southworth said. "We're not going all-out, but we will from now on, I assure you. You'll see a change in this ballclub." [15]

It had become the norm for any series between the Dodgers and Cardinals (or Dodgers and Cubs) to involve "dusters," hard slides, and vicious bench jockeying, which most often led to vocal and physical confrontations. This series was no different.

In the sixth inning of the June 18 game, Joe Medwick, who had walked, tried to take second on a pitch that got away from catcher Walker Cooper. But Cooper quickly recovered the ball and threw to shortstop Marty Marion to retire Medwick, who had slid in with his spikes high. Marion took exception to the slide, and he and Medwick prepared to settle the dispute with their fists. Cardinals second baseman Frank Crespi came between them, and soon he and Medwick were wrestling on the ground.

Dolph Camilli, the batter, raced out and jumped on Crespi, and Dixie Walker followed. Players from both teams joined in, initiating a full-scale melee around second base. Umpire Babe Pinelli ejected Crespi and Medwick, and the Dodgers also lost Walker, who had injured a leg in the brawl. Walker also suffered the indignity of being punched in the jaw by an unidentified Cardinals player.

Max Lanier, who was on the mound, told author Donald Honig he remembered Walker running right past him and diving at third baseman Whitey Kurowski. Kurowski and second baseman Jimmy Brown went after Walker, and soon players from both sides were rolling in the grass.[16]

Marty Marion later recalled the rivalry between the two teams and his personal rivalry with Pee Wee Reese (both men had come to the majors in 1940). Said Marion, "In those days it seems we were always battling the Dodgers for the pennant, and people were always comparing me with Reese. The Dodgers were our enemies. We hated them and they hated us, but it was nothing personal. It was just that we were fighting for the same prize."[17]

13

BECOMING A FULL-TIME RELIEF PITCHER

Leo Durocher had employed Casey in a dual role during his first three seasons, using him as a starter 53 times and a reliever 76 times. But his transition to a full-time reliever had begun in the second half of the 1941 season, when only two of his final 23 appearances were as a starter.

"Given his limited repertoire," Leo said, "I had done something with him that was unique at that time. I had assigned him the job of late-inning relief pitcher, the guy who came in over the last few innings to choke off a rally."[1]

Once he became a full-time reliever, the label "Fireman Casey" would be ascribed to him on a regular basis. The first mention of "Fireman Casey" had come from Roscoe McGowen in the June 16, 1939, *New York Times*. Casey had relieved Luke Hamlin in the fourth inning after St. Louis had scored two runs to tie the score at 3–3. "At this point," wrote McGowen, "Fireman Casey came in to put out the blaze by retiring the next three men."[2]

In 1942, Durocher had started him against the Phillies on April 18, a game in which Casey had pitched well but lost. He did not make another start until June 30, at home against Boston. He left after pitching four innings with the score tied, 3–3. It was to be his last start of the season and second-to-last start of his major league career.

After the 4–3 loss to the Braves, the Dodgers embarked on a 21-game road trip. They won 14 of 21, returning home with a record of 62–27 and a six-and-a-half-game lead over St. Louis. The trip was both

Figure 13.1.   Fireman Casey appeared in a career-high 50 games in 1942, and led the National League with 13 saves. *National Baseball Hall of Fame Library, Cooperstown, NY.*

successful and eventful. On July 11, at Cincinnati, Casey was the winner in a 3–2, 15-inning marathon that allowed the Dodgers to sweep a doubleheader. He was Brooklyn's fifth pitcher of the game, holding the Reds scoreless from the 11th through 15th innings.

The Dodgers moved on to Chicago, where their longtime feud with the Cubs erupted again on July 15. Kirby Higbe had a 5–0 lead in the fourth inning when he allowed home runs to Lou Novikoff and Jimmie Foxx. (The Cubs had purchased Foxx, the longtime American League slugger, on waivers from the Boston Red Sox on June 1.) The next batter was slugger Bill Nicholson. As Nicholson stepped in to hit, Durocher visited the mound, ostensibly to settle down his pitcher. Yet, he was barely back in the dugout when Higbe's first pitch went behind Nicholson's back.

The Cubs were aware that a pitch like that following two home runs was no accident and retaliated when the Dodgers batted in the fifth inning. Hi Bithorn knocked down Higbe, and Paul Erickson, in relief of Bithorn, knocked down Joe Medwick. As Bithorn was leaving after being relieved, he fired a ball into the Dodgers dugout. His target was Durocher, who had been riding him during his stint on the mound, but Mickey Owen stepped in front of his manager and deflected the ball. (National League president Ford Frick fined Bithorn $25 for throwing the ball at Durocher.) The Cubs rallied in the eighth, driving Higbe out, but Casey came to the rescue, preserving the 10–5 victory and earning his ninth save.

The next day he helped the Dodgers gain a split after Cubs lefthander Johnny Schmitz had shut them out in the first game. Casey picked up his 10th save in Brooklyn's 2–1 win with three scoreless innings in relief of Johnny Allen.

Under Durocher's leadership, the Dodgers had gained a well-earned reputation as bullies. He often instructed his pitchers to throw at opposing batters, making the Dodgers the most hated team in the league. In 1942 alone, six of the seven other teams complained about beanballs from Brooklyn pitchers.

Leo had been viewed as an aggressive agitator ever since he was a rookie with the 1928 Yankees. During World War II, when Casey was stationed at the Norfolk Naval Air Station, he was asked to comment on Durocher's loud and boisterous arguments with umpires. Leo was not Lippy, claimed Casey, defending his manager. "He just has one of those voices that carries well."[3]

The poorer clubs, in particular, resented Brooklyn pitchers knocking down their hitters, a move that struck Boston Braves manager Casey Stengel as counterproductive. After an August game against the Dodgers, in which beanballs had been thrown by both clubs, Stengel expressed surprise that Durocher would engage in such tactics.

"If I had a ballclub as good as Durocher's," he said, "I wouldn't throw at a ballclub as bad as mine. We're going to battle these guys all the harder from now on. I've talked to [Pirates manager Frankie] Frisch, [Cubs manager Jimmie] Wilson, and other managers who feel the same." Stengel also challenged the prevailing wisdom that the race was over. "Sure, they've got a big lead, but they're not in yet. In case you guys didn't notice it," he declared, "St. Louis is winning steadily."[4]

Stengel was particularly impressed with the Cardinals' speed, calling them a "track team that ran like uncaged rabbits."[5] Willard Mullin, cartoonist for the *New York World-Telegram*, had nicknamed them the "St. Louis Swifties." In 1937, Mullin had created the "Brooklyn Bum" cartoon, which came to personify the Dodgers.

The Cardinals' speed was "reflected more in how many bases they took audaciously rather than in stolen bases," wrote St. Louis baseball historian Bob Broeg.[6]

"Too much energy, entirely too much," complained Cubs manager Wilson. "No team can keep charging around a park the way they do and stay in one piece. The Cardinals knock you out of the way just for fun."[7]

Circumstances would soon change dramatically, but as of mid-July the National League pennant race was not as tight as it had been in 1941. Casey had been a major contributor to Brooklyn establishing its comfortable lead. Durocher, who had claimed the Dodgers could not have won in 1941 without Casey, could say the same about 1942, said Tommy Holmes, who commented, "[W]ith his fastball, his sinker and his curve, his control, his cold nerve, and his ever-ready arm, [Casey] is the best relief pitcher in the National League."[8]

So far, Holmes wrote, Casey had appeared in relief in 26 games, almost a third of the team's games played. His stints ranged from a third of an inning to eight full frames. Holmes went on to suggest a method of judging relief pitchers that would eventually come to pass—27 years later.

Acknowledging Casey's record of 4–2 was unspectacular, he said, "But a won and lost record is inadequate as a yardstick on a crack relief pitcher. Perhaps there should be some column in the big-league statistics labeled games saved."

After Chicago, the Dodgers, leading by eight games, went to St. Louis, where they would play back-to-back doubleheaders—on July 18 and 19—against the second-place Cardinals. The teams split the first pair, with Larry French—purchased from the Cubs in late August 1941—losing the first game, his first loss after opening the season with 10 straight wins. (He would finish the season 15–4, with a 1.83 earned run average.)

The bigger loss came after Casey relieved him in the sixth inning. The third batter he faced, Stan Musial, lined a ball back at Hugh that tore off the nail of the pinky finger on his pitching hand. When the Cardinals won both games the next day, Brooklyn's lead was down to six games.

While losing the opener on July 19, Les Webber, in relief of starter Whit Wyatt, brushed back Musial, who let the pitcher know he was peeved. Webber's response was to throw the next pitch behind Musial's head. The usually placid Musial headed to the mound, bat in hand, as players gathered round. Nothing happened, but Webber also had his own little war with winning pitcher Mort Cooper. Cooper hit Webber with a pitch, while Webber threw two pitches at Cooper's head.

The second game saw a key Dodger injured for the second day in a row. With the score tied, 6–6, in the 11th inning, Enos Slaughter led off the home half with a long drive off Johnny Allen to deep center field. Pete Reiser ran it down and caught it just as he crashed into the concrete wall, but the impact jarred the ball loose. Reiser retrieved it and started a relay home, but Slaughter slid in safely with a game-winning inside-the-park home run.

"It might have been the greatest catch I've ever seen," said left fielder Medwick. "I'll swear that Slaughter hit that ball beyond Reiser and that Pete overtook it. He was traveling like a bullet when he hit the fence."[9]

No stretcher was called this time, as Dodgers players guided a wobbly Reiser off the field. An ambulance took him to St. Louis's St. Johns Hospital. Dr. Robert F. Hyland, the Cardinals team physician, said Reiser had suffered a slight brain concussion and suggested he remain in the hospital until he recovered fully. Meanwhile, despite being ordered to rest, Reiser worked out in practice, much to the delight of Durocher and the dismay of Larry MacPhail.

Years later, Reiser spoke about Durocher playing him after his injury in July 1942:

> I have never, ever blamed Leo for keeping me in there. I blame myself. He wanted to win so badly it hurt, and I wanted to win so bad it hurt. I've heard a lot of guys knock Leo for all sorts of things, but I've always said this about him: If you don't know him, you hate his guts, but if you do know him, you love him. He was the best. He was aggressive, and he always fought for you. Always.[10]

An x-ray showed Casey, too, was injured more seriously than initially believed. He had fractured the little finger of his pitching hand. Dr. Hyland put a cast on the finger, and as the Dodgers traveled to Pittsburgh, Casey returned to Brooklyn. Dr. Hyland predicted Casey would be out from 10 days to two weeks, but it turned out to be close to three weeks.

Five years after it happened, Casey still talked about the "drive from Stan Musial's bat, which broke my pitching hand in four places, in the stretch drive of 1942. But for that accident we might have won another pennant."[11]

"An ironic twist to the present situation is that the absence of Hugh Casey . . . was needed to emphasize just how much that big moon-faced Georgian meant to the team with his consistently good relief performances," wrote Holmes.[12]

Casey's absence had affected the Dodgers pitching strategy more than the loss of a starter would have. They had no one to fill his role, although Durocher planned to try Curt Davis as his late-inning stopper. That would take Davis out of his regular turn in the rotation and necessitate other adjustments. As it developed, second-year man Ed Head would mostly fill Casey's former role in his absence.

Casey had been running to keep his legs in shape but had to give that up because the "jar of his beefy body pounding the turf" was enough to open the wound. During his absence, he lamented the lack of telephones in bullpens and suggested all big-league owners install them. Said Hugh,

Now you take a phone. Why don't they have a phone so they can tell us what's going on? Sometimes we can guess. We see a pitcher in a jam. And Chuck Dressen signals for one of us to warm up. Wagging his left hand means French; and right hand over head means somebody else; and side arm means me.

But the other night in Cincy I'd been told to warm up lightly in the eighth just in case Whit Wyatt weakened. Well, I didn't see him toss the ball in the dugout, and I didn't know what was going on when Leo started arguing with the umps. I thought he was stalling for time so I could get warmed up enough. So I pitched like all-get-out to find they didn't want me. All that work was for nothing.

Of course, I wouldn't mind except at night when you get all warmed up and then sit down your arm stiffens up, and you might not be able to loosen up in time if they need you later.[13]

On August 1, the Dodgers defeated the Cubs, while the Cardinals were splitting a doubleheader with the Giants. The Dodgers (71–29) now had a nine-game lead over the Cardinals (61–37). The lead reached 10 games on August 4, but from August 11 to 17, the Cardinals took three out of four from Chicago and four straight from Cincinnati. Although the Dodgers won a game from the Phillies and three of four from Boston, their lead was down to seven and a half games.

When Casey returned from his three-week absence, on August 6, Durocher inserted him to pitch the final inning of an 8–0 loss at the Polo Grounds as a quick tune-up. He returned to serious action the next day, at home against Boston. Casey came on in the eighth inning with Brooklyn trailing, 1–0, and pitched four excellent innings. He allowed just two hits, but one was a two-out, 11th-inning triple to Nanny Fernandez. Max West followed with a routine ground ball to short that should have been the third out. But Pee Wee Reese bobbled the ball, as Fernandez scored the eventual winning run.

"There is nothing wrong with the Dodgers that a few base hits wouldn't cure," Durocher said as he patted the head of Trusty, Casey's English setter, in the clubhouse before the August 19 game against Boston.[14] The club had lost two straight, to the Braves and Phillies, scoring a combined one run against Al Javery and Rube Melton. That afternoon, the Dodgers had 19 hits, crushing Boston, 11–1, as everyone in the lineup had at least one hit.

A four-game sweep of the Giants at Ebbets Field had Brooklyn seven and a half games ahead of St. Louis on August 24, as they began their last visit to Sportsman's Park. The series against New York had been testy, particularly Brooklyn's 10–5 win on August 22. The sixth inning alone came close to having two brawls: one between Dixie Walker and Mel Ott, and one between Joe Medwick and Bill Werber.

Many of the Dodgers already disliked Werber from previous encounters with him when he was with Cincinnati. When he got into it with Medwick, even easygoing Whit Wyatt came out to say a few words to him.

Higbe had started for Brooklyn that afternoon but was ineffective, leading Durocher to bring in Casey in the second inning. That was much earlier than Casey was used to seeing action, but he pitched the remaining six and two-thirds innings to gain his fifth win. (Umpires called the game because of rain with two out in the Giants eighth.)

In the series at St. Louis, Max Lanier, Mort Cooper, and Johnny Beazley allowed the Dodgers one run each in the first three games. Cooper's win was in 14 innings and Beazley's in 10. Curt Davis won the final game for Brooklyn. The lead was now five and a half games, and by the end of the month it was down to three and a half. The Dodgers had won 18 of 29 in August, but the Cardinals had been playing at a phenomenal pace, winning 25 of 33. MacPhail was not surprised by how close the race had become. He had warned about it, he said, but no one would listen.

"I didn't like the attitude of the team when I held that meeting a couple of weeks ago. They were blowing games they should have won because they were overconfident, and they should have known they were due for trouble later on. Guess that meeting I called didn't do any good," he continued. "Dixie Walker offered to bet that they'd win by the eight games; that was their lead then. I'm not singling out Walker but just emphasizing the fact that this was the spirit of the whole club." [15]

"It was in August," Walker later recalled, "and MacPhail came into a club meeting at Ebbets Field. We were nine games in front. Larry said, 'Men, you are going to lose this pennant just as sure as I stand before you.'" [16]

Walker offered to bet MacPhail $100 that the Dodgers would not only win the pennant, but also keep their present lead. Walker said his purpose was to get the players fired up, but MacPhail thought he was just being cocky and overconfident.

"I'll bet $100 you ought to win it by 20 games," was MacPhail's response. "Here's a club that has been in a slump and nobody worries about it except me. An eight-game lead in the middle of August isn't anything to sleep on. Leads like that have been lost."[17]

MacPhail made a move to strengthen his pitching staff for the stretch drive by purchasing veteran Bobo Newsom from the Senators. "Congratulations on buying the pennant," Newsom telegraphed Durocher when he heard the news. "Will report tomorrow in fine shape, rarin' to go."[18] But after shutting out the Reds in his first start as a Dodger, Newsom lost two of his next three decisions.

The lead was two games when St. Louis and Brooklyn met for the final time of the season, September 11 and 12, at Ebbets Field. Complete-game wins by Mort Cooper (3–0) and Max Lanier (2–1)—for each his fifth win of the season against Brooklyn—left the teams with identical 94–46 records.

"I think we're in," said Cardinals owner Sam Breadon, as he ordered his people to start preparing for the World Series. "We've won 29 out of 34, and those fellows have lost six of their last nine." Yet, neither Durocher nor MacPhail seemed outwardly discouraged. "All right, they caught up," Durocher said. "It took them five months to do it. Let's snap out of it and get after them now." MacPhail told his players he felt better than he had in a couple of days. "They're even with us, and I know you can win," he said. "Something's going to happen soon—a break that will start our rally."[19]

It had become a 14-game season. The Dodgers won 10, to finish with 104 wins, but the Cardinals won 12, to capture the pennant by two games. The 104 wins made the Dodgers the first National League team to have back-to-back 100-win seasons since the 1912–1913 New York Giants. They also tied the 1909 Chicago Cubs for the most wins by a second-place team. In the final four games, Casey added his 12th and (league-leading) 13th saves.

"You've got to give the Cardinals credit for a drive like that," Dixie Walker said. "There isn't anything you can take away from a bunch that can come far from behind when they should have known they were beaten. Remember—they won it. We didn't lose it."[20] Indeed they had, winning 43 of their final 51 games.

In April 1943, columnist Shirley Povich of the *Washington Post* asked Casey about the Dodgers' 1942 "collapse." Casey admitted there had been dissension. "There were fellows on the team that some of the guys didn't like," he said, without naming names. "MacPhail was right about some of the players loafing. We should have breezed in ahead of the Cardinals, but we tossed the pennant away."[21]

Brooklyn had spent 148 days in first place and St. Louis just 16. The Dodgers may not have won the pennant, but they did lead in bringing fans to the park. MacPhail's office announced that the paid home and road attendance of the Brooklyn club exceeded 2 million in both 1941 and 1942. That constituted approximately 45 percent of the total attendance of the National League.

In 1942, the Brooklyn club—at home and on the road—contributed more than 42 percent of the National League total and more than 20 percent of the entire amount raised by both leagues in relief games played for the war effort.[22]

Casey had picked up his final win of the season on September 19, a 5–4, 11-inning win against Philadelphia. The win, which cut Brooklyn's deficit to two and a half games, was won in a strange way. Reese had led off the 11th with a walk against Si Johnson. Billy Herman sacrificed him to second. Casey was to be the next batter, but with the winning run sitting on second base, everyone in the crowd expected to see a pinch-hitter. Instead, Durocher allowed Casey to bat, and he popped out to second base for the second out. Johnson then made Durocher's unorthodox move an afterthought when he walked the next three batters—Walker, Arky Vaughan, and Reiser—to force in the winning run.

Appearing in 50 games, all but two in relief, Casey led the league with 13 saves. Ten had come before his injury, along with a 1.80 earned run average. After he returned, he had three saves and a 3.25 ERA.

14

YOU'RE IN THE NAVY NOW

A month after the 1942 season ended, the *Brooklyn Eagle* reported that Casey, who was due to be drafted shortly after New Year's, might avoid the draft by joining the U.S. Coast Guard.[1] Casey seemingly confirmed the report when he announced in early January 1943 that he would soon report for active duty with the Coast Guard. As part of his announcement, Casey said he hoped to resume his baseball career after the war. "I am definitely not quitting the Dodgers," he related.[2]

But on January 30, Casey and Dodgers teammate Pee Wee Reese announced they had joined the U.S. Navy. Casey enlisted in Atlanta and was ordered to report to the navy's training station in Norfolk, Virginia. Reese enlisted in Louisville after gaining permission from his draft board in Brooklyn, which a few days earlier had ordered him to take his army physical.

The enlistments raised the number of players from the Brooklyn organization who were in the service to 16. "It looks that we are going to lose every man we thought we might lose," said new team president Branch Rickey.[3] The builder of the St. Louis Cardinals farm system had come to Brooklyn to replace Larry MacPhail, who had left to join the army.

The 1943 baseball season would feel the full impact of the war. Some of the game's greatest players, including Joe DiMaggio, Ted Williams, Johnny Mize, Pete Reiser, and Enos Slaughter, were now serving in the military, joining Bob Feller and Hank Greenberg, who were already serving.

Structurally, too, the game had changed to accommodate the wartime restrictions on travel. At the December 1942 Winter Meetings in Chicago, the owners had agreed to start the season a week later than usual and reduce from the customary four to three the number of series each club would play at the home parks of other clubs.

In addition, a compromise between Commissioner Kenesaw Landis and Joseph B. Eastman, director of the federal Office of Defense Transportation, limited spring training to locations north of the Potomac or Ohio rivers and east of the Mississippi River. St. Louis was the only major-league city west of the Mississippi River; however, the St. Louis Browns were allowed to train in Cape Girardeau, Missouri, 115 miles southeast of St. Louis and just west of the Mississippi River. The St. Louis Cardinals trained in Cairo, Illinois, east of the river.

The Dodgers chose Bear Mountain for their training camp. Located on the west bank of the Hudson River in frosty upstate New York, the site was seven miles south of the United States Military Academy at West Point, whose facilities they would use.

As did the managers of all teams, Leo Durocher had many holes to fill. Prominent among them was finding a reliable relief pitcher to replace Casey. One chilly mid-March afternoon, following a workout at the West Point Field House, Durocher announced he had found his man. "Les Webber will be the Dodgers' number-one relief pitcher this year. He keeps that ball down, and he throws a downer," Leo said, explaining why Webber would be a good reliever.[4]

"Well, Casey's shoes are going to be big to fill," said catcher Mickey Owen. "Webber could do it, but he might be one of our best starters . . . Casey's loss is a big one. Seldom do you see two kinds of fastball, like Casey threw; one jumped off to the side, the other fell away. Then his curve wasn't a big one, but it was a puzzler," Owen said, obviously speaking from experience. "Big thing was, however, that even when you knew Hughey's [sic] fastball was coming, you couldn't tell which one it was, how it would act."[5]

After the Dodgers wrapped up their stay at Bear Mountain with a 12–8 victory over the Army Cadets, Durocher pronounced their spring efforts a success. The club was in "as good condition as we would have been this long before Opening Day even if we had trained in Florida," Leo said. He was uncertain how strong his club would be but said the losses of Casey, Reese, Reiser, and Larry French would be difficult to overcome. Durocher also hedged some in declaring Webber the lone replacement for Casey. "For relief pitching, to replace Casey," he said, "I'm planning to use three men—Les Webber, Curt Davis, and [Bobo] Newsom."[6] (In the end it most often would be Webber, with a team-leading 54 appearances and a league-leading 10 saves.)

Casey began his navy career serving as a physical fitness trainer at the Norfolk Naval Training Station, which also happened to have an exceptionally strong baseball team—so strong, reported Shirley Povich of the *Washington Post*, they were comfortable sending Casey and Reese to the Norfolk Naval Air Station, managed by Homer Peel, a onetime National League outfielder.[7]

Eddie Robinson, who had played briefly with Cleveland in 1942, and had a long postwar career in the big leagues, wrote in his autobiography about the powerful Norfolk NTS team. The commanding officer was Captain H. A. McClure, who "wanted to have the best baseball and basketball teams in the navy."[8] The baseball coach was a chief warrant officer named Gary Bodie, and whatever he asked for his team, McClure would provide. Robinson remembered that getting rid of Casey and Reese suggested he was not a great judge of talent.

On April 4, Casey made his first appearance for Norfolk NAS in a start against the Washington Senators. It was an unimpressive debut, as the Senators pounded him for five runs in two innings. The Norfolk NAS team had just a few major leaguers, so while manager Peel had the game's best relief pitcher in Casey, schedules and conditions were such that he was forced to use him primarily as a starter.

In a game to benefit the War Bond Drive on April 26, Casey pitched a 4–0 no-hitter for the Norfolk NAS against the powerful Norfolk NTS, ending their 15-game winning streak. Phil Rizzuto, former New York Yankees shortstop, who NTS had kept rather than Reese, went hitless for the first time that season. The crowd of more than 5,000 at Norfolk's High Rock Park purchased almost $100,000 in war bonds.[9]

Casey faced the Norfolk NTS again on May 13. He pitched another strong game but walked in the winning run in the 11th inning to give NTS a 2–1 win. It was his only walk of the game, and it went to Eddie Robinson. The win raised the NTS juggernaut's record to 24–2.

In a game at Chapel Hill, North Carolina, on May 30, Casey held the Navy Pre-Flight Cloudbusters to no runs and three hits for the first seven innings. But an error in the eighth, followed by Johnny Pesky's single, Buddy Hassett's triple, and Ted Williams's single gave the Cloudbusters three runs and a 3–1 win. Joe Coleman, formerly of the Philadelphia Athletics, went the distance for the Cloudbusters. [10]

Meanwhile, in Brooklyn, the Dodgers, with only two players younger than 30 in their starting lineup, led the league from Opening Day until June 5, when they were passed by the Cardinals. By mid-July, Rickey, as he had done before and would do again, started unloading his veterans. He sold Joe Medwick to the Giants; traded Dolph Camilli and Johnny Allen, also to the Giants; traded Bobo Newsom to the St. Louis Browns; and released Fred Fitzsimmons.

Rickey would trade away several of his star veteran players during his years in Brooklyn, but Camilli was the first and the fans were irate. They were upset to see the slugging first baseman leave Brooklyn, and his going to the hated Giants only added to their sense of betrayal. Rather than report to the Giants, Camilli spent the rest of the season on his cattle ranch in California.

Years later, Rickey gave the reason for the trade, saying, "Failure to pull the ball to his own field with customary power is the first sign a player is slipping. It shows his reflexes are beginning to get dull. Camilli wasn't pulling the ball." [11]

In 1984, when Camilli was voted into the Brooklyn Dodgers Hall of Fame, he said, "I only wish I could receive the Dodgers' fans Hall of Fame plaque in front of those great fans who supported me during my stay in Brooklyn. All they cared about was their family, their job, and the Dodgers. And I don't know which was the most important." [12]

The Cardinals would romp their way to the pennant in 1943, but back in early July, when it was still a race, Chief Boatswain's Mate Casey, navy lieutenant Larry French, and army lieutenant Fred Frankhouse, who pitched for Brooklyn in the late 1930s, had visited Ebbets Field, where the Dodgers were playing the Cubs. They were there to cheer on their former teammates, who at the time were viable pennant contenders.

Casey confessed he was in Brooklyn on a mission. "My commanding officer told me not to go back to Norfolk unless I got the Brooklyn club to go down there later on for an exhibition game," he said. "And, incidentally, that's one game I want to pitch." He claimed he was in the best pitching condition of his life and added that Reese was a bigger and better shortstop than ever. [13]

While in New York, Casey became tangentially entangled in a near-mutiny by the Dodgers against their manager. It started after the Dodgers' 8–7 win over the Pirates on July 9. The Pirates scored two runs against Bobo Newsom in the third inning, only one of which was earned. The other came after Newsom struck out Elbie Fletcher with the bases loaded, but the ball got away from catcher Bobby Bragan. The Dodgers had obtained Bragan in a spring-training trade with the Phillies, where he had spent three seasons, primarily as a shortstop.

Durocher thought that Newsom's pitch was a spitball that had crossed up the inexperienced young catcher, and after the game he chastised Newsom for his actions. The argument ended with Durocher suspending his pitcher for three games. "A pitcher's hand gets wet from perspiration," Newsom said later, a polite way of saying the pitch had indeed been a spitter. [14]

As one anonymous Dodgers pitcher put it, "If you do not think that was a spitball Newsom threw to Bragan which caused all that trouble, and if you do not think that was a Hugh Casey spitball which got away from Mickey Owen for that third strike error in the 1941 Series, you are crazy." [15]

Durocher had told Tim Cohane, a reporter for the *New York World-Telegram*, about Newsom's suspension; however, he denied saying the suspension was because Newsom "tried to show Bobby Bragan up for missing a third-strike pitch to Elbie Fletcher." But Cohane said he had heard Durocher, while telling Hugh Casey about the incident, say, "[H]e was just trying to show the kid up." Cohane said Durocher then turned to him and said, "And I have suspended him for the season, if I can make it stick, and you can print that. Check with Branch Rickey." [16]

At a meeting of the players and reporters covering the team, Durocher admitted he had made a mistake in not telling Cohane the real reason for the suspension, which was insubordination during a late-inning argument about how Newsom should pitch to Vince DiMaggio.

"There is a feeling among the players that this is not the end of the affair," wrote Arthur E. Patterson of the *New York Herald Tribune*. Patterson believed Durocher had lost the loyalty of some of the veteran Dodgers and would be fired unless he could turn the discord on the team into harmony. He was accused of second-guessing his pitchers and accusing Joe Medwick of loafing. [17]

The players, especially Arky Vaughan, were upset with their manager. Billy Herman described what happened in the Dodgers locker room during pregame practice the next day. When Durocher admitted he had lied about the reason for the suspension, Vaughan went to his locker and removed his uniform, balled it up, and went back into Durocher's office.

"Take this uniform and shove it right up your ass," he said, and he threw it in Leo's face. "If you would lie about Bobo you would lie about me and everybody else. I'm not playing for you."[18]

Durocher tried to explain his position to the rest of the players, but Dixie Walker, the acknowledged leader of the team, sided with his teammate Vaughan against his manager. "I don't see why this boy should suffer, and if he's out, I guess I'm out too," said Dixie.[19]

Durocher was now faced with a full-blown strike; only pitcher Curt Davis and catcher Bobby Bragan had agreed to take the field for the July 10 game against the Pirates. To make a bad situation even worse, it was Kitchen Fat Day at Ebbets Field. In addition to the 8,748 paying customers, there were more than 4,000 women who had been granted free admission for bringing a pound or more of household fats to the park. Also in the crowd were 930 servicemen and 441 blood donors. Ballplayers striking in the middle of a war would have been a public relations nightmare for the Brooklyn club.

Finally, Branch Rickey intervened and settled the dispute. Durocher agreed to take no disciplinary action against Vaughan, and the players agreed to call off their strike. Casey was also on hand and helped convince the players to take the field. The Dodgers proceeded to take out their anger and frustration on the Pirates, scoring 10 runs in the first inning and 10 more in the fourth to win, 23–6.

The following day, Durocher and Vaughan explained their positions. "I had a talk with Vaughan, and he explained his reasons for turning in his uniform to me," Durocher said. "Now that I see those reasons, I can understand them. But I cannot tell you what Vaughan's reasons were for getting so mad and wanting to quit."

Vaughan said, "I boiled over because I thought Newsom was wrongly treated, and I thought to myself the same thing could just as well happen to me. I could be the next victim."[20] Four days later, Rickey traded Newsom to the Browns.

The Cardinals ran away with the race in the second half, finishing 18 games ahead of Cincinnati and 23 and a half games ahead of Brooklyn. They had upset the Yankees in the 1942 World Series, but the Yankees got even this year. The Dodgers voted to award their former players now in the military a half-share of their third-place Series money, so Casey, Reese, Reiser, French, and Lew Riggs each received $378.30.

Meanwhile, Casey had a World Series of his own to play. His Norfolk NAS team was playing the Norfolk Naval Training Center team in the navy's 1943 World Series. The teams had met 43 times during the season, with the sailors winning 24 and the airmen 18, with one tie. The sailors had Freddie Hutchinson, Charley Wagner, Dom DiMaggio, Eddie Robinson, Phil Rizzuto, and Don Padgett. Casey and Pee Wee Reese were the stars of the NAS team.[21]

Casey, who had pitched in 45 games for NAS in 1943, pitched in five of the seven games against NTC, winning Game One, Game Four, and Game Six. He won the first game with a six-hit, 3–0 shutout. NTC won the next two games. In Game Four, Casey pitched a complete game in a 10-inning, 5–3 win to tie the Series at two games apiece. After a two-day rest, NTC won the fifth game, but the next day Casey got NAS even again, winning, 4–1.[22]

Casey started the seventh and deciding game, pitching six innings of two-hit shutout ball. But manager Peel lifted him for a pinch-runner in the seventh. NTS eventually won, 1–0, on a ninth-inning double by Don Padgett. Emil Lochbaum, who relieved Casey and gave up the run, was charged with his third defeat of the Series. Lochbaum had been a successful minor leaguer but had no big-league experience.

That game brought Casey's Norfolk career to an end. On February 25, 1944, he was among five major leaguers detached from their duties at the NAS to be posted elsewhere. After traveling to San Francisco, Casey shipped out to Hawaii, where he was stationed at Kaneohe Bay Air Base in 1944, and Aiea Naval Hospital in Oahu in 1945.

Dissension on the 1943 Dodgers, highlighted by the Vaughan rebellion, made many in the press believe Rickey would not retain Durocher as his manager. Among those rumored to replace him in 1944 were Dixie Walker and Billy Herman, plus Burt Shotton and Ray Blades, both of whom had managed for Rickey in the Cardinals system. Eventually, Durocher kept his job, while Herman, if he had been seriously considered, was now in the military and unavailable. Also in the service was star pitcher Kirby Higbe, while Vaughan had chosen to sit out the season at his California farm. Rickey made a strong financial case to Vaughan to get him to change his mind, but Vaughan refused.

Vaughan did not say he was staying at his ranch because of Durocher, but he stayed out of baseball until 1947, the year of Durocher's suspension. After three years of idleness, he hit .325 as a part-time outfielder, third baseman, and pinch-hitter.

As the 1944 major-league season approached, teams were unsure of their rosters. "All I can say is that we will have a large number of human beings at the training camp," Rickey said when spring training began in March.[23] An early indication of how terrible a season it would be in Brooklyn came in the first game of an April 30 doubleheader at the Polo Grounds. Led by Phil Weintraub's 11 runs batted in, the Giants pounded five Brooklyn pitchers for 18 hits and 26 runs. "I had nothing but humpty-dumpties on my staff that year," Durocher later wrote.[24]

At the close of play on June 25, the Dodgers were in fourth place, with a 33–30 record, as they began a western trip. The road trip turned out to be the worst in franchise history. They lost 16 straight, 13 before the All-Star break and three afterward. (Loss number 14, at Pittsburgh, was halted by curfew and completed later.) The 1944 Dodgers finished in seventh place, 42 games behind St. Louis, who breezed to their third-consecutive pennant. Brooklyn's lone bright spots were the June 6 trade of pitcher Bob Chipman to the Cubs—which brought them second baseman Eddie Stanky in return—and Dixie Walker's league-leading .357 batting average

15

BASEBALL ENTERS A NEW ERA

Casey had pitched well enough for the Aiea Naval Hospital team in Hawaii to be selected for the 1944 All-Star Team by the managers of the Central Pacific service baseball league. One of his All-Star teammates, Barney McCosky, a former Detroit Tigers outfielder, had almost come to blows with Casey that summer during a game in Hawaii. "That fiery temper hasn't deserted Hugh Casey," wrote Ben Gould in the *Brooklyn Eagle*, explaining that the cause of the confrontation was McCosky's claim that Casey had dusted him off.[1] After the war, McCosky gave his account of what had transpired:

> Hugh Casey was with the air base, and I could hit him like I owned him. This one game, the first time up I hit a home run off him. This was a big game; we were going right down to the championship. The next time up, I bent down to get some dirt in my hand, with my back turned to the pitcher, and bang! He threw the ball while I was bending over and got me right in the middle of the back. So I walked right out to the mound, and said, "Did you mean that?"

When Casey answered in the affirmative, McCosky said, "I hauled off and whacked him right in the mouth. We had a fight right on the mound."[2]

Casey had also pitched in the Army–Navy World Series, the so-called pineapple series, played in Honolulu. Both teams were made up of the best players from their branch of the service. In addition to Casey, the navy team included Phil Rizzuto, Pee Wee Reese, Johnny

Mize, Dom DiMaggio, Virgil Trucks, and Schoolboy Rowe. Their manager was Bill Dickey.

After Admiral Chester W. Nimitz, commander in chief of the Pacific Fleet, threw out the first ball, Trucks won Game One with a four-hit shutout. The navy also won the second game. Casey made his first appearance in Game Three. He relieved former Cleveland Indians pitcher Tom Ferrick with two out in the 10th and held the army scoreless. The navy scored a run in the 12th to win, 4–3. When the navy won the fourth game, the Series was officially over, but the teams played the final three games for the benefit of the servicemen.

After the Cardinals defeated the Browns in the 1944 World Series, the *Midpacifican*, a service newspaper, began a campaign to have the Cardinals meet the navy team—winner of the Army–Navy World Series. "How about a real World Series," it asked, "an all-around-the-world championship series between the winning team at home and the winning team here?"[3] The paper suggested the game be played in Oahu for the entertainment of the servicemen.

Cardinals manager Billy Southworth liked the idea but said it should have been put forth six weeks earlier. "Then there might have been a chance to consider it," he said. At that point, players had made other plans. Luke Sewell, manager of the American League champions, said, "We'd be glad to play the navy boys. They have a lot of stars, but they wouldn't find us easy."[4]

From 1942 to 1944, the Cardinals had won three consecutive pennants and two World Series. Yet, Brooklyn's Kirby Higbe believed the Dodgers would have done as well as the Cardinals during those years, after the two teams had battled so closely in 1941 and 1942. "They didn't lose the men to the service the Dodgers did. They sure didn't," said Higbe. "We had pretty nearly an All-Star Team. The best infield in baseball. Until the war."[5]

But while Higbe was looking backward, Dodgers manager Leo Durocher was looking to the future. In a postseason interview with Bob Considine of the *Washington Post*, Durocher made a few amazingly accurate forecasts. He said the Cardinals figured to dominate the National League for the next few years. "Then it will be Brooklyn's turn," he said, citing the young players Branch Rickey had signed within the span of a few years. "I'll guarantee you this: Once Branch Rickey wins a pennant Brooklyn'll win six times out of 10 thereafter for as long as he wants. I think our next pennant will come about 1947."[6]

Leo was right on target. Brooklyn's first postwar pennant would come in 1947, and they would win six of the next 10. The Dodgers won pennants in 1947, 1949, 1952, 1953, 1955, and 1956. They also finished second in 1950 and 1951, losing on the last day of the season in both years.

After Durocher praised the future Dodgers—and, of course, he did not know that group would include Jackie Robinson—he was asked about some of the veterans who had helped win the 1941 pennant. "If the war is over in a year we might still be able to use Billy Herman on second base, but if it goes two more years . . .," he just shrugged. "The same is true of Hugh Casey."[7]

In its 1945 preseason issue, *Time* magazine predicted the Cardinals would again win the National League pennant, but it reminded readers about the quality of baseball they would see. "With most rosters as full of unknown names as YMCA hotel registers," noted *Time*, "everybody agreed that the caliber of big-league 1945 baseball would be somewhere between AA and A—but it would still be baseball."

Time wagered that St. Louis's challengers would come from the three other western teams: Chicago, Cincinnati, and Pittsburgh, while the "four Eastern clubs, which formed a solid second-division block in 1944, are filled with long ifs and forlorn buts." Brooklyn was dismissed as having to "get along on fanatical fan-enthusiasm and the league-leading bat of Dixie Walker."[8] The sale of Casey's longtime friend, pitcher Whit Wyatt, to the Phillies, on March 28, left the Dodgers with only Walker, Augie Galan, Mickey Owen, and Curt Davis from the 1941 pennant winners.[9]

Baseball historian David Jordan, who has studied wartime baseball extensively, said, "It was a serious game played by serious professional ballplayers."[10] Nevertheless; *Time*'s assessment "that the caliber of big-league 1945 baseball would be somewhere between AA and A" was accurate. More so than the early war years, "big league teams were a mixture of legitimate major leaguers, players past their prime, and youngsters not ready for the big league stage."[11]

That was one reason the nation welcomed the opening of the 1945 season with a low level of enthusiasm. An even greater reason was the earthshaking events taking place that spring. At the Elbe River, south of

Dresden, Germany, U.S. soldiers, advancing from the west, had linked up with Russian soldiers, advancing from the east. Meanwhile, the U.S. Ninth Army was fewer than 50 miles southwest of Berlin.

If the news from Europe was hopeful, the news from the Pacific was not. After capturing Iwo Jima, the U.S. military's next target was Okinawa, where thousands would die on both sides before the island was finally secured. Meanwhile, the U.S. Army Air Corps continued to bomb airbases on Kyushu, one of Japan's main islands, while the Allied leaders planned for the grim task of invading the home islands. The casualty estimates for Operation Olympic and Operation Coronet—the invasion of Japan—were catastrophically high.

Dwarfing even the war news was the shocking death of President Franklin Delano Roosevelt. The president had succumbed to a cerebral hemorrhage on April 12, at his vacation home in Warm Springs, Georgia. Roosevelt's death had stunned the nation and left many Americans unsure if his successor, Vice President Harry S. Truman, was up to the task of ending the war and securing the peace.

Men were dying and being physically, mentally, and emotionally maimed by the war, but for Hugh Casey and many other former professional ballplayers, officially classified as "physical instructors," their wartime duties were devoted to playing baseball. The powers that be obviously approved, considering these exemptions from battle necessary to keep up the morale of the servicemen who watched these games. Of course, many prewar and postwar star athletes did see combat, including Ted Williams, Bob Feller, Warren Spahn, Yogi Berra, and Cecil Travis.

Casey was still pitching for the Aiea Naval Hospital in Oahu, in April 1945, when in an April 24 article datelined "Somewhere in the Pacific," Marine T/Sergeant Bill Goodrich described him as being anxious to return to the Dodgers. Goodrich had spoken to Casey after a recent game in which he had pitched a shutout against a marine raider team. Goodrich described the 32-year-old Casey as appearing in excellent shape and hoping he was not too old when the Japanese were finally beaten. Casey claimed he could "step nine innings of Major League Baseball anytime," and those who played with and against him agreed.[12]

Casey was the winning pitcher when the National League All-Stars defeated the American League All-Stars in the opening game of the navy's World Series in Honolulu, a series the National Leaguers won.

More than 26,000 servicemen attended the game at Pearl Harbor. Casey, who was set to return to civilian life, broke an ankle while sliding into home plate with the winning run.[13]

He was flown back to the mainland in October, landing in Oakland, California, and then to the Naval Hospital in Charleston, South Carolina, for treatment and recuperation. He wore a cast on the foot until late November, and the ankle had healed completely by the end of the year.[14]

Casey received his discharge at Charleston on December 12, 1945. He returned to Atlanta and civilian life, having served 35 months in the navy, reaching the rank of chief specialist. (The specialist designation was used in the navy and had the same pay structure as the petty officer.) *Yank* magazine had reported in their March 10, 1944, edition that Casey and Reese had been promoted to that position while at Norfolk.[15]

Eager to reconnect with the Dodgers, Casey said he planned to go to New York in early January to meet with Leo Durocher about his future and discuss his 1946 contract. A note in the December 10, 1945, *Syracuse Herald-Journal* reports Durocher's reaction to news that Casey's weight had ballooned to 247 pounds. "Boy, I'll have to sell him by the pound," Durocher allegedly said.[16]

In a year of relative mediocrity, Brooklyn had bounced back from its disastrous 1944 season to win 87 games in 1945 and finish third behind the pennant-winning Cubs. Yet, the most noteworthy event in Brooklyn that year had happened off the field. On October 23, Rickey had signed Negro League shortstop Jackie Robinson to a contract to play for the International League's Montreal Royals in 1946. Robinson, a star in four sports at the University of California, Los Angeles before the war, would be the first black player in organized baseball since Fleetwood Walker played for the Toledo Blue Stockings of the American Association in 1884 (the American Association of 1884 is recognized as a major league).

There was no official edict against black players playing in organized baseball, just a "gentlemen's agreement" that mirrored the segregation that permeated much of the country. As recently as August 1942, *Sporting News* had published an editorial defending segregation in baseball. It argued that members of each race "prefer to draw their talents from their own ranks," and that "both groups know their crowd psychology and do not care to run the risk of damaging their own game."[17]

But the war was bringing social change to all facets of American life, including the broad recognition that segregation was immoral. Commissioner Kenesaw Landis, a staunch defender of segregated baseball, had died in November 1944, to be replaced by Albert "Happy" Chandler, a former governor and senator from Kentucky. Chandler was supportive of Robinson's signing. "I'm for the Four Freedoms," he said. "If a black boy can make it in Okinawa and Guadalcanal, hell, he can make it in baseball . . . I don't believe in barring Negroes from baseball just because they are Negroes."[18]

Rickey's signing of Jackie Robinson elicited mixed reactions from those connected to the game. Manager Connie Mack of the Philadelphia Athletics and owner Powel Crosley of the Cincinnati Reds had no comment, nor did Jack Zeller, general manager of the world champion Detroit Tigers; however, Zeller's first baseman, Alabama-born Rudy York, applauded the move. "I wish Robinson all the luck in the world and hope he makes good," said York, who, according to York family lore, was part Cherokee Indian. (On January 3, 1946, the Tigers traded York to the Boston Red Sox for shortstop Eddie Lake.)

Horace Stoneham, president of the New York Giants, approved of Rickey's action and said his club would begin scouting Negro players. "It is an affair of the Brooklyn and Montreal clubs whom they sign, whether white or colored," was the opinion of Pittsburgh Pirates president Bill Benswanger. And Hector Racine, owner of the Montreal Royals club for whom Robinson would be playing, gave another good reason for offering Robinson this opportunity. "Negroes fought alongside of whites, and shared foxhole dangers. They should get a fair trial in baseball," argued Racine.[19]

In a foreshadowing of the trouble that lay ahead, Dixie Walker, the unofficial team leader of the Dodgers, said, "As long as he isn't with the Brooklyn club I'm not worried."[20] Pirates coach Spud Davis and Reds pitcher Elmer Riddle had similar reactions. Signing Negroes was fine with them, they said, as long as they were with teams other than theirs.

But several other baseball people were more vocal in their opposition. Rogers Hornsby, former star second baseman, said that Negro players ought to stay in their own league, where they belonged. George Digby, a scout for the Boston Red Sox, said, "Personally I think it is the worst thing that can happen in organized baseball. I think a lot of southern boys will refuse to compete with Negroes in baseball."[21] "Southern boy" Hugh Casey was recuperating in Charleston at the time of Robinson's signing, and his immediate reaction is unknown.

The United States had emerged from World War II as the world's preeminent military and economic power. Aside from being the sole possessor of the atomic bomb, the United States was the only major participant that had not experienced the war's devastation at home. Infrastructure and transportation systems were intact and, in most cases, even stronger than before the war. American industry, which had turned out the planes, ships, and tanks so instrumental in achieving victory, was converting back to peacetime production. Businesses old and new, competing to satisfy the public's pent-up demand for goods and services, would launch the country into an extended period of unprecedented growth.

Baseball, too, was entering one of its greatest eras. After four years in which the quality of play had steadily worsened, fans were eager to welcome back the game's returning heroes. Some, like Hank Greenberg, had already returned. Greenberg rejoined the Detroit Tigers during the second half of the 1945 season and was a major factor in their capturing the pennant and World Series. Now, as baseball's first postwar season got underway—and its last in which all the major-league players were white—almost all were back.[22]

In late January, Branch Rickey said he expected his Dodgers would be a much better ballclub in 1946. "We'll have a bunch of infielders back from the service headed by Pee Wee Reese. And we'll have a whole covey of outfielders headed by Pete Reiser. Both our infield and outfield are bound to be better," he concluded;[23] however, he was less optimistic about his pitching staff.

Rickey added, "So far there has been no conclusive evidence presented that it will be any better than it was last year. That hurts because the pitching of every other club is bound to be improved." He was concerned that neither Kirby Higbe, whom he expected would be his ace, nor promising youngster Rex Barney had as yet returned home.

"Of course, we'll have some pitchers back in time for spring training," he said, mentioning Ed Head and Casey. "Apropos of Casey," Rickey cautioned, "I cannot see how a man can weigh 280 pounds and be in condition to pitch baseball. Well maybe 280 is an exaggeration, but my information is that Casey has grown extremely large." If Casey had gained that much weight, he had lost most of it by the start of spring training. He reported to camp at Daytona Beach looking like the old Casey, probably overweight but certainly not "extremely large."

After watching a day of practice in civilian clothes, Casey signed his 1946 contract the next day. Normally an "obstinate gentleman when it comes to money," he signed in less than two minutes after conferring with Rickey, his new boss.[24]

Casey had not actually signed his contract when he worked out for the first time but said he and Rickey had agreed to terms that morning. "It took only about a minute and a half," he said. "I told him I wasn't holding out, I just wanted to clear up a little misunderstanding." The misunderstanding was concerning the bonus arrangement in Casey's contract during the Larry MacPhail regime. The contract he received from Rickey contained no such clause. "He told me," Casey said, "'Young man you don't need to worry about anything. I know you can pitch every day, and I know what kind of relief pitcher you are.'"[25]

As to the ever-present concerns about his weight, Casey claimed he weighed only 215 pounds. "That's the lightest I ever came to camp. I'm ready," he said. "All they have to do is put a cushion for me out in the bullpen. Everything's fine otherwise." He described his salary negotiations and his first meeting with Rickey.

"He looked at me over his glasses and said he'd heard that I'd been known to take a drink. I confessed that I like to lift a few beers. 'That's all right young man,' said the teetotaling Rickey, 'but don't overdo it because I'm counting on you.' And he gave me what I wanted."[26]

Brooklyn's third-place finish in 1945 had earned Leo Durocher a new one-year contract and ended rumors that his old boss, Larry MacPhail, now running the Yankees, would hire him to replace Joe McCarthy.

Spring training in 1946 had a very different look from the war years, and even the prewar years. Each club's training camp was overcrowded with players anxious to secure a job. Alongside the rookies were those who had been there in 1945, those who had been big leaguers before the war, and the many who were returning from the service.

"Sportswriters were wiring home 6,000,000 words a week from the Florida and California baseball training camps," reported *Time* magazine. "But all the words they wrote could be summed up in two: job jitters. Nobody felt safe, and everybody hustled."[27]

Unlike most clubs that had foregone signing new players during the war, Rickey had signed youngsters by the dozen. Now they were in camp competing for jobs against the veterans. Even such Dodgers legends as Dixie Walker and Pete Reiser were not guaranteed their old jobs back as Durocher lauded several of his young outfielders.

"When I see these kids run, throw, and hit for extra bases the way [Dick] Whitman, [Carl] Furillo, and [Gene] Hermanski have done," Durocher said, "I don't care if they've got famous names or none at all."[28] These three would comprise Brooklyn's starting outfield on Opening Day: Whitman in left, Furillo in center, and Hermanski in right.

16

THE RETURN OF PEACE BRINGS
THE RETURN OF WARS WITH ST. LOUIS
AND CHICAGO

Signing Jackie Robinson was the most notable move Branch Rickey had made since coming to Brooklyn. Robinson, now a member of the Dodgers' top farm team, the Montreal Royals, was at second base on March 13 when the Dodgers worked out against Montreal on Kelley Field in Daytona Beach. Casey was on the mound for Brooklyn in the last three innings of a game free of racial incidents.

On March 17, the Dodgers played Montreal at Daytona Beach, in an actual game. Robinson was in the Royals lineup, marking the first appearance of an integrated team in organized baseball in the twentieth century.[1] Again, there were no incidents on the field or in the stands, which were segregated by Florida law. More than a thousand black fans in attendance were crammed into the Jim Crow section in right field, which had seating for only about 800.

"The precedent-breaking participation of a Negro in a baseball game with white players here this afternoon seemingly was taken in stride by a majority of the 4,000 spectators," wrote Roscoe McGowen in the *New York Times*.[2]

The local paper, the *Daytona Beach Evening-News*, did not mention Robinson until the third paragraph of its story. "All eyes were focused on Jackie Robinson, hefty Montreal second-sacker and the first Negro to appear in an organized baseball game," wrote the *Evening-News*'s Bernard Kahn.[3]

Rickey's fears about the strength of his pitching staff were temporarily erased during spring training, as Hal Gregg, 20-year-old Ralph Branca, and highly touted rookie Joe Hatten looked impressive. "Hatten, a 28-year-old southpaw, looks like the nearest thing to a freshman Dizzy Dean," declared *Time*. "He has a deadly sidearm motion that should baffle right-handed hitters and has a curveball that can turn a corner."[4]

The Knothole Gang Dinner, held at Brooklyn's Hotel St. George just before the opener, gave Leo Durocher a chance to crow about his hurlers. "It's become the strongest department on the Dodgers," he said. "Wherever we go this year it will be on our pitching."[5] Because of returning veterans, teams would be allowed to carry 30 players after the June 15 cut-down date, instead of the traditional 25. Durocher said he expected to keep 13 pitchers.

On Opening Day, while the measles epidemic in New York City continued, with more than 1,500 cases and three deaths reported, the Dodgers were in Boston. The Braves, under new owner Lou Perini and his two partners, had lured former Cardinals skipper Billy Southworth to Boston. In the game, a 5–3 loss, Casey saw his first major-league action in almost four years. He pitched the final two innings in relief of Gregg, allowing one unearned run.

Four days later, he made his first postwar appearance at Ebbets Field. He relieved Higbe—making his first start in Brooklyn since 1943—with two on and no one out in the eighth inning. Despite being touched for an inside-the-park home run by Mickey Witek on a ball that Carl Furillo and Gene Hermanski allowed to roll between them, Casey was the winner in a 9–8 victory over the Giants. Fans were also treated to a pregame ceremony, in which Dixie Walker and several others received the Asiatic-Pacific campaign ribbon for their USO work entertaining the troops in the China–India–Burma Theater. It was a big day for Dixie, whose eighth-inning, pinch-hit home run onto Bedford Avenue had tied the score.

Win number two for Casey came two days later, 5–4, at home against the Braves. After he pitched a scoreless ninth inning, Billy Herman's single in the home half drove Pee Wee Reese home with the game-winner. Ed Head's no-hitter against the Braves the next day, followed by a win at Philadelphia and two at New York, gave the Dodgers eight consecutive wins following their Opening Day loss.

This was the first start of the year for Head, who had missed the 1945 season. Earlier, before his military service, he had worked on a new pitch in batting practice, an adaptation of the slider patterned after Whit Wyatt's. He asked the Dodgers batters for their reaction, and Dixie Walker had been the most encouraging. "Pretty good, but stay with it and you'll make it better," he answered. "And that's all you need—a pitch with some quality of deception to go with your other stuff. You've got everything else."[6]

Brooklyn's 8–1 record had them in first place, but the Cardinals, preseason favorites to win another pennant, were right behind at 8–2. When they returned home after their first trip west, Casey's 2–0 record had dropped to 2–2, after losses at Chicago and Pittsburgh.

The April 30 loss to the Cubs was directly attributable to Casey. Head, in his first start since the no-hitter, took a 1–0 lead into the home ninth. The Dodgers' run had come on Eddie Stanky's single off Emil Kush in the eighth inning. Kush had come on in the fifth to replace starter Hank Borowy, who left with a blister on the middle finger of his pitching hand. Head was one out away from his second shutout in a row, when Heinz Becker, pinch-hitting for Lennie Merullo, hit a blooper that fell in front of rookie center fielder Furillo, who was fooled on the trajectory of the hit. That allowed Eddie Waitkus, running from second base on contact, to score the tying run.

After Don Padgett batted for Head in the top of the 10th, Durocher called on Casey. Hugh left two runners on in the 10th but could not survive the 11th. In addition to throwing to the wrong base on a sacrifice bunt, he walked Dom Dallessandro on four pitches to force in the winning run.

The May 5 loss in Pittsburgh was in the second game of a doubleheader, called after six innings because of the Pennsylvania Blue Laws. (Vic Lombardi had lost the opener in 11 innings.) Brooklyn's three runs in the top of the sixth had tied the score at 3–3. With the clock ticking, Casey could have preserved a tie and the game's later completion when he relieved Les Webber in the bottom of the inning, but he surrendered a two-out, game-winning double to Frank Gustine. The double loss, combined with the Cardinals' split with Boston, left the teams tied for first with 10-6 records.

Eddie Dyer, who had spent years in the Cardinals system as a player and manager, had replaced Billy Southworth as the team's manager.

Brooklyn and St. Louis, bitter rivals who had staged season-long battles for the pennant in 1941 and 1942, were setting the stage to do it again.

A split in Cincinnati gave the Dodgers a 3–4 record for their trip west. Their highly anticipated first battles with the Cardinals fell victim to two rainouts; however, they did score an important victory off the field. The Mexican League, led by the wealthy Jorge Pasquel and his brothers, was attempting to sign as many big-league players as it could. It was the first raid on organized baseball since the Federal League in 1914, and among those to whom they had made tempting offers were Pete Reiser and young infielder Stan Rojek.

Rickey, who had already lost Luis Olmo and Mickey Owen to the Mexican League, flew to St. Louis to meet with Reiser and Rojek, and used his vaunted powers of persuasion to convince them to reject the offers.

Brooklyn was 15–7 and two games ahead of the Cardinals when the clubs finally met for the first time on May 14, the start of a two-game series. The Cardinals quieted the Ebbets Field crowd by winning both games. Max Lanier improved his record to 5–0 with an 11-inning win in the first game, and Howie Pollet pitched a 1–0 shutout the next day. (Lanier would win his next decision and then jump to the Mexican League.)

In the fifth inning of the second game, Enos Slaughter responded to a Les Webber pitch he thought came too close to him by bunting up the first-base line and crashing into Webber, who was attempting to field the ball. The benches emptied, "indicating another free-for-all indicative of Dodgers–Cardinals relations."[7]

That was just the preview of a two-day brawl that began a week later. On May 22, the defending National League champion Cubs paid their first visit of the season to Ebbets Field and renewed the "long, bitter, and bloody feud of fistfights, beanballs, and fractured skulls" between the teams.[8]

The *Brooklyn Eagle*'s Harold C. Burr dated the feud back to the 1931 season and the on-field brawl between Brooklyn's Mickey Finn and Chicago's Billy Jurges. The teams had clashed several times in 1945, mostly relating to pitchers throwing at batters. Chicago's Phil Cavarretta, the eventual National League batting champion, was hit twice, once in the face. On August 18, Cubs shortstop Lennie Merullo had a heated exchange with Dodgers catcher Johnny Peacock and later in the game slid hard into third baseman Augie Galan.

Perhaps Merullo remembered these 1945 incidents when he ignited this battle. In the top half of the 10th inning of a 1–1 game, Eddie Stanky, attempting to complete a double play, "was bumped by Merullo," in the words of Joseph M. Sheehan in the *New York Times*.[9]

Tommy Holmes of the *Eagle* described the play much differently: "Stanky . . . got the ball away . . . and stepped off the bag. Merullo ran right into him, knocking him down."[10]

Not surprisingly, Irving Vaughan of the *Chicago Tribune* saw the incident in a completely differently way. According to Vaughan, "Stanky, after throwing the ball, leaped on the Cub infielder, even before the latter reached the bag."[11]

Stanky and Merullo, who had clashed before when they were teammates as the Cubs' double-play combination in 1943, started throwing punches. After Reese and umpire Dusty Boggess stepped in and broke it up, Reese allegedly punched Merullo, and Cubs pitcher Claude Passeau separated Durocher from his jersey. The Dodgers eventually won, 2–1, in 13 innings, when Walker's double off Johnny Schmitz, who had pitched the entire game, drove in Dick Whitman with the winning run.

Merullo was also the catalyst for the even bigger brawl the next day. "During pregame batting practice, Merullo walked into the batting cage to show Reese his black eye, reportedly telling him that if he wanted to hit him again to do it while he was looking so that he could break Reese's neck," wrote Chicago baseball historian Art Ahrens. "Sneaking up from behind, Dixie Walker slugged Merullo on the back of the head and then headed for the home dugout." Ahrens continued, "Lennie grabbed Walker, tripped him to the ground, and knocked out one tooth, while breaking another in half. By now everybody on either side of the fence had become involved in the melee."[12]

While admitting he struck the first blow, Walker denied hitting Merullo from behind and then running away. "After I hit him, Merullo attacked me," he said. "It was a regular football tackle, and it knocked me down and took all the breath out of me. Then he started pummeling me, using his knee and his fists."[13]

Cubs outfielder Peanuts Lowrey recalled that after Walker hit Merullo, Cavarretta went after Walker, but Cubs pitcher Paul Erickson got there first. Erickson, who was 6-foot-2 and weighed 200 pounds, dragged Walker to a clear patch of ground and Merullo followed.

"Players from both clubs made a big circle around Merullo and Walker," Lowrey remembered, continuing,

> We all spread out our arms and touched them to the next guy's shoulders, and pretty quickly we had ourselves a nice ring and a nice little fight to watch. I couldn't say who won the fight, but they were both going at it real good. They'd both be on the ground and then up and down again, and all the time swinging and cuffing or wrestling. A little park cop broke through the ring, but Clyde McCullough grabbed him and tossed him right out again. Finally a whole bunch of cops broke through, and that was it.[14]

After the fireworks, the teams played 11 innings, with Brooklyn again winning, 2–1. Casey came through with three scoreless innings, from the eighth to the 10th. There were no more confrontations between the teams, but there was much arguing and sniping at one another and the umpires, mainly from the Brooklyn side, with Durocher and four of his players—Augie Galan, Joe Hatten, Hal Gregg, and Stan Rojek—being ejected.

Walker and Reese had their shirts torn so badly in the pregame fighting they had to get new ones for the game. Reese had a spare number 1 jersey, but Walker had to wear number 9 instead of his familiar number 11. League president Ford Frick fined Walker, Cubs coach Red Smith, and Merullo $150 each, and suspended the former two for five days and the latter for eight. Reese and Cavarretta also contributed $100 each.

"The Dodgers are running this league," said Cubs general manager Jim Gallagher, clearly unhappy with Frick's sense of justice.[15]

This two-day free-for-all was the final battle in the war that had raged between the Dodgers and Cubs since 1931. Beginning in 1947, Leo Durocher would be gone from Brooklyn, except for the first half of the 1948 season, and while the Dodgers were in their ascendancy, the Cubs were sinking into a long period of mediocrity.

Casey picked up his third win at Philadelphia on May 26. He pitched six and two-thirds scoreless innings in an 11-inning victory. The Dodgers ended the month of May with a two-game lead over St. Louis. They stretched the lead to three and a half games with a doubleheader sweep at Cincinnati on June 2. Dodgers pitching allowed the Reds only one run in 20 innings; the second game went 11. Brooklyn won the first game, 2–1, behind Les Webber, who pitched 10-and-a-third innings, and Vic Lombardi, who got the final two outs.

Forty-year-old Art Herring (five innings) and Casey (four innings) combined for a 1–0 shutout in the nightcap. Herring, who had to leave with a sore arm, despite not yielding a hit, got the win, while Casey picked up his first save of the season. Casey's own fielding blunder, however, cost him a loss two days later in Pittsburgh. He relieved Lombardi in the ninth frame of a 3–3 game and never retired a batter. A walk and an error by first baseman Howie Schultz on an attempted sacrifice bunt put runners at first and second. Bob Elliot also attempted a sacrifice bunt, but when Casey threw to third in an attempt to get the lead runner, his throw sailed past third baseman Billy Herman, allowing Frankie Zak to score the game-winner.

In the aftermath of the brawls, the Dodgers had lost their last four games against the Cubs before topping them, 6–3, on June 15. Casey, who replaced Joe Hatten in the second inning and pitched into the seventh, was the winner. He was not needed on June 19, when Hatten shut out the Pirates, 7–0, preserving the Dodgers' game and a half lead. That evening, the navy veteran did what so many other returning servicemen did. He joined the American Legion, specifically Brooklyn's J. W. Person Post No. 14.

Two days later, the Dodgers' lead went to two and a half games after a win over the Cardinals in the opener of a three-game series at Ebbets Field. In front of the largest nighttime crowd of the season, Lombardi started for Brooklyn but was touched for two runs in the first inning and removed with one out after an Enos Slaughter liner caught him on the leg. Casey replaced him and pitched the rest of the way, although St. Louis reached him for three runs and 11 hits.

The eight and two-thirds innings pitched was Casey's longest stint of the season. Hugh raised his record to 6–3 on June 24, against the Reds. This time he logged four and two-thirds innings as Brooklyn's fifth pitcher in a 13-inning win. Higbe started but was knocked out early, putting his sparkling 7–0 record in jeopardy. "With my luck and your stuff, how can we lose?" Higbe said to Casey after the game. Between them, the roommates now had won 13 games.[16]

The next afternoon, Casey suffered the only ejection of his career during a loss to the Reds. The Brooklyn bench had been heckling umpire Bill Stewart from the start of the game. By the fourth inning, Stewart decided Casey and Stanky were the main culprits and tossed them. Durocher, who was ejected by first-base umpire Tom Dunn, was fined $100, while Casey ($50) and Stanky ($25) also had fines levied against them.

The two Southerners—Casey from Georgia and Higbe from South Carolina—were alike in that both were heavy drinkers. But "unlike Higbe, who was talkative, friendly, and gregarious, Casey was a loner."

"Hugh was kind of a loner," agreed Higbe, adding,

> Outside of me, he didn't care too much about messin' around with other ballplayers, not that he didn't like them. He was just that type of fella. He would go up to his room after a ballgame and read a Western magazine or Western book and smoke them big cigars. That's about all Hugh would do. And drink. He'd have a few drinks, as most people did back in them days. [17]

Supposedly it was in 1888 that Mike "King" Kelly of the Boston Beaneaters had first suggested that the team in first place on July 4 would win the pennant. After the doubleheader split with the Giants on July 4, 1946, the Dodgers had a comfortable seven-game lead on the Cardinals. [18]

The lead was five games at the All-Star break, when sportswriter Dan Daniel questioned Dixie Walker about Brooklyn's chances of winning the pennant. "They are wrapped up in Reiser," Walker said. "Every day, sitting around in the clubhouse, we ask each other, 'Can Pete play through the season?' If you have the answer to that question, you need ask no more."

Walker went on to say that he thought Brooklyn had the most balanced team in the league, but he would make no predictions. "I have seen the Dodgers on top in July and beaten in October too often to get cocky," he commented. [19]

At the All-Star Game, played in Boston's Fenway Park, several members of the Cardinals contingent taunted Walker and Higbe about the shakiness of the Dodgers' lead.

"We're going to catch you guys before you leave St. Louis!" promised Marty Marion. That did not sit well with Higbe, who had not pitched well in the game. He gave up one of Ted Williams's two home runs and was battered for four runs in one-and-a-third innings in the American League's 12–0 victory.

"Catch us before we leave St. Louis!" an indignant Higbe told the New York press. "Why, we'll be seven games out in front when we get through with those Cardinals!" said Higbe, who after opening the season at 8–0 had lost his last two decisions.[20]

Marion would prove to be a much better prophet than Higbe with regard to the progress of the National League pennant race.

17

A RESTAURANT LAUNCHED AND
A PENNANT LOST

Playing in the west immediately after the All-Star break, the Dodgers lost two of three in Chicago, in a series played without beanballs or base-running incidents. Casey earned a save in Brooklyn's lone win, although he had the radio audience back home holding their breaths. Hank Behrman had held the Cubs to one run through eight innings and took a 4–1 lead into the ninth. But when Clyde McCullough led off with a double and Billy Jurges walked, Durocher called on Casey.

Stan Hack's single scored McCullough, and Eddie Waitkus's double scored Jurges, cutting the lead to one run. With runners at second and third, and two outs, Durocher ordered an intentional walk to the dangerous Phil Cavarretta. Casey then left the three runners stranded and the crowd of more than 40,000 disappointed when center fielder Carl Furillo caught Peanuts Lowrey's fly ball with his back to the wall.

Meanwhile, the Cardinals had opened the second half of the season by splitting four games with the Giants. They trailed the Dodgers by four and a half games when the clubs began a crucial four-game series with a July 14 doubleheader in St. Louis. A crowd of more than 35,000, the largest of the season to date at Sportsman's Park, watched with delight as the home team won both games, cutting Brooklyn's lead to two and a half games. Ted Wilks, in relief, beat Rube Melton, also in relief, 5–3, and Murry Dickson defeated Vic Lombardi, 2–1, a fierce, 12-inning battle in which both men went the distance.

The Dodgers scored a first-inning run in game two, but Dickson shut them out the rest of the way, retiring in order Brooklyn's final 16 batters. Lombardi blanked the Cardinals until Stan Musial led off the eighth inning with a triple and scored the tying run on Whitey Kurowski's fly ball. Musial then won the game with a leadoff home run on Lombardi's first pitch in the 12th. Musial had also played a key role in the opener. His two-out single in the eighth inning of a 3–3 game was followed by an Enos Slaughter home run.

About a third of the way through the season, Cardinals manager Eddie Dyer had benched highly touted rookie first baseman Dick Sisler and moved Musial in from the outfield to play first base. Musial made the move in his usual gracious manner and kept on with his sensational hitting. On the way to his second Most Valuable Player Award, he would lead the league in batting (.365), runs (124), hits (228), doubles (50), triples (20), and slugging percentage (.587). Musial led all Cardinals batters against Brooklyn in 1946, with a .418 average—.429 at home and .408 at Ebbets Field—and 18 runs batted in. Among his 41 hits were 8 doubles, 6 triples, and 3 home runs.

It was during this season that Musial earned the nickname, "The Man," an expression of honor and respect that would remain throughout his life. The story goes that on June 23, at Ebbets Field, Dodgers fans took to chanting, "Here comes the man" when Musial stepped to the plate. *St. Louis Post-Dispatch* writer Bob Broeg heard the chant and mentioned it in his next column.

The doubleheader loss to St. Louis so upset Leo Durocher, he took the unusual step of bypassing scheduled starter Joe Hatten and starting Casey against Harry Brecheen in game three. For Casey, who had not started a National League game since June 30, 1942, it would be his only start of the season and the final one of his major-league career.

Durocher's gamble proved disastrous. Casey faced five batters. Four of them hit safely and two scored before Durocher replaced him with Ed Head. The only batter Casey retired, Enos Slaughter, launched a 400-foot drive that Furillo caught. Sparked by four hits from Musial—who raised his batting average to .367—the Cardinals romped to a 10–4 victory.

Beating Durocher was especially satisfying to Musial and the Cardinals. He "tried to intimidate the other team," Musial said of the Dodgers' manager, "but I think it backfired on him more often than not. He was just stirring up a nest of hornets. When Durocher came to town, I was so charged up I could go up there and climb six fences. I wasn't the only one. Our whole team was up."[1]

"I will never forget that night for many reasons," Casey told J. G. Taylor Spink in recalling his one 1946 start. "One of them concerns our kid catcher, Bruce Edwards. He worked in spite of a fever of 103. He did not know where he was or what he was doing," Casey said, continuing,

> In the middle of the game, he called our other receiver, Ferrell Anderson, and said, "You take over. I am going in for a drink of water." Durocher raised merry hell with Edwards and hollered, "I am the manager and I am the one who will tell you when to leave, and who is to take your place." Leo did not realize that Edwards was in a delirium.[2]

Edwards had been Brooklyn's first-string catcher since being called up from the Mobile Bears of the Southern Association in June. After the season, New York sportswriter Jimmy Cannon asked Durocher what single player had helped the Dodgers most. "Bruce Edwards. He's the reason we're up there," responded Durocher.[3]

Casey also talked about his start against St. Louis in a 1950 interview with Furman Bisher of the *Atlanta Constitution*, calling it a desperation move by Durocher. "The young pitchers had been letting him down, and Leo asked me to start one day in Cincinnati. 'These kids can't get anybody out,' he told me. 'I need somebody to go out and stop 'em.'" Thinking about it made Casey smile. "Know what happened? I got knocked out in the first inning, and that was the last time I started."[4] Casey's memory was partially correct. He pitched just a third of an inning and allowed four hits and two runs before Ed Head relieved him. But the game was in St. Louis, not Cincinnati.

Recalling his 1946 pitching staff, Durocher, a manager who liked to control every aspect of the game, gave especially high praise to Casey. "Casey was the only pitcher I allowed to use his own judgment," he wrote. "For the others, we called the pitches from the bench. I would tell Dressen, 'curve,' or 'fastball,' and he would signal the pitcher. Edwards, in turn, would get the sign from the pitcher."[5]

If the first three losses to the Cardinals had been disheartening, the loss in the final game was devastating. Joe Hatten took a 4–2 lead into the last of the ninth, but pinch-hitter Erv "Four Sack" Dusak justified his apposite nickname by slugging a three-run homer to give St. Louis a 5–4 win. The mob scene at home plate congratulating Dusak, a rookie outfielder, was the kind usually seen only after a team had won the World Series.

The Dodgers, their lead now down to a half-game, then lost their first two in Cincinnati. They recovered to win the getaway game and ended the trip by sweeping a three-game series in Pittsburgh.

While in Cincinnati, a thief entered the unlocked hotel room Casey shared with Kirby Higbe and stole their wallets, which contained a combined $316 in cash—$300 of which was Higbe's—along with both men's salary checks.

"I woke up and saw a light in the bathroom," Casey said. "But I thought it was Kirby and got up and pulled down the shade and went back to bed."[6]

The next morning the thief went to the Lincoln National Bank when it opened and was able to convince the teller, a 26-year employee , to cash both checks, estimated at $2,000.

"Going to pitch against the Reds today, Kirby?" the bank clerk asked the impostor claiming to be Higbe. "I'll beat 'em too," he responded, and then asked the clerk if he would mind cashing Casey's check too.[7] The clerk eagerly obliged.

After discovering the loss, Casey and Higbe notified traveling secretary Harold Parrott, who ordered a stop payment on the checks. The bank had to absorb the loss.

The second-largest crowd of the season was at Ebbets Field for the July 27 doubleheader with Pittsburgh. It was supposedly Leo Durocher's 40th birthday, and when he came out to coach at third base in the first game, the fans serenaded him with a chorus of "Happy Birthday." It was really his 41st birthday. As is the case with many athletes and entertainers, Durocher was pretending to be younger than he was.

The Dodgers treated the large crowd to two exciting 4–3 wins, with Casey figuring prominently in both, as he earned his eighth win and fourth save. He pitched three and two-thirds scoreless innings in relief of Hank Behrman to win the first game, won in the last of the ninth on an Eddie Stanky single. In the second game, he pitched the ninth inning in relief of Higbe, allowing two hits and a walk but only one run.

The Cardinals had faltered some since their four-game sweep of the Dodgers two weeks earlier. When they opened a three-game series at Ebbets Field on July 30, they trailed Brooklyn by two and a half games.

Figure 17.1.   Second baseman Eddie Stanky congratulates Casey after he nails down another Dodgers win. *National Baseball Hall of Fame Library, Cooperstown, NY.*

The Dodgers won the opener, 2–1, but the Cardinals, who had totaled 10 runs in their previous seven games, broke out for a 10–3 victory in the second game. The Cardinals won again the next day and were now just a game and a half out of first place.

That game was on August 1, less than a month after Dixie Walker had wondered whether Reiser could play through the season. In the fifth inning, Reiser crashed into the left-field wall attempting to catch a drive hit by the Cardinals' Whitey Kurowski. Reiser, who had to be carried off the field, was taken to Peck Memorial Hospital but returned to action a week later.

It seemed no meeting between these two teams went by without at least some bickering. Several St. Louis players—Musial, Slaughter, Marion, and Dusak—complained that Dodgers pitchers had dusted them off in the second game of the series. Marty Marion and Casey had yelled at one another during the ninth inning of that game, when a Casey pitch hit Marion on his left hip. "I've warned my players that they will have to take care of themselves," said manager Dyer, invoking the game's long-held code of conduct.[8]

Political columnist and baseball fan George F. Will wrote in 2010,

> The codes are frequently enforced from the pitcher's mound. When a fastball hits a batter's ribs, he is reminded to stop peeking to see where—inside or outside—the catcher is preparing to receive the pitch. In 1946, Dodger Hugh Casey threw at Cardinals shortstop Marty Marion while Marion was standing out of the batter's box— but closer to it than Casey thought proper—in order to time Casey's warm-up pitches.[9]

No one ever doubted Hugh Casey was a mean competitor on the field and a hard drinker off the field. But he did have another side. He had a love for playing bridge. Harry J. Roth, the *Brooklyn Eagle*'s bridge columnist, devoted a column to those members of the Dodgers who played the game to while away the hours spent on trains and in hotels. Casey, he says, usually partnered with Pee Wee Reese to play against Higbe and Harold Parrott, the former *Eagle* sportswriter who Branch Rickey had hired to be the Dodgers traveling secretary. Other bridge enthusiasts on the club, wrote Roth, were Howie Schultz, Ed Head, Cookie Lavagetto, trainer "Doc" Wendler, and even manager Durocher.[10]

Back on the field, Casey had one of his best outings of the season against the Reds on August 4. He picked up his ninth win by pitching scoreless, two-hit baseball from the 10th through the 14th innings.

His 10th win came at the Polo Grounds four days later with a similar performance—three and two-thirds innings, no runs, and two hits. Win number 10 tied him with Vic Lombardi for the club lead. Casey also contributed a couple of hits in the game. His leadoff single in the 10th inning started Brooklyn's two-run rally, which gave them the 3–1 win. Durocher had Dick Whitman run for Casey and then brought in little-used 20-year-old Ralph Branca to nail down the victory.

The Dodgers and Cardinals had identical 73–45 records when they began a four-game series at Sportsman's Park with a doubleheader on August 25. Rather than have them leave Cincinnati with the team, Durocher sent Hatten and Branca to St. Louis early to have them rested for the twin bill. The Dodgers won the opener but lost the nightcap, as the Cardinals pounded Hatten and five others, including Casey, for 14 runs.

The next day, the Cardinals scored two runs in the first inning against Rube Melton, and Murry Dickson made them stand up the rest of the way, as St. Louis moved into first place with a 2–1 win. Higbe's complete-game victory in the series finale moved the Dodgers back into a tie for the lead.

After splitting a Labor Day doubleheader at Philadelphia, the Dodgers had slipped two and a half games behind St. Louis. And although they won the next day, which started a six-game winning streak, they were able to pick up just a half-game on the front-runners.

Melton's 8–0 shutout of the Reds at Ebbets Field on September 10 was Brooklyn's ninth win in 10 games. But the Cardinals had won eight of 10, and at the start of play on September 11, they maintained a two-game lead. That afternoon, a crowd of about 15,000 got their money's worth—19 innings and four hours and 40 minutes later, darkness ended the game with neither the Reds nor the Dodgers having scored.

Johnny Vander Meer went the first 15 innings for Cincinnati, with Harry Gumbert pitching the final four. Brooklyn starter Hal Gregg pitched 10 innings, followed by Casey's five, Herring's three, and Hank Behrman, who pitched the final inning.

The Dodgers never came close to scoring, while the Reds mounted two threats. In the fifth, Eddie Lukon hit a drive off the right-center

wall that caromed away from center fielder Carl Furillo and right fielder Dixie Walker. Pete Reiser, the left fielder, retrieved the ball and
threw it to shortstop Reese, who relayed to catcher Bruce Edwards,
who tagged Lukon to prevent an inside-the-park home run.

In the 19th inning, the Reds had Dain Clay on second base with one
out. Bert Haas lined a single to right, sending Clay around third, heading for home. But Walker charged the ball and made a perfect throw to
Edwards, cutting down the potential winning run. Darkness was set-
tling in, and when the Dodgers went down in order in the bottom of the
inning, umpire George Barr called the game. The 19-inning scoreless
tie remains the longest scoreless tie in major-league history. The game
was replayed nine days later, with Brooklyn winning, 5–3.

The next day, the Dodgers and Cardinals met at Ebbets Field for the
final time (or so they thought) for three games, September 12–14. The
Cardinals, who led by a game and a half, had won 13 of the previous 18
against the Dodgers and five of eight in Brooklyn.

Manager Dyer and his players were aiming for a sweep, which they
believed would all but end the race. Winning at least two of the three
was a must. "We've got to win at least two," said Enos Slaughter.
"There's just no use in kidding ourselves. No other club seems able to
beat them here. And even if we do win two, we'll have to keep playing
at a fast pace after that."[11] The teams split the first two games, but
Brooklyn took the third on Ralph Branca's three-hit shutout—just his
second win of the season.

As the pennant race remained tight, Casey embarked on his career
as an entrepreneur. He purchased, in partnership with Mrs. Rose Buery
and her husband, what had formerly been an Italian restaurant at 600
Flatbush Avenue, not far from Ebbets Field, and renamed it Hugh
Casey's Steak and Chop House.[12] The Casey name and presence would
be the magnet to draw patrons, but it would be the culinary-talented
Rose Buery who ran the place.

According to a description in *Sporting News*, the long and narrow
restaurant was

> softly lighted, with a 30-foot mirrored bar at the front. There are
> booths for cozy dining, a gaudy juke box is near the door, and photo-
> graphs of famous Brooklyn players cover the walls. Casey and wife
> Kathleen live in an apartment on one of the two floors above the

restaurant. During the offseason, "I crawl right out of bed and get right down to work," he said. [13]

Flouting any thoughts of superstition, he scheduled the opening for Friday, September 13. Following Brooklyn's 4–3 win over the Cardinals that afternoon, the restaurant, which seated 90, opened, with Casey on hand to greet patrons. Several hundred friends and fans came by to wish him well in his new venture. The place was not as yet decorated, but plans called for a number of sports mementoes, including "numerous pictures of Brooklyn stars in baseball, football, and boxing circles." [14]

The bar had a full selection to choose from, but one thing was missing—food, which could not be delivered due to a trucker's strike, so there was not enough meat and vegetables on hand to start regular dining service. Labor unions had been mostly quiet during the war years, so as not to appear to harm the war effort. But in this first year of peace, strikes had plagued the nation, as workers tried to make up for their years of remaining strike free despite the lack of pay raises.

Casey got his fifth and final save of the season against Cincinnati on September 20, and it was a big one. With St. Louis idle, Brooklyn's 5–3 win moved them to within a game of the Cardinals. After three games in Boston, the Dodgers played their last five games at home, three against the Phillies and two against the Braves. They won three and lost two.

In the September 25 game, Casey was one of eight pitchers Durocher sent to the mound in an 11–9 loss to the Phillies. The eight pitchers used set the National League record and tied the major-league record for most pitchers used by one team in a game. That morning, the Rev. Benney S. C. Benson had knelt on the steps of Borough Hall, asking for heavenly help for the Dodgers. "Oh Lord, their chances don't look so good right now, but everyone is praying for the Bums to win," he told the crowd gathered around him. "We ask you not to give . . . St. Louis any better break than you give us." [15] Unfortunately, the only break the Dodgers got was to Pete Reiser's left leg. The injury-prone Reiser broke it the next day on a slide back to first in an attempted pickoff play, ending his season.

Meanwhile, the Cardinals had gone into a collective batting slump. They scored only 16 runs in their last eight games, against the Reds and Cubs, and were fortunate to win four of the eight.

The 1946 pennant race had come down to the final day, with the teams tied for first place. The Dodgers would play Boston at Ebbets Field, and the Cardinals would face Chicago at Sportsman's Park. Neither team would have an easy task. Only one game separated the Cubs and Braves in their battle for third place, giving each team a monetary incentive to win, in addition to one of pride. The teams who finished in the top four in each league shared in the World Series money. The individual payoffs for members of the third-place team would be higher than those for the fourth-place team.

Braves manager Billy Southworth started Mort Cooper, whom he had used in many big games against Brooklyn when both were with St. Louis. Cooper reprised some of his glory days as a Cardinal by shutting out the Dodgers, 4–0. Vic Lombardi, Brooklyn's starter, almost matched Cooper through eight innings, allowing just one run. Looking for a run to tie the game, Durocher used Joe Medwick to pinch hit for Lombardi in the eighth and sent Kirby Higbe to the mound in the ninth.

Boston took much of the pressure off Cooper by adding three runs against Higbe, and Casey, who allowed two inherited runners to score. Casey had already finished a league-leading 27 games; nevertheless, Durocher brought in Joe Hatten to get the third out. The home fans sat in silence until midway through the game. Their first opportunity to cheer came when the scoreboard showed the Cubs had scored five runs in the sixth inning at Sportsman's Park to take a 6–2 lead.

After Brooklyn first baseman Ed Stevens made the final out, groups of fans gathered in front of the scoreboard in right field. They stood mostly in small groups, awaiting the final score from St. Louis, which, to their delight, proclaimed an 8–3 Cubs victory. Brooklyn and St. Louis had each finished the regular season with 96 wins and 58 losses, necessitating the first playoff in major-league history.

According to National League rules, the teams would play a best-of-three series, with a coin toss to decide where the games would be played. The winner of the toss could choose to play either the first game at home or the second and third (if necessary) games at home. Brooklyn won the toss and chose to play the second and third games at home.

In game one, at Sportsman's Park, Dyer opened with his ace, Howie Pollet, with a 20–10 record and a league-leading 2.10 earned run average. Durocher countered with 20-year-old Ralph Branca, who had won only three games during the season. But Branca had pitched two shut-outs down the stretch, including one against St. Louis.

This time, the Cardinals knocked Branca out of the box in the third inning, while Pollet went the distance to win, 4–2. Veteran center field-er Terry Moore and rookie catcher Joe Garagiola each had three hits for the winners. Moore had played only 91 games during the season, but he remained the captain and team leader.

"You could say that he was the father of the ballclub," said Whitey Kurowski about Moore. "If we had any troubles or anything, we would go to Terry. He's the one that kept us in good spirits." Harry Walker agreed. "Terry was our captain and was respected by everyone on the club," he said. "He would do more talking to players than the manager did; everyone respected him for that." [16]

The Brooklyn fans that followed the radio broadcast, including those at Hugh Casey's restaurant, understood their team was in a difficult position. They were down a game, and to get to the World Series they had to win the next two. [17]

After a travel day, the playoff resumed at Ebbets Field, with the Cardinals winning easily, 8–4. The game was even more one-sided than the score indicates. Murry Dickson allowed just two hits until the ninth inning, when the Dodgers scored three runs. Joe Hatten, the first of six Dodgers pitchers, was the loser. Brooklyn had been in first place or tied for first for 124 days of the season, but not at the end. The Cardinals went on to defeat the Red Sox in seven games to capture their third World Series in the last five seasons.

As author Thomas Oliphant wrote, "A powerful team being slowly assembled under Branch Rickey had been beaten by a St. Louis Cardi-nals team that Rickey had already helped build." [18]

The Dodgers' decision to play the first game on the road rather than at Ebbets Field came in for much second-guessing. The Dodgers had compiled a phenomenal .727 winning percentage at Ebbets Field, win-ning 56 of 77 games. On the road they had been a so-so team, winning 40 and losing 37. A win in that first game, critics argued, would have shifted the pressure to the Cardinals.

In this first postwar season, the Dodgers had set a National League record by drawing 1,796,824 people. The fans were loyal and vociferous in their support. Author Wilfrid Sheed wrote of the joy Brooklynites found in going to that wonderful old park:

And just walking from the subway to the ballpark past the Botanical Gardens reminded one of what an elegant, mellow, old city Brooklyn was in those days. The jokes which made it sound like a saloon attached to a bowling alley in no way prepared you for the range and variety of the architecture or the populace. [19]

Sheed also lovingly describes Ebbets Field: "The spanking blue seats gave your heart a lift on sight, and they seemed to have been gathered close to the field, the way people pull up their chairs to get a better look at something."

"There was a feeling in that ballpark that probably will never be recaptured again," Dixie Walker told the *Los Angeles Times* in 1974. "The people loved the Dodgers as if they were a part of them." [20]

Durocher faced some criticism of his own for opening the playoffs with the inexperienced Branca. Meanwhile, Branca had some criticism of Durocher, blaming the Brooklyn brain trust for the team not winning the pennant outright.

"The three of them, Rickey, Dressen, and Durocher, blew the pennant," Branca declared, "'cause I had pitched very effectively in '45, but I had held out, and they didn't pitch me in '46. If they had pitched me, you know we would have won at least one more game than we did." [21]

Unlike Branca, Casey's comments on Durocher's handling of pitchers were in praise of Leo. "In 1946, I got into the habit of relieving as early as the first inning," he told Spink. "That was a new wrinkle for me. You will recollect how we patched together pitching jobs and used a lot of pinch-hitters, and somehow came within an ace of winning the pennant." [22]

After the season, Walker told Jimmy Cannon he believed Durocher was the best manager in baseball and had pulled off a small miracle in getting the Dodgers into the playoff. He also believed that Durocher had changed throughout the years. "In the old days, Leo said he could not manage young ballplayers," Walker said, adding,

But this season his patience with young ballplayers improved a hundred percent. That's the most important change in him as a manager. In other years there was tenseness about the ballclub all the time. We had older ballplayers then. Now we have young ballplayers who figure to blow sky high. But Leo really builds the young fellow up.

Gets them ready, makes the whole team feel as though it would fight through 50 hells.[23]

Casey was one of several Dodgers who played for the National League All-Stars, managed by Charlie Dressen, who went to Cuba for a series of games following the season. The others were Ralph Branca, Rex Barney, Kirby Higbe, and Eddie Stanky. Dodgers traveling secretary Harold Parrott accompanied the team to scout hotels for a possible Dodgers stay in Cuba for spring training in 1947.

Casey also continued with his civic activities in Brooklyn. He, Fred Fitzsimmons, and former National League star Rabbit Maranville were guests at a luncheon held on Saturday, October 12, by Brooklyn's leading department store, Abraham and Straus. The event, which took place at the Hotel St. George, was to honor the 20 Brooklyn boys, ages eight to 17, who had written prize-winning essays in a nationwide contest on "My Favorite Baseball Player." Casey presented the prizes, which consisted of money, autographed baseballs and photographs, certificates of merit, and subscriptions to *Calling All Boys* (the magazine that sponsored the contest). Casey expected lots of questions from the boys, which is as it should be, he said, "because there is nothing like getting the boys started right in baseball."[24]

Just before Thanksgiving, he and two members of the Brooklyn Football Dodgers of the newly formed All-America Football Conference, Glenn Dobbs and Bill Daley, attended an American Legion social held at the St. Francis of Assisi school in Brooklyn. The proceeds from the event would be used to purchase Christmas gifts for paralyzed veterans.

On November 29, Casey was presented with the American Legion pin, cap, and membership card at the J. W. Person military post ball at the Hotel St. George. And he continued to stay active in Legion social events. On January 10, 1947, he was a guest at the Bill Brown Post, for a dance to the benefit of the March of Dimes.

With his successful baseball career, a restaurant that had proved extremely popular, and his involvement in civic life, Casey had become one of the best-known and best-loved citizens of Brooklyn.

18

A HISTORY-MAKING ADDITION

In its October 1946 pre-playoff article, which looked ahead to the World Series, *Time* magazine did not think highly of either the Dodgers or the Cardinals. It expected that whoever won would not pose a serious threat to the powerhouse Boston Red Sox, who had easily won the American League flag.

The Dodgers did not have a single 20-game winner (Kirby Higbe was tops, with 17), noted *Time*, while the Cardinals had one, Howie Pollet. The Dodgers had two regulars who batted above .300 (Dixie Walker and Augie Galan); the Cards had three, including Stan Musial, who led the league. "But," the magazine claimed, "when it came to managers, the Dodgers had a big edge: at getting the most out of his mediocre material. The Cards' polite little Eddie Dyer was no match for flamboyant, volatile Leo 'the Lip' Durocher."[1]

Buried in their pre-Series analysis, however, *Time* made a prescient prediction. "Whether Brooklyn wins or loses this week's playoffs, Dodger fans have a really rosy future to contemplate during the long winter months," it wrote. "The 12-club farm chain collected by President Branch Rickey is busting with young talent. Most likely to succeed: Negro Jackie Robinson."[2]

Robinson had exceeded even Rickey's expectations at Montreal. Before the season, Royals manager Clay Hopper had begged Rickey to not assign Robinson to Montreal. "Please don't do this to me," he pleaded. "I'm white, and I've lived in Mississippi all my life. If you do this, you're going to force me to move my family and my home out of Mississippi."

But after Robinson won the International League batting championship and led the Royals to the pennant and victory in the Little World Series, Hopper had changed his mind. "You're a great ballplayer and a fine gentleman," he said to Robinson. "It's been wonderful having you on the team." Hopper also told Rickey that Robinson was a "gentleman" and also the "greatest competitor" he had ever seen.[3]

Rickey was now determined to bring Robinson to Brooklyn in 1947, despite what Happy Chandler claimed was the unanimous opposition of the other owners. Chandler recalled (probably incorrectly) that at the Winter Meetings in January 1947, none of the other 15 owners were in favor of Robinson joining the Dodgers. An ownership group, headed by Larry MacPhail of the Yankees, had met during the 1946 season and issued a secret report on the business ramifications of Robinson's coming to Brooklyn. The report warned of dangers to the "physical properties of franchises"[4] —a polite way of saying crowds of black fans in the park would cause many white fans to stay away.

"Horace Stoneham was a good baseball man and one of my best supporters," Chandler said, but the Giants owner predicted that if Robinson played for the Dodgers, the Negroes in Harlem, site of the Polo Grounds, would burn down the park. MacPhail, Lou Perini of the Braves, and Clark Griffith of the Senators spoke against Robinson's coming to Brooklyn. "They voted 15 to one not to let him play," said Chandler. The reason for their opposition was not so much racism— although there was no doubt that was part of it—as it was a "business decision."[5]

Dodgers broadcaster Red Barber, who was born in Mississippi and raised in Florida, recalled a lunch he had with Rickey in March 1945, when Rickey first revealed his plan to integrate baseball. "I don't know who he is, or where he is, but I'm going to put a Negro on the Brooklyn Dodgers," Rickey told him.[6] Barber, who was immensely popular in Brooklyn, said Rickey's announcement had shaken him to his foundations.

Rickey's plan had so upset him, he considered walking away from a job he loved. A conversation with his wife Lylah caused him to reconsider. Yet, that an educated man like Barber, whose job would not be to play on the same field as a black man, but simply to broadcast the games, would consider quitting was an indication of how deeply ensconced segregation was in the United States in 1947.

For Casey, who spent the winter in Brooklyn, the "problem" of dealing with Robinson was months away. He devoted most of his days to overseeing his restaurant, although he still found the time to make seemingly weekly appearances at fund-raising events for the American Legion, the March of Dimes, and various other charities.

Tommy Holmes visited Casey at his restaurant one evening in January and had this evaluation: "The big pitcher is applying himself conscientiously to his new venture, is doing a good business with a fine clientele, and should, if he wants to, set himself up in our town for life."[7]

Casey was one of several Dodgers who signed their 1947 contracts on February 10. Speaking from his Montague Street office, Rickey had high praise for two of them: rookie catcher Gil Hodges and Casey.

"He wants to beat you," Rickey said of his veteran relief pitcher. "He doesn't lazy in from the bullpen. He has only one thought in his mind—to get the hitter."[8]

The most encouraging news Rickey had to report was Arky Vaughan's return to the Dodgers. After three years spent on his California ranch, the 35-year-old Vaughan and Leo Durocher had put the hard feelings from the mini-revolt of 1943 behind them.

After the 1946 All-Star Game, Holmes had taken the train from Boston to New York with Al Lang, the father of spring-training baseball in St. Petersburg, Florida. "Is Branch Rickey going to bring Jackie Robinson up to the Dodgers?" Lang asked Holmes. When told he most likely would, Lang shook his head and said, "Well, it was nice knowing you Dodgers, anyway." He knew that Florida would not welcome a black player. "The people down there wouldn't stand for it," he said.[9]

To ease Robinson's transition and avoid Florida's Jim Crow laws, the Dodgers returned to Havana for spring training in 1947, where they had trained in 1941 and 1942. The Montreal team, including Robinson, would be there too, with the Dodgers and Royals playing a series of exhibition games against one another.

In January, Rickey had announced that Robinson would appear for the Royals in two spring-training exhibition games against the Dodgers at Ebbets Field. In that same announcement, Rickey made it known that Dixie Walker would be with the team for the year. The *New York Amsterdam News*, New York City's major black newspaper, wrote that Rickey's statement "throws down the gauntlet to Dixie," whom the paper called (incorrectly we would learn that spring) the "one anti-Robinson man in the Dodgers fold."[10] Rickey had scheduled these games in the hope that after seeing Robinson in action, the Dodgers players would demand he be promoted to the big-league roster.

The Dodgers had veteran Eddie Stanky at second base, so on top of everything else Robinson had to handle, he would have to learn a new position—first base. Ed Stevens and Howie Schultz had split the first-base duties in 1946, but they did not figure in Rickey's long-term plans. Stevens, in his autobiography, related one interesting incident involving Casey that spring.

The Yankees, who were training in Venezuela, were in Havana for a game against the Dodgers one afternoon when Stevens spied a bunch of players in full uniform chatting in the hotel lobby.

Wrote Stevens,

> Bill Dickey, who had just gotten off the elevator, walked up to Casey and said, "Hugh, I understand you have a problem with me, and we need to settle a few things."
>
> Casey looked Dickey square in the eye and said, "If I had anything against you, Bill, I would come to you—you wouldn't have to come to me."
>
> Dickey said, "Well this is as good a time as any to settle all this and get it straight. You sure there's nothing you want to talk to me about?"
>
> "Not a thing," said Casey.
>
> "Fair enough," said Dickey.

Everyone was relieved, said Stevens, that these two big, burly men had settled peacefully whatever there was between them.[11]

Casey was one of the veteran Dodgers who had been in Havana in 1941 and 1942, but he seemed in no rush to return. His trunk had been at the Hotel Nacional for three days before he finally arrived on February 23. He said he had stopped in Jacksonville and run into an old friend who convinced him to go quail shooting in Moultrie, Georgia. "And if the weather hadn't been bad, I wouldn't be here yet," he added.[12]

"I weigh 214 pounds," said Casey. "I've reported at 216 and didn't have any trouble getting down to weight." He said some of the players had told him that the playing surface at Grand Stadium (Gran Estadio de La Habana, to be exact) was hard from baking in the sun so long.

"But I'd rather have it that way than the sand of Florida. At Daytona Beach last spring the soft footing raised a lump on the calf of my leg as big as an Easter egg."

Casey had not worked out with the club on his first day in Havana; instead, he got his exercise from unpacking his trunk, wrote Harold C. Burr of the *Brooklyn Eagle*. "It was good bending exercises for a 214-pounder fat man."[13]

19

BURT SHOTTON REPLACES
LEO DUROCHER

Except for his three years in the U.S. Navy, Hugh Casey had been attending spring training every year since 1932. At Havana, in 1947, he reflected on the changes he had seen in training camps, particularly in the number of players each club brought south. Rather than the 30 men it had been back then, most camps now resembled a mob scene.

"You got more work, more chance to whip into shape," he said about the early camps he attended. "This is my second visit to Havana. It's the best camp of all. You do so much running," he continued. "Why in 1941, when we were here before, Freddy Fitzsimmons did so much shagging of flies his hands were all swollen and cut up, and he had to wear golf gloves for weeks after we broke camp. It all goes back to the way you run down here and like it. Cuba's great for a ballplayer's legs."[1]

Leo Durocher's column, "Durocher Says," ghostwritten by Harold Parrott, appeared regularly in the *Brooklyn Eagle*. In one column, subtitled "Hugh Casey Smart Codger on Mound," Leo discussed the pitcher who had come to Brooklyn in 1939, his first year as manager.

"There is not much that Old Hugh Casey misses when he is out there throwing 'em," he wrote. Leo gave as an example instructions Casey had given to Bruce Edwards, a second-year catcher, on how to hold his glove:

"I'm a low-ball pitcher. And I need those close calls when I'm trying to pitch low to get a hitter to ground into a double play," Casey explained. "Now if you catch me with your arms low and your glove up, the whole frame of your body is lower, and the umpire is deluded into thinking the pitch is lower than it is. One call or two like that could cost us a ballgame."[2]

Durocher revealed Casey advised even veterans like Hal Gregg and Kirby Higbe, his roommate, in the art of holding runners close, though he had about given up on Higbe. He also took it on himself to instruct the younger pitchers in the art of holding baserunners. "With two out and a man on first, I will defy the man to steal," he said. "At least, he will not steal on me; he may steal on the catcher, but I will do my part holding him on. He will not get a break on my delivery once in ten times."[3]

Casey also spent time with the young pitchers, advising them to abandon trick pitches. "If I could throw as hard as some of these guys I would be begging to pitch every day," he said. "And I would throw only a curve, fastball and let up. I would scrap those knucklers, screwballs, and sliders." Casey, who now relied more on guile than speed, had a pet peeve—the slider. "It's just a curve that doesn't break," he said. "And no kid should throw it because he doesn't know where to put it. It is a mistake pitch that goes over the fence when it comes up there fat."

Unlike most pitchers, Casey said he liked the bullpen. "I've learned plenty there just warming up," he said. "I've learned how to make the ball spin and rotate, and break different ways just by altering the way my fingers go across the seams."[4]

Casey was also adept at alternating the pace between his pitches. One time he would deliberately hold onto the ball and another time he would get rid of the ball so fast it was almost a quick pitch. While Durocher did not say as much, it seemed Casey had the makings of an excellent pitching coach when his playing days were through.

On St. Patrick's Day, the Dodgers and Montreal Royals played in Panama City, Panama. Montreal's Jackie Robinson got two hits and fielded flawlessly at first base. He had three more the next day, two of them on bunts that had embarrassed and frustrated the Dodgers infield. Casey was on the mound when he came to the plate again, and the Royals expected Robinson would see a brushback pitch at the very least.

The Dodgers expected worse. "Everybody said he'd knock his own mother down," rookie Spider Jorgensen said of Casey. "Instead," remembered Jorgenson, "Casey went right along and pitched to him."[5]

Perhaps Casey was in a good mood, having spent the morning with seven teammates fishing in Panama Bay. He was the only one who had success, catching three fish, including a 15-pound corbina.

Another fishing trip, in Havana, was less successful. On March 25, an offday, Casey again headed a deep-sea fishing party in search of tarpon. With him were Carl Furillo, Gene Hermanski, Harry Taylor, Ed Head, and Ed Heusser. Rainy weather and rough seas made for a long and difficult day. The players set out in the morning and did not return to the hotel until 9:30 that night, empty-handed.

"I'll bet this was the first fishing trip ever made where fishermen used boat, bus, train, and taxi," Casey said. "That ocean got a little too rough, so we had to leave the boat and finally return to Havana on a train. I still don't know the name of the town where we got off the train."[6]

Baseball historian Irv Goldfarb described the Dodgers' modern hotel and ballpark facilities in Havana. Of Gran Stadium, he wrote, "Built only the year before as part of Havana's burgeoning modernization, the ballpark reportedly included a playing field and lighting system of major-league quality." Of the Hotel Nacional, the best resort in the city, he said,

> These opulent quarters boasted beautiful swimming pools, fine restaurants, and the players were quartered with visiting diplomats and international businessmen. The Class Triple-A Royals were housed at the Havana Military Academy, a prep school attended by the wealthy offspring of government employees.[7]

The Dodgers black minor leaguers—Robinson, catcher Roy Campanella, and pitchers Don Newcombe and Roy Partlow—were housed at the less-luxurious Hotel Boston in "old" Havana. Robinson protested, but when he was told Rickey thought it best they be quartered separately, he went along with it.

Yet, some Dodgers were not satisfied with having the black players staying at a different hotel—they did not want them as teammates. Reacting to rumors that Robinson would soon be a member of the Dodgers, a group of players supposedly drew up, or were preparing to draw up, a petition expressing their opposition.

Dixie Walker was allegedly the organizer, and second baseman Eddie Stanky, outfielder Carl Furillo, backup catcher Bobby Bragan, and

pitchers Casey, Kirby Higbe, and Ed Head were generally acknowledged to have been involved to one degree or another. Furillo, a Penn-
sylvanian, always claimed he had been wrongly implicated and that his
only opposition to Robinson was the same as it would have been toward
any rookie vying for his spot on the roster.

"There has been much made of that petition, but I never saw it," said
Ed Stevens, who would lose his first-base job to Robinson. "Never
heard talk of it, and I don't know who in the world started the rumor,
but then I was just a young player and nobody let me know anything."[8]

Traveling secretary Harold Parrott found out about the petition
while the team was in Panama for a series of exhibition games. He ran
into an inebriated Higbe in a bar, where the pitcher, as he so often did,
had been drinking heavily. "Ol' Hig just won't do it," he said to Parrott.
"The ol' man [Rickey] has been fair to Ol' Hig. So Ol' Hig ain't going to
join any petition to keep anyone off the club."[9] Parrott immediately
informed Rickey and Durocher of what he had heard.

Durocher wasted no time in heading off this potential crisis. Although it was the middle of the night, he had the players gather in the
kitchen of the army barracks where the team was staying. When he
entered the room, wearing his pajamas and bathrobe, "he looked like a
fighter about to enter the ring," Parrott remembered.[10]

"Listen, I don't care if this guy is white, black, green, or has stripes
like a fucking zebra. If I say he plays, he plays," declared Durocher. "He
can put an awful lot of fucking money in our pockets. Take your petition
and shove it up your ass. This guy can take us to the World Series, and
so far we haven't won dick."[11]

In his memoir, *Nice Guys Finish Last*, Durocher elaborated on what
he had said to the players that night.

> I hear some of you fellows don't want to play with Robinson and that
> you have a petition drawn up that you are going to sign. Well, boys,
> you know what you can do with that petition. You can wipe your ass
> with it. Mr. Rickey is on his way down here and all you have to do is
> tell him about it. I'm sure he'll be happy to make other arrangements
> for you.
>   I hear Dixie Walker is going to send Mr. Rickey a letter asking to
> be traded. Just hand him the letter, Dixie, and you're gone. *Gone!* If
> this fellow is good enough to play on this ballclub—and from what

I've seen and heard, he is—he is going to play on this ballclub and he
is going to play for *me*.

Leo then warned his players that Robinson was only the first and soon
there would be other black players in the league. "So," he said, "I don't
want to see your petition, and I don't want to hear anything more about
it. The meeting is over; go back to bed."[12]

Rickey later met individually with each Robinson protestor. "Hugh
Casey, our best relief pitcher, was indispensable but curiously insecure
for a great competitor," Rickey told Roger Kahn years later. "When I
told him he might end up relieving in the minor leagues, he simply
wilted."[13]

Eventually, those who had originally opposed the addition of a black
player learned to appreciate Robinson's ability and competitiveness,
particularly Casey. "The enigmatic pitcher from Atlanta spent hours
during the early season batting balls to Robinson to help him adjust to
the first-base position and gently chided Robinson about his fielding
after the games," wrote author Jules Tygiel.[14]

Yet, sometimes Casey's drinking would lead him to make outrageous
statements. He always drank when he played cards—actually, he always
drank. One time during a poker game with Spider Jorgensen, Marv
Rackley, and Robinson, he reached over and rubbed Jackie's head.

"I got to change my luck, Jackie," he said. "In Georgia, when my
poker luck got bad, I'd just go out and rub me the teat of the biggest,
blackest nigger woman I could find."[15]

Robinson turned to Jorgensen and said, "Deal the cards," letting it
go in a way he might not have if he thought Casey meant any harm.[16]

Moreover, writes Robinson biographer Arnold Rampersad, "Casey
was one of the older players who liked to help Robinson in practice; he
was also quick to back him more than once that season in rough episodes with opposing players."[17] Robinson, in turn, called Casey "one of
the swellest guys I've met."[18]

Durocher started Casey in an April 2 game against the Royals. Robinson, playing first base for Montreal, faced Casey three times and
failed to get the ball out of the infield. Casey pitched six innings and
gave up just one run. But in the fourth inning he was hit on his right
biceps by a George Shuba line drive. He chased after the ball and threw
Shuba out. Although he remained in the game for two more innings, his

arm began to bother him the next day, and the club decided to rest him. Casey sat out for 10 days, before returning to pitch in the traditional final exhibition series against the Yankees.

During that series, in which Robinson played first base for the Dodgers, the team quietly announced on April 10 that they had purchased his contract from Montreal. He would be the first black man in the major leagues since Fleetwood Walker in 1884. As big a story as that was, and despite the eventual historical significance it would have for the country, its impact on the fans of Brooklyn was secondary to the previous day's announcement that Leo Durocher had been suspended for the 1947 season.

Commissioner Happy Chandler had suspended Durocher, citing his "string of moral shortcomings: gambling debts, associations with known gamblers and nightlife figures, and a scandalous marriage with charges of adultery, bigamy, and contempt of court."[19]

Chandler also took into consideration the feud between the Yankees and Dodgers that had simmered throughout spring training. The fracas generated charges and countercharges by Durocher, Rickey, and the Yankees' Larry MacPhail, Rickey's former friend and Durocher's one-time boss. Durocher and MacPhail made the most damaging allegations, accusing one another of gambling and consorting with known underworld characters. Brooklyn also claimed that MacPhail was tampering when he signed two of Durocher's coaches, Charlie Dressen and John Corriden, to Yankee contracts for 1947. In addition to suspending Durocher, Chandler suspended Dressen for the season's first 30 days, and he fined each club $2,000.

Rickey named coach Clyde Sukeforth to manage the club until he could get a permanent replacement for Durocher. The Dodgers, playing at home, won their opener, as Casey saved the win for Hal Gregg. Robinson had a mostly uneventful debut, going 0-for-3 with a run scored. Brooklyn's star of the day was Pete Reiser, whose eighth-inning double drove in the winning run.

In the ninth inning, Sukeforth replaced Robinson defensively with Howie Schultz. The Dodgers soon realized Robinson needed no help at first base. Schultz played in only one more game before Brooklyn sold him to the Phillies. Twenty-two-year-old Ed Stevens, the Dodgers' other first baseman, played in just one game before they sent him back to the minors.

Sukeforth made an interesting decision in the ninth inning, one that had those in the press box wondering if Durocher would have handled it the same way. The Dodgers were ahead, 5–3, when the Braves put two runners on with one out. Casey and left-hander Vic Lombardi were warming up, and with Boston's next two batters being left-handed, Lombardi seemed the logical choice to relieve Gregg. But Sukeforth went with Casey, who got Bama Rowell on a foul pop to first baseman Schultz and struck out rookie Earl Torgeson looking. Two days later, in Brooklyn's second game, Casey saved a win for roommate Higbe with two and two-thirds innings of scoreless relief, twice pitching out of bases-loaded situations.

Rickey's first choice to replace Durocher had been Joe McCarthy, the former Yankees manager who had quit the team in 1946. When McCarthy turned him down, Rickey turned to a longtime friend and associate, 62-year-old Burt Shotton. Now retired and living in Florida, Shotton, excepting one game in 1934, had not managed in the major leagues since 1933, when he led the Phillies. Because he managed in civilian clothes, Shotton was not allowed out of the dugout. Sukeforth, who remained as a coach, would represent the team in on-field disputes.

Shotton had been offered the job at approximately 10:30 a.m. on April 18. The appointment became official at noon. The announcement was brief and succinct: "Burton Edwin Shotton has accepted the management of the Brooklyn Dodgers and will take charge of the team today." By 1:30 p.m., the new skipper, dressed in a topcoat and a gray fedora, was sitting in the visiting team's dugout at the Polo Grounds, where the Dodgers were losing to the crosstown Giants, 10–4, in New York's home opener.

John Drebinger of the *New York Times* observed that Shotton "appeared on the scene like something whisked out of a magician's closet by Prof. Branch Rickey."[20] When asked to comment on the day's events, Shotton only could utter, "It was a complete surprise to me."[21]

The new manager made immediate use of his veteran reliever—on the field and off. Casey warmed up in six of Brooklyn's first seven games and was called on in four of them. He appeared in seven of the first 13 games, saving four and winning two.

After the Dodgers defeated the Cubs on April 29, a game in which Casey recorded his fourth save of the young season, he and four of his teammates—Dixie Walker, Tommy Tatum, Gene Hermanski, and Hank Behrman—participated in a bowling match to benefit the Red Cross. "All of them are experienced hands at the sport," reported the *Brooklyn Eagle*, "especially Casey, who makes a specialty of benefit contests."[22]

Casey's save that afternoon had not been one of his better efforts. He relieved Joe Hatten in the eighth inning with Phil Cavarretta on second, two outs, and the Dodgers clinging to a 3–2 lead. He ended the threat by retiring Dom Dallessandro on a groundout to Pee Wee Reese. Brooklyn scored seven runs in the bottom of the inning. When he returned for the ninth, Casey, perhaps affected by the extended stay in the dugout, allowed four runs, three of them earned.

He sloughed off the ninth, saying he would rather come into a game to protect a slim lead and see enemy runners on base than come in with an eight-run lead. He also had a ready explanation for why he often walked leadoff batters in innings. "I just don't have good control when I wind up," he said. "I am so used to pitching with men on the bases. I never wind up in the bullpen. Don't even throw hard anymore. I save all I have for the game. I figure the more games I can get in the more I can help. I need only a few tosses to loosen up my arm. Think maybe I'll quit the windup entirely."[23]

The obvious solution here would have been for Casey to always pitch from the stretch position, but it was not done that way during his time. Pitchers used a full windup, except in cases where runners were on base and a steal situation presented itself. Only then would they pitch from the stretch position.

When Casey was not on the mound, Shotton depended on him and coaches Sukeforth and Ray Blades to get a reading on the assets and liabilities of the club he had inherited. Casey would sit by his side in the shade of the dugout, usually until the seventh inning, when he would trudge to the bullpen.

Conversely, Casey would go on to have a good season and credited Shotton for much of his success. "Barney handled me perfectly," he said. "He asked me how much work I thought I could do, and I told him I could work three innings almost every day if necessary. So Shotton told me he would never call on me before the seventh."[24]

Nevertheless, Shotton would have several detractors. Pitcher Ralph Branca remembered thinking Shotton had never overcome his years away from the game. "We would sit on the bench, and we'd laugh at some of the moves Shotton made," Branca said. "[A]fter having Durocher, who was three or four steps ahead of everybody—to have this man who was a step behind or two steps behind as far as strategy went, it was a big comedown to me."[25]

Shotton also had critics in the press. Red Barber said most of the writers covering the Dodgers cared little for Shotton, particularly Dick Young of the *Daily News* and Harold Rosenthal of the *Herald Tribune*. Yet, according to Barber, Shotton was the "unsung hero of 1947." He brought calm to an unsettled situation, won the pennant, and carried the Yankees to seven games in the World Series.[26]

Dixie Walker also praised the job Shotton had done in replacing Durocher. "We seem to be doing well enough and drawing the fans in as great numbers as we did in 1946. And don't forget this," he said, in what could be construed as a shot at Leo, as well as praise for Robinson. "The 1947 Dodgers are as aggressive as any club you have ever seen in Brooklyn."[27]

20

THE HUGH CASEY THEORY
OF RELIEF PITCHING

The first week of May 1947 was a wet one in Brooklyn. Four consecutive days of rainy weather wiped out two scheduled two-game series, one with Cincinnati and one with Pittsburgh. On one of those offdays, May 3, Rickey traded Casey's friend and roommate, Kirby Higbe, and four other players to the Pirates for outfielder Al Gionfriddo and a reported $100,000.

Accompanying Higbe to Pittsburgh were pitchers Hank Behrman and Cal McLish, infielder Gene Mauch, and catcher Dixie Howell. The Pirates, unsatisfied with Behrman's performance, sold him back to Brooklyn on June 14.

Despite his 2–0 record, the 32-year-old Higbe had not pitched well the first month of the season. In addition, he allegedly had been one of the most vocal Dodgers in his opposition to playing with Jackie Robinson. Rickey had also tried to trade Dixie Walker, the purported leader of the opposition to Robinson. But Walker was Brooklyn's best offensive weapon, and Rickey was not satisfied with what the Pirates had offered in return.

Higbe had won many games for Brooklyn throughout the years, and he was popular among his teammates. To head off any resentment, manager Burt Shotton called in Walker and Casey to explain the reasoning behind the deal and asked them to explain it to the other players.

The Dodgers returned to action on May 6, defeating the Cardinals, 7–6, in the first meeting between the teams since the 1946 playoff.

Casey entered the game in the seventh inning, with the score tied, 6–6, and pitched three scoreless innings to earn his second win. At 10–3, the Dodgers had a two-game lead over the Braves and Cubs. The Cardinals, at 3–12, were in last place, already eight games behind Brooklyn.

The Cardinals won the next two games in the series, starting the Dodgers on a run of eight losses in 10 games. By May 16, their record had slipped to 12–11, when they faced former teammate Higbe at Pittsburgh's Forbes Field. Higbe allowed only four hits in eight innings in losing, 3–1, but one of the hits was a two-run home run by Pee Wee Reese. Casey earned his fifth save with two-and-a-third scoreless innings in relief of Ralph Branca. Two days later, he pitched three scoreless innings to save a 4–2 win for Joe Hatten at Chicago.

Robinson's presence in the Dodgers lineup continued to generate attendance records, as a crowd of more than 46,000 saw Robinson's first game at Wrigley Field. Cubs left-hander Johnny Schmitz had a 2–0 lead after six innings. But Pete Reiser's bases-loaded double highlighted Brooklyn's four-run seventh. At that point, Shotton turned the game over to Casey.

The 12th appearance of the season by the "pleasantly plump pitcher" had the *Brooklyn Eagle*'s Harold C. Burr "begging" Shotton for mercy on his behalf. "If manager Burt Shotton doesn't give Hugh Casey some rest soon," wrote Burr, "the Dodgers' number-one relief pitcher won't have any strength left to serve those succulent steaks to the customers of his Flatbush restaurant when the team returns to Brooklyn."[1] Casey had been in 12 of Brooklyn's 26 games, winning two and saving six, with one loss.

Watching from the stands, Casey's pitches did not seem to pose a problem to hitters, which led one reporter to ask him the secret to his success. "None of your business," he replied. "There are other games coming up, and I've got to keep on fooling those guys. If I told you they would find out it's a nothing ball and lay back and let me have it right between the eyes."[2]

Casey got his third win at St. Louis on May 21, as the team concluded an abbreviated first swing through the west in which they won only three of eight games. The Dodgers scored a 10th-inning run to win, 4–3, and defeat nemesis Harry Brecheen. They returned home to face Ben Chapman and the Phillies, the manager and team that had been so vicious in their verbal assaults on Robinson in their first visit to Ebbets Field.

Led by Chapman, the Phillies hurled the vilest racial insults at Robinson. It grew so hateful that Walker, a lifelong friend of Chapman, told him to stop. Stanky, another Dodger who had not originally welcomed Robinson, called Chapman a coward and dared him to "pick on somebody who can fight back."[3]

For Rickey, the Chapman incident proved to be a positive, both for Robinson and the Brooklyn team. "Chapman did more than anybody to unite the Dodgers. When he poured out that string of unconscionable abuse, he solidified and united 30 men, not one of whom was willing to sit by and see someone kick around a man who had his hands tied behind his back—Chapman made Jackie a real member of the Dodgers."[4]

In the series opener, the Dodgers rallied from a 4–0 deficit to win, 5–4. Two seventh-inning bases-loaded walks issued by relievers Ken Heintzelman and Tommy Hughes accounted for the tying and winning runs. Casey's two innings of scoreless relief allowed Rex Barney to win his first game of the season.

The crowd at Ebbets Field the next afternoon, Saturday, May 24, witnessed history of a sort. They saw a play that happened for the first time in the major leagues and has not happened since. Philadelphia's starting pitcher was right-hander Al Jurisich, while at the same time Chapman had left-hander Oscar Judd warming up in the bullpen. The idea was to get Shotton to replace the left-handed hitters he had started. After Jurisich struck out Reese and walked Robinson, Chapman made the switch.

Two batters later, the Dodgers had two men on and two out, when with left-handed-hitting Gene Hermanski due up, Shotton sent Carl Furillo up to pinch-hit for Hermanski. The right-handed-hitting Furillo responded by driving Judd's first pitch into the left-field seats to give the Dodgers a 3–0 lead.

It was the first and only first-inning pinch-hit home run in major-league history. But in a reversal of the previous day's events, this time the Phillies rallied and won, 4–3, in 10 innings. Casey came into the game in the 10th inning and allowed a run, giving the Phillies the victory. But that was not the worst part of his day. At 11:00 that night, he was driving home to his apartment, at 406 East Eighth Street, a multifamily house with two units, built in 1925, less than two miles and 10 minutes from his restaurant. Casey, who claimed he was going only about 20 miles per hour, struck and killed Alex Azarewicz, a blind, elderly pedestrian.

According to detectives from the Fifth Avenue Station in Brooklyn, Azarewicz had gotten off the Fifth Avenue trolley, near Seventh Street, and was being led across the street by his sister Stella. They were crossing in the middle of the block when Casey's car, a Nash, struck them. Casey followed as Azarewicz was transported to Methodist Hospital, where the 62-year-old Manhattan resident was pronounced dead on arrival.

Casey did not say from where he was coming, although he often spent his evenings at his bar and grill. He was told he would be required to appear in Traffic Court the next day, but the police were convinced the accident had been unavoidable, and they would bring no charges against him.[5] We can only speculate whether Casey had been drinking at his bar and, if so, how much; furthermore, we can only speculate whether the police would have handled the incident differently if he had been an ordinary citizen and not Hugh Casey, the star reliever of the hometown Brooklyn Dodgers.

A doubleheader loss at Boston on Memorial Day dropped the Dodgers to fourth place, although only two games behind the surprising first-place New York Giants. Seven wins in eight games moved them to the top of the standing by June 8, only to fall out of the lead the next day. The Reds ended Brooklyn's five-game win streak and knocked them out of first place with a 9–6 win. Four Dodgers pitchers followed starter Harry Taylor, who lasted just one-and-a-third innings.

Casey, who had not pitched in nearly a week, allowed Cincinnati's big blow: Benny Zientara's three-run home run in the eighth. The Dodgers were ahead, 6–5, when Casey relieved Vic Lombardi with two on and one out in the eighth. The first batter he faced was the normally weak-hitting Zientara, who reached him for the first home run of his career. The Reds added another run against Casey before Ed Chandler got the third out.

Brooklyn lost two of three to the Reds to finish the homestand. Following an offday, they traveled to St. Louis to begin their second western swing. The disappointing Cardinals were still in last-place, but seeing their perennial rivals seemingly awoke Eddie Dyer's crew. They won all four games, outscoring the Dodgers, 31–8. Howie Pollet's win in the final game was his third of the season without a loss against Brooklyn, while he was just 1–7 against the rest of the league.

Brooklyn left town three games behind the Boston Braves and without catcher Bruce Edwards, who had injured his hand in the June 13 series opener. Rookie Gil Hodges would do most of the catching for the next two weeks. The Dodgers snapped out of their slump by winning seven of eight games in Chicago, Cincinnati, and Pittsburgh. Casey picked up his ninth save in Chicago and fourth win in Cincinnati. On June 26, the club returned home, where they defeated the Braves to move back into first place by half a game.

The now-departed Kirby Higbe would later describe the aura that surrounded Casey when he came into a game:

> When old Hughie walked in from the bullpen, it would look like he was walking uphill. Leo would say something like, "Case, the tying and winning runs are on base with one out, so you have to get them out."
>
> Old roomie would say, "I can see skipper. I been here all day too." And he would never change his expression. In those tight situations he never showed anything except that he was going to give it everything he had. He always did.[6]

In early June, J. G. Taylor Spink of *Sporting News* subtitled his weekly "Looping the Loops" column, "Bull Session with a Bullpen Ace." Few of his readers would have any doubt this would be a column about Hugh Casey. As the 1947 season progressed, Joe Page of the Yankees would emerge as the American League's best relief pitcher, and arguments about whether he or Casey was the game's greatest reliever would ensue. But at this point in the season, Page was one bad outing away from manager Bucky Harris returning him to the minors.

"My arm is in great shape," Casey told Spink, "and that restaurant of mine is going great. A man just offered me 60 grand for it. Not bad on an investment of $15,000. But Hughie isn't selling."[7]

Casey said owning the restaurant made him a better pitcher. "You know you pitch better if you have what you might call an anchor to the windward," said the former sailor. "If, as a veteran, you go into the box and say, 'They can't do me any real harm, because I can walk out of here into a paying restaurant business,' your sense of independence is reflected in your work."

It was a long interview, in which Casey laid out his theories on relief pitching and how he prepared himself. He would prefer to be a starting pitcher, he said, but understood he had greater value to the Dodgers as a reliever.

"I am a good team man. I am willing to do what is best for the club. To begin with, I am like ol' Stubblebeard, Burleigh Grimes," Casey said, invoking the hard-nosed former Dodgers pitcher and manager, "a mean guy on the mound. I like mean guys for pitchers. It is me or it is the opposition."

He continued,

> Now don't get me wrong. I am not the sort of man who will throw at a guy's head and say, "To hell with him. Let him watch out." I don't want anybody to get hurt.
>
> But when I go into the game I say, "The batters want to beat your brains out. Well, don't let them. Don't be soft and easy. Act tough."
>
> This is the first essential in the construction of a first-class relief pitcher. He must be tough. He must realize that he knows what he is going to do and the batters don't.
>
> Never get excited. Get complete control over yourself, then control over the ball. You were sent in to stop the opposition, not to help them. So don't beat yourself.
>
> Have confidence in yourself. Be so confident that your fielders will share that feeling. Make them feel glad when they see you walk out of the bullpen.
>
> A good part of relief success lies in getting the hitters nervous and jittery. Knock one down. Not too close. But knock him down. Show you mean business. Don't go out there and throw your heart out. Because you may be called again the following day, and then again. Pace yourself. Watch your timing and coordination; conserve your energies.

Casey explained some of the style adjustments he had to make in becoming a reliever:

> When you relieve, you cannot afford to experiment. You cannot afford to waste anything. You cannot fool around with deliveries of which you are not the complete master. . . . A fine curve is important

in any kind of pitching. In relief it is the first essential. What a terrific feeling if you walk in, throw a sharp curve, and see the batter jam into a double play to retire the side and kill the threat!

He said the conditioning necessary for relief work is no different than for a starter. "You have to run every day, get your sleep, watch your diet. Sometimes, if the weather is cool, I will give myself a day off from running," he said, adding that he seldom did any running before night games because the damp air stiffened his joints.

Casey added,

> The will to win is, of course, very essential for every ballplayer. But it seems to me it is extra important for the relief pitcher. You see, he never is called if things are running smoothly. The only time he is thrown into the game is when things are tough. Never a lot of smiling fielders, but always grim guys facing an emergency. Don't think that is too pleasant. But you get used to it.
>
> Insofar as I am concerned, relief hurling entails no special mental angle. If you are inclined to be the worrisome type—well, if you are, you don't get to be a relief pitcher.

When Spink asked him to name the essentials of relief pitching, Casey listed the following five qualifications:

1. Be calm, cool, and collected.
2. Make control the primary requisite.
3. Throw only sharp stuff. Don't waste effort or motion.
4. Have that old team spirit, without which you just can't be a relief man.
5. Study your hitters. Know them. Know what they are likely to do in certain spots. Don't just loaf around the bullpen. Watch those hitters all the time. They have little tell-tale movements, little giveaways.

Casey told Spink he was working with Rex Barney, the hard-throwing young right-hander whose main problem was lack of control. "I am trying to correct Barney's pitching stride, getting him to work into a 'groove.' Rex may turn out to be the key to the pennant," Casey said. "If I can teach him a few things, improve his control, among other matters, he may win the flag for us. He is fast, intelligent, and has a world of stuff." He also was working with other young hurlers, teaching them the fine points of the art of pitching, which had earned him the nickname "The Professor" among his teammates.

On July 6, the final game before the All-Star break, Ralph Branca blanked the Braves on three hits for his 12th win of the season. Brooklyn's 4–0 victory moved the Dodgers past Boston and back into first place.

Casey had notified the members of the press covering the Dodgers he would host a dinner for them at his restaurant following the July 15 doubleheader against the Pirates. The dinner was held, although the two games had resulted in easy wins for Pittsburgh, and Casey's first game appearance was among his worst of the season. He allowed four runs, the result of rookie Wally Westlake's grand slam. The lead over Boston was shaved to two and a half games.

Almost 70 years later, the 95-year-old Westlake still had fond memories of this game, which included not only his first grand slam, but also an earlier bases-loaded double. About the grand slam, he said he had "faked like he was going to right, and Casey threw one in his wheel house and he was able to hit it out."[8]

In late July, the Dodgers ran off a 13-game winning streak, during which Casey picked up his 11th and 12th saves. In both games, July 23, at Cincinnati, and July 27, at Pittsburgh, he pitched two scoreless innings to preserve victories for Hank Behrman.

In the July 27 game, the first of a doubleheader, he faced pinch-hitter Hank Greenberg in the eighth inning with two outs, the bases loaded, and the Dodgers ahead, 8–4. With everyone at Forbes Field rooting for big Hank to hit a game-tying grand slam, Casey fell behind, 2–0. After the second ball, he called time and walked to the Dodgers dugout and began toweling sweat off his arms and face.

"I could have called for a towel," he said later, "but Greenberg made me wait when he came to bat and now he can wait." While he was in the dugout, he said Shotton told him it would be all right for him to walk Greenberg and pitch to the next hitter, leadoff batter Billy Cox. "Nope," Casey said he replied, "I won't walk Greenberg, and he won't hit me either."[9] He then returned to the mound and threw Greenberg three consecutive curveballs. Hank swung at and missed all three, silencing the crowd of more than 42,000.

Casey had notched his seventh win the day before, against the Pirates. He relieved Ralph Branca in the eighth inning of a 4–4 game with Pirates runners on first and second, and Ralph Kiner and Hank Greenberg due up. Casey retired the two sluggers, and after the Dodgers went ahead with two runs in the ninth, one the result of his RBI bunt single, he retired the Pirates in order in the home half. Brooklyn's winning streak, which extended to the last day of the month and concluded with a three-game sweep at St. Louis, moved them a season-high 10 games ahead of the Cardinals and the surprising Giants, who were tied with St. Louis for second place.

21

HOLDING OFF THE CARDINALS

Unlike the season-long battles with the Cardinals in 1941, 1942, and 1946, which featured multiple lead changes, the Dodgers would remain in first place for the rest of the 1947 season, with their lead never falling below three games.

Their late July win streak ended at Wrigley Field on the first day of August. Cubs catcher Clyde McCullough hit a ninth-inning, two-out, two-run home run off Casey to give Chicago a 10–8 victory. Two more losses at Chicago followed, accompanied by three Cardinals wins, which reduced the Dodgers' lead to seven games.

Casey returned to form the next day, at Boston, when he pitched four and two-thirds scoreless innings in a 10-inning, 4–2 win. But Brooklyn lost the next three to the Braves, while St. Louis was winning three from Cincinnati. When the Dodgers opened a series against the Phillies on August 8, the lead was down to four games. The Giants were five games behind, but a losing streak soon dropped them out of contention.

St. Louis was four and a half games behind when they came to Brooklyn for a crucial four-game series, beginning with a day–night doubleheader on August 18. Before the game, a reporter had informed Cardinals manager Eddie Dyer that the Dodgers were saying the pressure was on his club.

"Well, we've got to catch them," Dyer replied, adding,

If that's pressure, well, I don't know. These fellows give me what they've got. Whether they've got enough to catch Brooklyn, that's something else again. Now if it worries the Dodgers to be in front, maybe that's pressure. I don't know. But I'd trade places with them. A lead of four and a half games, I'd take that.[1]

The Dodgers won the afternoon game, 7–5, with Casey rescuing Vic Lombardi in the ninth inning. He came in with pinch-runner Bernie Creger on second and Ron Northey on first. On his first pitch to Red Schoendienst, Creger wandered too far off second base and was picked off by catcher Bruce Edwards. Schoendienst took the next pitch, but on Casey's third delivery he grounded into a game-ending double play. Casey had needed only three pitches to get the three outs and earn his 13th save of the year.

Brooklyn also won the night game, a replay of a July 20 protested game that National League president Ford Frick had ruled should be played in its entirety. In the top of the ninth inning of that contest, with the Cardinals ahead, 2–0, Northey hit a high fly to deep right-center. Center fielder Pete Reiser failed to make the catch, and the ball dropped onto the field. Right fielder Dixie Walker picked it up and relayed it to Eddie Stanky, whose throw to catcher Bruce Edwards nailed Northey at the plate.

First-base umpire Larry Goetz ruled the ball in play, but third-base umpire Beans Reardon had signaled to Northey that it was a home run, causing him to slow down, which contributed to his being out at the plate. In the bottom of the ninth, the Dodgers scored three runs to "win" the game, 3–2.

The basis of the Cardinals protest was that Northey had been deceived by the umpire and would have scored if he had not slowed down. Frick upheld the protest and awarded Northey a home run; however, he did not order the game resumed in the top of the ninth with St. Louis ahead, 3–0, which would have been the normal procedure called for by the rules. He allowed the Dodgers' runs to stand and ruled the game a 3–3 tie. All the records in the game counted except for the pitchers' win and loss. Casey would have been the winner and Murry Dickson the loser.

In defeating the two Cardinals left-handed aces—Howie Pollet and Harry Brecheen—the Dodgers raised their first-place lead to six and a half games. St. Louis won the next two games to earn a series split and cut Brooklyn's lead back to four and a half games. In the last game, on

August 20, Ralph Branca had a one-hitter and a 2–0 lead through eight innings. But he walked Schoendienst to lead off the ninth, and after getting two outs, he walked Enos Slaughter. When Branca's first two pitches to Northey were balls, Shotton replaced him with Casey. Both runners eventually scored before Casey got the third out, sending the game into extra innings.

Casey pitched the final three-and-a-third innings, allowing only one run. Hot-hitting Whitey Kurowski led off the 12th inning with a home run that proved to be the game-winner. "If that first ball is in there, I'll put it into the stands," Kurowski had told his teammates upon leaving the dugout.[2]

Despite the myriad of obstacles put in his way, Jackie Robinson was having a sensational season, one that would earn him the *Sporting News* Rookie of the Year Award. He had won over his teammates with his hitting, fielding, daring baserunning, and ability to withstand the abuse he had taken from opponents, fans, and some of his own teammates.

Dixie Walker, the alleged leader of those who had opposed Robinson joining the Dodgers, said of him, "No other ballplayer on this club, with the possible exception of Bruce Edwards, has done more to put the Dodgers up in the race than Robinson has. He is everything that Branch Rickey said he was when he came up from Montreal."[3]

This August 20 game, however, was Robinson's most difficult since those April games with the Phillies. In the top of the 11th inning, with Stan Musial on first, Slaughter hit a ground ball to Robinson at first base. After determining he had no play on Musial, who was running on the pitch, Robinson raced to first to retire Slaughter. But instead of Slaughter's foot landing on the bag, it landed on Jackie's right foot, which was not even on the base, but flush against the inside of the bag. Robinson began hopping around on his injured foot, as the Ebbets Field crowd loudly booed the Cardinals outfielder.

Slaughter's spikes had opened a cut on Robinson's foot, but after treatment by trainer Doc Wendler, Robinson stayed in the game. He led off the home 12th with a single off Pollet. The Cardinals were ahead, 3–2, and Shotton, satisfied to play for the tie, had Pete Reiser sacrifice Robinson to second. Jackie's difficult day ended when, as the potential tying run, he took too big a lead and pitcher George Munger, who had replaced Pollet, picked him off.

The Cardinals clubhouse was a scene of jubilation after the game. "The cokes [and presumably the beers] are on me," yelled Dyer, trying to be heard above the shouting and celebrating. "It's just like I've been telling you all along," he said, "this is going down to the last day, and we'll win it."[4]

Dyer turned serious regarding Slaughter's spiking of Robinson. "Listen," he said,

> I've particularly told my boys to be very careful when playing this club, so there will be no chance of an incident. Not once this year has Robinson even had to duck a ball thrown by one of my pitchers. So you may be dead sure it was an accident when Enos spiked him. Enos runs mighty hard, and with his head down. He didn't see Robinson's foot.

Yet, when Dyer had come out of the Cardinals dugout to ask about him, Robinson's pent up anger came pouring out.

"Get away from me, I don't want anything to do with you," he said.

"What's the matter? What happened?" Dyer asked.

"You heard him," yelled Casey. "He said get away from him."

"Get along, Dyer," Eddie Stanky shouted. "We'll take care of this and your ballplayers, too."[5]

After yelling at Dyer, Stanky turned his attention to Robinson. "You've got to watch your step now," he said, speaking more as a veteran to a rookie than as a white man to a black man. "This is the money month up here. They're going to be out to get you. . . . If you don't watch out now, they'll tear you apart."

Robinson said he thought he had given Slaughter plenty of room and was ready to come off the bag when Slaughter spiked him. "It may have been intentional. I don't know," he said. Robinson's teammates mostly agreed that the spiking was not accidental.

Ralph Branca had no doubt it was intentional, noting that Slaughter had attempted to spike Robinson earlier in the game. "I went over and told Jackie then that Enos had barely missed him and that I'd get him the next time he came up. But Jackie told me that he didn't think Slaughter had tried to cut him. I'm sorry as hell I didn't get him like I wanted to."

To his dying day, Slaughter vehemently denied spiking Robinson intentionally. "The throw to Robinson was low," he explained, continuing,

> He had to step forward to scoop up the throw, and when he stepped back on the base for the putout, his foot was right in the middle of the bag. . . . I had always played by the rule that the basepaths belong to the runner, and I don't believe I have to apologize for not making an exception to this for anyone. On this occasion, my spikes clipped his ankle.[6]

Slaughter was guilty of either lying or, to be more generous, having a faulty memory. His ground ball was hit directly to Robinson. There was no need for him to "step forward to scoop up the throw" and step back on the base.

Yet, as ugly an incident as this was, it had a positive outcome. Sam Lacy covered Robinson in 1947 for the *Baltimore Afro-American*. The following spring, he wrote an article about Leo Durocher's recently released book, *The Dodgers and Me*. According to Leo, Rickey had predicted the terrible treatment Robinson received from other clubs would only serve to bring the white Dodgers to his side and make them a more cohesive team.[7]

"It worked that way too," Leo wrote in *The Dodgers and Me*. "When Enos Slaughter spiked Robinson's outstretched foot in a play at first base that wasn't even close, Hugh Casey, who lives in Georgia, charged at the Cardinals' outfielder."

"I saw a Georgia cracker defend a Negro boy!" marveled one writer. "It can be said that Robinson 'made' the team today!"[8]

The "stout innkeeper," as the *Brooklyn Eagle* had taken to calling Casey, picked up back-to-back saves in wins against Pittsburgh on August 24 and 25, in two very different games—3–1 and 11–10.

Bob Cooke of the *New York Herald Tribune* never passed up an opportunity to make a crack about Casey's weight. Hugh had saved the August 24 game for Branca when he was called on to protect a two-run lead in the eighth inning with one out and the tying runs on base. He retired Frank Gustine and Ralph Kiner and then set down the Pirates in the ninth.

The opening sentence of Cooke's August 25 article read,

Hugh Casey, Brooklyn's large right-hander, who eats so many of his own steaks that he finds it easier to slip into the box score than he does his clothing, transformed a nasty Pittsburgh threat into an exciting tonic for 33,207 people yesterday as he kept Pirate hands off Brooklyn's 3–1 victory.[9]

Later in the article, he described Casey's entrance into the game as filling it with his "ample anatomy."

Casey's save in the August 25 game was not as efficient. He relieved Clyde King in the seventh inning and pitched the rest of the way. He allowed two runs in the ninth inning before retiring Pittsburgh sluggers Kiner and Hank Greenberg to strand the potential tying run at third base. This was Casey's 33rd game finished, breaking the team's single-season record, set by Jack Quinn in 1932. He would add four more in the final month of the season.

Save number 16 came against the Giants at Ebbets Field on August 30. After the Dodgers had scored three in the eighth, he pitched a three-up-three-down ninth inning, needing only four pitches to save a 3–1 win for King.

Casey's 17th save, a 7–6 win at the Polo Grounds on September 5, was not so pristine. He allowed two runs in two innings, both runs coming on Johnny Mize's two-out home run in the ninth inning. He preserved the win for rookie Phil Haugstad, the first and only win of Haugstad's big-league career, by getting Walker Cooper on a ground ball to Pee Wee Reese for the final out.

"I wasn't worried with Big Coop coming up in the ninth," Casey told *New York Post* sportswriter Jimmy Cannon. "I don't think he ever got a hit off me since he came into the league. If he gets 50-for-50 I'll still be even." (Walker Cooper had two hits in 16 at-bats against Casey in his career, a .125 batting average.) Casey further related, "Little Johnny Hopp hits me pretty good. So does [Phil] Cavarretta. . . . But in a jam I can get everyone out. The record shows every one hits me pretty good. But I get them out when I got to."[10]

Throughout the season, Burt Shotton had used Casey only to protect a lead or in a tie game. (His 76 and two-thirds innings in 1947 was a full-season career low.) That was the way Casey liked it. It would depress him, he said, to pitch in games that were lopsided. "In the spots I come in, any bad play and I'm in real trouble," he said. "I never get excited. Bad days. Good days. If I don't do it, I feel bad. I watch all the hitters, study them. But I don't go to the bullpen until the seventh inning. I work three innings. Once in a while four. No matter what happens, I go home and relax. All the good athletes relax."

Casey claimed it was not necessary for him to warm up before pitching. "I can walk off the bench and pitch," he said. "I just stretch my muscles and I'm ready." Durocher liked him because he did what he was told, he recalled. "If Leo said knock him down—I'd upset the hitter. If he said hit him—I hit him." He did not say anything about Shotton issuing such orders.

Cannon could not resist a reference to Casey's girth in describing his entrance into a ballgame. "There is an odd contentment in the way Hugh Casey comes strolling in from the bullpen," he wrote, adding,

> It is the gait of a fat man who has eaten well and saunters down a quiet and familiar street after dinner. You expect him to be smoking a cigar when he gets to the pitching mound, and until he throws the first ball he does not seem in any way connected with the commotion his appearance creates in the park.[11]

That same day, Casey said he usually weighs 215 during spring training but goes up to 222 during the season.

Late in the season, J. G. Taylor Spink wrote a column praising Dodgers catcher Bruce Edwards. In it, he asked Edwards to discuss catching the different pitchers he had to handle. "Well, the softest hurler on the club to catch is Hugh Casey," he said. "Hughie is around the plate all the time. He knows what to pitch. He shoulders the mental burden. I just grab what he throws. It's a very fine arrangement. Casey's sinker is almost a screwball," he added. "Hugh has control, always. Daring, too."[12]

Casey earned his 18th and final save of the season on September 10, when he pitched two-and-a-third scoreless innings to save a Joe Hatten win at Chicago. His 18 saves set a National League record, topping Giants moundsman Ace Adams and Phillies hurler Andy Karl, who each had 15 in 1945. Fred Marberry, with 22 for the 1926 Washington Senators, held the major-league record.

The next day, the Dodgers were in St. Louis for the final series of the season between the teams. Brooklyn's lead was four and a half games, making it a near necessity for the Cardinals to win all three games. Instead, they lost two of the three to fall five and a half games behind.

Ralph Branca defeated Harry Brecheen, 4–3, in the opener for his 20th win of the season. No Brooklyn pitcher had won 20 games since Whit Wyatt and Kirby Higbe in 1941, the Dodgers' last pennant-winning season. The game featured another incident between Robinson and a Cardinals player. This time it was second-year catcher Joe Garagiola, and like the Slaughter incident, Garagiola spiking Robinson at first base was the cause.

Garagiola had hit into a rally-killing double play in the home second and stepped on Robinson's foot in his attempt to beat the throw. Robinson thought it was intentional, and when he came to bat in the top of the third, he told Garagiola what he thought of him. The tension in the stands was as great as it was on the field. When the two men moved toward one another, plate umpire Beans Reardon wisely stepped in and quieted them.

Some of the cast had changed since before the war, but the hostility between these rivals continued. The Dodgers and Cardinals were bitter enemies, and no one on either team liked anyone on the other team. "I don't think we had any personal love for anybody on the whole club," Marty Marion, a Cardinal since 1940, told author William Marshall, "and I'm sure they didn't for us."[13]

St. Louis won the middle game of the series, a wild affair in which the Dodgers scored four runs in the top of the ninth to take a 7–6 lead, only to have the Cardinals score two in the bottom of the ninth on Slaughter's double to win, 8–7. (Shotton had brought in Branca, who had pitched seven-and-a-third innings as the previous day's starter, expressly to pitch to Slaughter.)

Casey had replaced Hal Gregg in the seventh inning, with the score tied at 2–2. He walked three men and then gave up a two-out, bases-clearing triple to Musial that put the Cardinals ahead, 5–2. After the game, his 46th and final appearance of the season, he revealed he was suffering from a lame shoulder and a kink in his right elbow. Casey said he had sustained the injuries in a game five days earlier while pitching to Johnny Mize of the Giants. The Dodgers won the final game, also by a score of 8–7, and the countdown to the clinching of the pennant began.

Twenty-one-year-old Ralph Branca's 21st win, at Cincinnati on September 16, combined with the Cardinals loss to the Giants, raised the Dodgers lead to eight and a half games and reduced their magic number to four. The number dropped to two the next day, when they won at Pittsburgh, while the Cardinals were losing to Boston. Despite a loss to Pittsburgh on September 18, the Dodgers clinched at least a tie for the pennant when the Cardinals again lost to the Braves.

On Saturday, September 20, the club had two opportunities to clinch the pennant outright. Neither occurred. At Ebbets Field, Boston's Johnny Sain secured his 20th victory, with five Brooklyn errors contributing to an 8–1 loss in front of a disappointed home crowd. That night, George Munger of St. Louis shut out the Cubs to keep the Cardinals alive for another day.

The fans had celebrated Hugh Casey Day before the game and presented the popular pitcher with a new Chrysler sedan. Casey accepted the gift while standing at home plate. A field microphone had been set up, which he used to thank fans for "making this the happiest day of my life," a statement that Roscoe McGowen called an "excusable overstatement."[14]

On Sunday, Warren Spahn shut out the Dodgers, 4–0, matching Sain's feat of the day before by winning his 20th game. For Brooklyn, it was their third-consecutive loss and third-consecutive failed opportunity to clinch the pennant. They received no help from the Cardinals, who were rained out.

22

THE MAINSTAY OF THE 1947 WORLD SERIES

The pennant-clincher came on Monday, September 22, an offday for the Dodgers. After beating the Cubs in an afternoon game, the Cardinals lost the night game, eliminating them from the race. "When the word came the citizens of Flatbush poured into the streets, forming impromptu parades and filling the night air with howls and shrieks of joy" that continued well past midnight, reported the *New York Times*.[1] A stretch of Flatbush Avenue, the borough's main thoroughfare, was jammed with people celebrating their home team's triumph.

For some of the players, and their wives, the place to be that evening was at Casey's bar and grill. There were three booths, occupied by Casey and wife Kathleen, Pete Reiser, Bobby Bragan, Harry Taylor, Vic Lombardi, and Spider Jorgensen, all accompanied by their wives, along with bachelors Bruce Edwards, Gene Hermanski, and Hank Behrman.

When news of the Cardinals loss became final, they let out a collective roar and the players began pounding one another on the back. It had been a long, difficult struggle, and now that it was over the pent-up emotions were gushing out. "We did it, we did it," shouted Lombardi, who had contributed several key wins down the stretch. "And we'll take the Series, too," added Taylor.[2]

The Dodgers played out the string of remaining games as manager Shotton prepared his team for the World Series. Casey had been idle since September 12, and would remain so for the rest of the season. Nevertheless, he added his 10th win, without throwing a pitch, on September 25, at Philadelphia. Before the regularly scheduled game against the Phillies, the Dodgers won what was the completion of the August 17 game. That game had been halted after six and a half innings with Brooklyn ahead and Casey the pitcher of record.

Brooklyn's opponent in the World Series would be the New York Yankees, just as it had been in 1941. If Brooklyn's beating out the Cardinals had been a mild surprise, the Yankees running away with the American League pennant had been a major upset. They had finished 12 games ahead of the Detroit Tigers and 14 games ahead of the Boston Red Sox.

The Red Sox had been expected to repeat as American League champions, while most preseason forecasts had consigned the Yankees to a middle-of-the-pack finish. These Yankees were not the dominating team they had been before the war, but led by their new manager, Bucky Harris, and the league's Most Valuable Player, Joe DiMaggio, they won 97 games.

Allie Reynolds, acquired in a trade with Cleveland for Joe Gordon, won 19, and Frank "Spec" Shea, a 26-year-old rookie, won 14. During the season, Harris turned left-hander Joe Page, a high-living, failed starter, into a reliever, and Page responded with 14 wins and a league-leading 17 saves. He was in every way the Yankees' counterpart to Hugh Casey, in the same way Johnny Murphy had been in 1941. Of course, Bucky Harris backed his man. "I never saw a better pinch pitcher than Page," he said.[3]

Experts judged the two teams as far inferior to the Cardinals and Red Sox, the previous year's champions. "Their pitching strength rests largely in the bullpen," wrote Tommy Holmes, "or to be more specific, on the left arm of Joe Page and the right arm of Hugh Casey."[4]

Casey was one of five Dodgers who had faced the Yankees in the 1941 Series. The others were Dixie Walker, Pete Reiser, Pee Wee Reese, and Cookie Lavagetto. Yankees holdovers from 1941 were DiMaggio, Phil Rizzuto, Tommy Henrich, and Spud Chandler. (Charlie Keller was injured and not on the Series roster, and Frank Crosetti was now a coach.) Only three pitchers had Series experience: Casey for the Dodgers and Chandler and Bobo Newsom for the Yankees.

The World Series was the nation's most glamorous sporting event, as reflected by some of those in attendance for Game One at Yankee Stadium. Political dignitaries included former president Herbert

Hoover, Secretary of State George Marshall, and New York governor Thomas Dewey. Governor Dewey was joined in the box seats by the governors of New Jersey, Rhode Island, Connecticut, and Pennsylvania, as well as more than 50 disabled war veterans. New York mayor William O'Dwyer, an admitted Dodgers fan, threw out the first ball.

Among those at the game from the baseball world were Commissioner Happy Chandler, Ty Cobb, Babe Ruth, Tris Speaker, Cy Young, and Leo Durocher, with his "wife" Laraine Day. Laraine Day's 1947 marriage to Durocher was declared invalid by the California judge who had granted her an interlocutory divorce on January 20, 1947, which required a year's wait before she could legally remarry. The judge had declared her Mexican divorce and subsequent Texas marriage to Durocher invalid. She then (re)married Durocher in California on February 18, 1948.

Ralph Branca started strong for Brooklyn. He retired the side in order in each of the first four innings before the Yankees erupted for five runs against him in the fifth. The idea of a "closer" had not yet been born. The game plan where managers used several relief pitchers as a bridge between their starter and their ace reliever was 40 years in the future. So after Frank Shea held the Dodgers to one run through five innings, Harris turned the game over to Page.

The hard-throwing Page allowed single runs in the sixth and seventh innings but earned the save in New York's 5–3 win. Hank Behrman had replaced Branca with no one out in the fifth and pitched through the sixth, whereupon Shotton brought in Casey, who pitched the seventh and eighth.

Bringing in one's closer with your team two runs behind is inconceivable in the way the game is played in the twenty-first century. It was also contrary to the way Shotton had used Casey during the season. Still, Shotton believed Casey was the man most likely to keep the Yankees from adding to their lead, and he was right.

Casey gave up a seventh-inning leadoff single to Phil Rizzuto, who worked his way around to third base with two outs. At the plate was Tommy Henrich, and anyone whose memory dated back to 1941 could not help but remember Casey's pitch to Henrich that got away from Mickey Owen in Game Four that year. One member of the press box said, "If he strikes him out again and the ball goes through [catcher Bruce] Edwards, we will really have a story."[5]

To the relief of Brooklyn fans, Casey got Henrich to ground out to second baseman Eddie Stanky. After retiring all six men he faced following the Rizzuto single, Casey assured everyone that despite the loss, things would get better. "What have they got?" he asked. "They can't hit," he said, answering his own question. "We might win the next four in a row."[6]

Game Two was a Yankees romp. Allie Reynolds, aided by a Series record-tying three triples by the New Yorkers and sloppy fielding by the Dodgers, pitched a complete-game, 10–3 victory. Shotton started Vic Lombardi and followed with three relievers—Hal Gregg, Hank Behrman, and Rex Barney—making this the only game of the Series he did not use Casey.

The Series moved to Ebbets Field for the third game, where the Dodgers chased starter Bobo Newsom with six runs in the second inning. The score was 7–2 by the end of the third inning and 9–4 after four. Meanwhile, the Yankees kept chipping away at Joe Hatten and Ralph Branca, who relieved Hatten in the fifth. The Yankees had narrowed the gap to 9–7 with a run in the top of the sixth, leading Harris to call on his ace reliever. Page came on in the Brooklyn sixth and would keep the Dodgers scoreless the rest of the way.

Branca was still in there for Brooklyn in the seventh inning when Yogi Berra, batting for catcher Sherm Lollar, hit the first pinch-hit home run in World Series history. With the lead down to 9–8, Shotton called for Casey, who shut down the Yankees the rest of the way. Hugh pitched the final two and two-thirds innings, holding the Yankees scoreless.

He survived a Yankees threat in the eighth by getting DiMaggio to hit into a double play after he had walked Henrich and allowed a Johnny Lindell single to open the inning. The official scorers, taking into account Casey's effectiveness and Hatten and Branca's ineffectiveness, awarded Casey the win. The contest, which lasted three hours and five minutes, was the longest nine-inning game in Series history to that point.

Sportswriter Herb Goren noted that Casey had retired seven of the nine batters he faced in Game Three, and none of the last six had a ball called on them. "His performance in the Series was all the more remarkable," wrote Goren, "because Casey himself had said that a sore

Figure 22.1. Winning pitcher Hugh Casey, Pee Wee Reese, Joe Hatten, and Eddie Stanky surround a seated Dixie Walker after Brooklyn's 9–8 win in Game Three of the 1947 World Series. *National Baseball Hall of Fame Library, Cooperstown, NY.*

arm and a bad cold had made it 100 to 1 he would be able to pitch in the Series. Penicillin had saved the day for the Brooklyns."[7]

Because of his sore arm, Casey was taking 20 minutes of diathermy, followed by a 10-minute arm rub, each day during the Series. "My arm aches all over—every inch of it," Casey said in the trainer's room. "But I'll be all right tomorrow." Harry Taylor, the expected starter for Game Four, was counting on it. "He'll do it if he has to," said Taylor.[8]

Casey's win in Game Three inspired Grantland Rice to invoke again Ernest Lawrence Thayer's memorable 1888 poem, "Casey at the Bat." This one is centered on the escape by the Dodgers ace reliever from the eighth-inning jam by inducing DiMaggio to hit into a double play. It began:

> The outlook wasn't brilliant for the scrappy Dodger band—
> The score was 9 to 8 with DiMaggio on hand.
> When Henrich walked and Lindell hit all Dodger hopes fell flat,
> For there was Joe DiMaggio advancing to the bat.

And ended:

> So Casey whirled and cut one loose—in Casey's able way
> As Big Joe hit to Stanky for the winning double play.
> And from that mighty Dodger throng with all its roaring flocks
> They should have known that they were safe with Casey in the box.[9]

Game Four of the 1947 World Series, played on Friday, October 3, is remembered for the most dramatic ending in Series history. Brooklyn came to bat in the last of the ninth, trailing, 2–1. The Yankees had scored a run in the first off starter Harry Taylor, who left without getting an out, and another in the fourth on a Billy Johnson triple and a Johnny Lindell double off Hal Gregg.

New York appeared ready to blow open the game in the ninth when they loaded the bases against Hank Behrman with just one out. With Tommy Henrich due up, Shotton called on Casey to again face his old nemesis. This time Casey won. Henrich hit his first pitch back to the mound, where Casey started an inning-ending pitcher-to-catcher-to-first double play.

"It was a low curveball," Casey replied, when asked what pitch he had thrown to Henrich. "It was a perfect pitch—went right where I wanted it to go, and it was a strike. What the heck," he said with a smile, "you throw it and you hope it works the way you intended it to work."[10]

But the big story, one that had been building all afternoon, was Yankees pitcher Bill Bevens. No pitcher in World Series history had ever thrown a no-hitter. But Bevens had held the Dodgers hitless through eight innings, although they had scored a fifth-inning run due to his wildness. The sellout crowd and those watching on television knew they were three outs away from witnessing history. "East Coast bars and taverns from Schenectady to Washington reported land office business during television broadcasts of the Series."[11] This was the first World Series to be televised—although the signal was limited to New York City; Schenectady, New York; Philadelphia; Washington, DC; and some of the suburbs surrounding those cities.

Bevens opened the home ninth by getting Bruce Edwards on a fly ball to left fielder Lindell. After walking Carl Furillo, his ninth walk of the game, he got Spider Jorgensen to foul out to first baseman George McQuinn.

With the Dodgers down to their last out, Shotton made two simultaneous moves. He sent in little-used Al Gionfriddo to run for Furillo and an injured Pete Reiser as pinch-hitter for Casey. After Gionfriddo stole second, Harris made the most daring move of the Series. He disregarded the unwritten rule of never intentionally putting the winning run on base by ordering Bevens to walk Reiser. Pete, who could barely walk, hobbled down to first base, where Shotton replaced him with Eddie Miksis.

Shotton continued making moves. He sent Harry Lavagetto in as a pinch-hitter for Eddie Stanky. The 34-year-old Lavagetto, affectionately known to his fans as Cookie, was the longest-serving Dodger on the roster. He had been with the team since 1937, minus four years in the military, but had played in only 41 games in 1947. After a swing and a miss, Lavagetto drove Bevens's second pitch over Henrich's head and off the right-field wall, scoring Gionfriddo with the tying run and Miksis with the winning run.

> In that instant, Bevens lost his no-hitter and the game, as Brooklyn won, 3–2, and tied the Series. Delirious fans poured onto the field. Jubilant teammates pounded Lavagetto on the back, while supporters surrounded the celebrating players. One fan snatched Cookie's baseball cap, ignoring the police who were escorting the hero to the dugout. Later, in the outfield, Brooklynites gathered beneath the point on the wall where Lavagetto's drive had struck. In the bedlam, Bevens walked in glum silence to the Yankees' clubhouse. On the radio, Red Barber said, "Well, I'll be a suck-egg mule!"[12]

Life called the ninth-inning confrontation the "most exciting two minutes in the history of the World Series."[13]

Speaking in the locker room after the game, Lavagetto revealed he was surprised he had gotten the call. "When Shotton called to me on the bench I thought he wanted to send me in as a pinch-runner. He had to tell me twice before I realized that he wanted me to go up and hit for Ed Stanky."[14]

Casey got the win, his second, although he had made but a single pitch. He became the first-ever pitcher to win World Series games on successive days.[15]

The crowd at Casey's restaurant was even more raucous than usual after the dramatic win. "The best things happen in Brooklyn like nowhere else on earth," said one fan. "Those Yanks pulled the biggest boner they ever pulled by walking Reiser. That poor cripple couldn't run anywhere, but do you think they could see it?" Another patron said, "You could live a hundred years and never see anything like yesterday's game."[16]

Other fans began chanting, "Who won the game?" Casey had the most frequently heard reply, although many in the crowd held out for Lavagetto. Casey himself appeared to be the calmest person in the restaurant. "It was just a day's work, that's all. We looked bad there a couple of days, but we snapped out of it." He voiced his agreement with the rest of the crowd on the Series' eventual outcome. "Sure, I think we'll take the Series," he said.

Mrs. Rose Buery, Casey's partner in the bar, said the place was overflowing with fans despite not having a television set like other bars. "We can't have television like other bars because we've got too many customers to encourage any more," she said, a sentiment not often heard from proprietors of restaurants.

New York Times columnist Arthur Daley describes driving back to Manhattan in a cab with National League president Ford Frick and former star second baseman and manager Frankie Frisch. "What has he got, Frank?" Frick asked Frisch with regard to Casey. "Stomach," replied Frisch, and, as Daley explained, that was not a reference to Casey's girth, but to the "inner fire, which the purists refer to as guts."[17]

Harris went with Frank Shea and Shotton with Rex Barney in Game Five. Shea, making his second start, pitched a complete-game victory. As they had the day before, the Yankees took a 2–1 lead into the last of the ninth. With two outs and a runner on first, Lavagetto again came to the plate as a pinch-hitter with the game on the line. But there would be no miracles at Ebbets Field this afternoon. Shea fanned him to end the game. Lavagetto had batted for Casey, who had contributed two scoreless innings as Brooklyn's fourth pitcher.

The teams returned to Yankee Stadium for Game Six, a slugfest won by the Dodgers, 8–6. New York used six pitchers, including Joe Page,

Figure 22.2.   Casey tags Tommy Henrich at the plate in the ninth inning of Game Five of the 1947 World Series. *National Baseball Hall of Fame Library, Cooperstown, NY.*

who was the loser. The Dodgers used four, including Casey, who saved the win for Ralph Branca. The game is best remembered for Al Gionfriddo's sensational catch that robbed DiMaggio of a possible three-run, game-tying home run. With Brooklyn ahead 8–5 in the home sixth, the Yankees had Yogi Berra on first and George Stirnweiss on second. DiMaggio drove Joe Hatten's pitch on a trajectory that appeared would take it into the seats in left-center, at the 415-foot marker.

Gionfriddo, who had just entered the game, described the catch in Roger Kahn's book *The Era, 1947–1957: When the Yankees, the Giants, and the Dodgers Ruled the World*: "I didn't think I had a chance . . . I put my head down and I ran, my back was toward home plate and you know I had it right. I had the ball sighted just right."[18] DiMaggio, not known for showing emotion on the field, kicked at the basepath dirt in frustration.

The catch preserved a three-run lead that Brooklyn carried into the bottom of the ninth. When the first two Yankees reached base against Joe Hatten, Casey was summoned to the mound once again. The day before, Henrich had bumped him while he attempted to score on a short passed ball. Before this afternoon game, Casey doubted he could pitch. "My arm hurts and I've got a pain in my side," he lamented.[19] But when Shotton called on him, he answered the bell and retired the side.

One of the runners eventually scored on a fielder's choice, but with the tying runs on base, Casey got Snuffy Stirnweiss, who represented the potential Series-winning run, on a comebacker. "I figured I could give 'em one run, even two runs, but that they'd never beat us. . . . I'll go all the way tomorrow if Barney [Shotton] wants me to."[20]

23

A WORLD SERIES HERO AND
A SUCCESSFUL RESTAURATEUR

Casey had now pitched in five of the first six World Series games, winning two, losing none, and allowing no runs and four hits in eight-and-a-third innings. The *New York Sun* took note of this accomplishment and the calming effect Casey had on Brooklyn fans by reprinting a Grantland Rice poem that had appeared in the paper during the summer. Interestingly, exactly six years earlier, following Game Four of the 1941 World Series, H. L. Phillips of the *Sun* had written a poem with the same name, "Casey in the Box":

> The score was four to three for the Dodger bunch that day
> The score was four to three with two innings left to play
> For Branca—brilliant Branca—had blown a two-run lead,
> And Hatten, who had followed Ralph, was now in direst need.
> No Brooklyn bum got up to go—each proudly held his seat.
> They'd seen the Dodger lead cut down—with Brooklyn in retreat.
> And then a mighty cheer went up from Brooklyn's rabid flocks,
> As Casey—mighty Casey—was advancing to the box.
> A sneer was fixed on Casey's lips—his teeth were clenched in hate.
> As Casey, mighty Casey, cut the corner of the plate.
> And then from thirty thousand throats there came a roaring sound—
> "We knew they never had a chance with Casey on the mound."[1]

The Brooklyn club had been a member of the National League since 1890, but it had never gotten this close to winning a World Series. Bucky Harris's choice to pitch the seventh and deciding game was

Frank Shea, the rookie who had won Game One and Game Five. Shotton, faced with the most consequential pitching decision of his career, chose Hal Gregg, who as a reliever in Game Four had allowed only one run in seven innings. But neither Shea nor Gregg lasted long. Harris replaced Shea with Bill Bevens in the second inning, and Shotton replaced Gregg with Hank Behrman in the fourth.

The Dodgers had jumped out to a 2–0 lead but trailed, 4–2, after six. The Yankees added a fifth run off Casey, who had come on in the seventh, and won, 5–2. It had been a wonderful season for the Dodgers, but when it was over the fans were left with the now-familiar cry of, "Wait 'til next year."

Unlike Shotton, Harris had gone to Joe Page earlier in the game. His ace reliever entered in the fifth inning and allowed no runs and just one hit in the final five frames. Page, the loser the day before, was the winner. He also had a save in the Series opener, but before his outstanding performance in Game Seven, he had allowed six earned runs in eight innings in his three previous games.

Meanwhile, Casey pitched in six games, with a 2–0 record, a save, and an 0.87 earned run average. He set records by appearing in six of the seven games and pitching five games in a row, the last five.

Through six games, Casey had been the more effective of the two, wrote columnist Joe Williams. "And take it from a guy who saw both [Fred] Marberry and [Wilcy] Moore, Casey's just as good as either, maybe better than both. Certainly in this man-to-man contest he's run away and hid from Page."[2]

After the Series, the *New York Mirror* devoted a column a day to participants from both sides. In his column on Casey, Gus Steiger wrote that the bulky right-hander could take "unpardonable pride in a scintillating mound performance unmatched in the history of baseball's title event."[3]

Casey had appeared in six games, the most games ever by a pitcher in a World Series. In 10-and-a-third innings, the Yankees had only five hits and never more than one in any game. His earned run average was 0.87, and had it not been for a generous scorer, who credited Billy Johnson with a triple rather than charging an error to left fielder Eddie Miksis in Game Seven, it would have been 0.00. "He's worth his weight in gold," said Billy Herman, recently released as manager of the Pirates, about his onetime teammate.[4]

The *Brooklyn Eagle* paid special tribute to Casey's efforts in a post-Series editorial:

> Hugh Casey's performance on the mound was positively sensational. He was the winning pitcher in the third and fourth games. He appeared in the late innings of all but the second encounter and saved the Dodgers in several of their most serious crises. He was a complete enigma to the Yankees, and if even one other Dodger pitcher could have equaled his performance it would have been another story.[5]

More than a quarter-century later, sportswriter Bob Broeg paid tribute to Casey and Page, not only for their performances in the Series, but also for what they did to demonstrate the importance of relief pitchers.

"In the long list of distinguished relievers, a few deserve special mention," Broeg wrote. "By their brilliance, the Yankees' Joe Page and the Dodgers' Hugh Casey, who made the 1947 World Series their private preserve, broke down club owners' reluctance to pay relievers as much as or more than starters."[6]

The 1947 World Series was the crowning achievement of Hugh Casey's career. He would never again come close to achieving such glory. And yet, it almost did not happen. In 1949, Dan Daniel, of the *New York World-Telegram*, revealed how close Casey had come to missing the Fall Classic. Casey had developed a sore arm 12 days before the season ended and spent those days having his arm treated with a diathermy machine.

The day before the Series opened, as the players gathered for the team picture, Vic Lombardi jokingly accused Casey of faking the injury and fired a ball at him. An angry Casey fired the ball back, and to his surprise and delight, he felt no pain. The soreness was gone from his arm. "I had torn something in my shoulder a fortnight previous, against the Giants, and aggravated it a few days later in a game with the Cardinals," Casey said in 1949. "I was sure it would not have healed so soon."[7]

"The day the series opened I had only a light workout," he said, reflecting on the Series. He continued,

> I got into a pepper game but did no throwing. . . . Well, you know the rest of the story. I got into the first game, and I pitched in five more.

Once I faced the Yankees I found that I could throw anything I ever had. My curve was good, and I was pretty fast . . . I never will forget the seventh and last game. In the third inning we had the lead, but the Yankees were ganging up on us. I begged Barney Shotton to let me go in. I said, "This is a big park, and I can stop those birds."

Shotton explained that he wanted to save him for later in the game, which he did, but by that time the Yankees had taken the lead and had Joe Page to protect it.

In a post-Series interview, Mary O'Flaherty, of the *New York Daily News*, spoke with Kathleen Casey, who she described as "blonde and blue-eyed, and soft-voiced, with shoulder-length hair." Mrs. Casey used the interview to remind people that the exciting seven-game classic had taken its toll on the players' wives as well.

"I wouldn't say the Series was tougher for the wives than for the players," she said. "But the Series was certainly equally as hard for the wives. For the reason that the men can get out there on the field and expend their energy and do something about it. We want to win as much as they do," she pointed out, "but we just have to sit and wait, and see what happens."

Kathleen described the Series as being almost too exciting for her. "I couldn't seem to relax," she said. "I went to bed early during the Series, but it was a restless sort of sleep. I'd wake up during the night and begin thinking of yesterday's game and wondering will we win today, and I'd pray . . . my goodness, I think I prayed more than I ever prayed all the rest of my life put together."[8]

She said she had neglected the housework in their six-room apartment and now had a lot of catching up to do, after which they would relax for a while. "All either one of us want now is just quiet. We're getting so many invitations to go out, but Hugh would just rather be quiet and not go out any place at all." Kathleen said that Casey had told her after the Series, "Honey, we are going away for six weeks where we won't see one soul. Just you and I."

Shortly before Christmas, Ward Morehouse, a New York City drama critic writing for *Sporting News*, spent an afternoon with Casey at his restaurant, observing his normal routine. "Casey is there shortly after the noon opening, spends part of the afternoon there, and is almost always around to greet and mix with the evening crowds," Morehouse reported. "He takes great pride in his steaks and chops, but the Baptist

Casey does satisfy much of his Catholic clientele by serving fish on Fridays."

Before the Second Vatican Council (1964–1965), Catholics were obliged to abstain from meat on Fridays throughout the year, which forced restaurants to have fish on the menu on Friday year-round. Such abstinence is now mandatory only on Fridays during Lent.

"Hell, sure I'm making out all right," Casey proclaimed, while puffing on a big cigar, adding,

> I have a partner, you know, and a good one—Mrs. Rose Buery. We were out shopping for a place when the United States got on my tail. I went into the navy, but I didn't forget about going into business. So when I got out of the service, Mrs. Buery and I looked around some more and found this site—and here we are.[9]

"It was always crowded," wrote Kirby Higbe. "He would go around with her (Kathleen) greeting people—average people, poor people, gangsters, millionaires—wearing a big red carnation and looking like the happiest person alive."[10]

Casey said he numbered many doctors and lawyers among his customers, and that the restaurant did especially well during the baseball season, when players from visiting clubs would dine there.

"The Phillies are great customers," he said, citing one example—a seemingly odd one considering the animosity between the Phillies and the Dodgers generated by the Phillies' vicious verbal attacks on Jackie Robinson. "The fellows you see on the walls are mostly boys I've known and played with." Gazing at the photographs, Casey settled on a few for comment.

"There's Joe DiMaggio . . . great ballplayer if I ever saw one. . . . That's Dolph Camilli right over there. He was one of the best first basemen the game ever had and one of the greatest guys I ever knew." About Jackie Robinson he said, "A fine boy. I'm a Southerner, a Georgian, but I enjoyed playing with him. He never said a word, he minds his own business, and he had some tough going in those early weeks. He'll be even better next year."

"We're trying to run a nice family sort of place, and I want it to be a hot-stove league for the players during the offseason," he said. "I think a lot of them will be dropping in here during the winter. Branch Rickey hasn't been in yet, but nearly everybody else has. Burt Shotton several times."[11]

Lighting up a fresh cigar, Casey told Morehouse,

> I'm a Protestant, a Baptist. I hunt and fish, and I like to play ball. My idea in playing is to win, and if I can help my team more by being a relief pitcher, that's all right with me. I keep in good shape, and I warm up quickly. I could go out and pitch three or four innings right now, and when I report for spring training I'm ready to pitch.

But life was not all work. "I'll do a lot of hunting in Georgia after the first of the year," he said, "quail and wild turkey around Dover Hall."

When asked if he would be content to finish his career working out of the bullpen, Casey replied,

> Why not? As I told you my idea is to win—and get paid for it. I pitched in 46 games last season; I've done as many as 50. I like it out there in the late innings. I've liked playing ball ever since I was a kid when I first learned to throw rocks. That's the way kids start in the South. Learning early to play ball and to handle a gun. First you get a B.B. air rifle and then a .22 and then a single-barreled shotgun and finally a double-barrel. I love hunting. Enjoy watching the dogs work, and I can get 21 or 22 quail out of every 25 shots. . . . Sure this bar's fine, and it's been fun running it, and we may make a little money, but baseball is still my trade, and I'll be playing it just as long as I get paid.

Ever the entrepreneur, Casey lent his name to a baseball board game called "Casey on the Mound." He spent one Saturday afternoon in November signing autographs and demonstrating the game on the fourth floor of Namm's Department Store, at Fulton and Hoyt streets in downtown Brooklyn. He continued to remain active in the J. W. Person Post of the American Legion, which honored him with Hugh Casey Night on November 19, awarding him a gold lapel button for his Americanism.

The ex-navy man was also appointed an honorary recruiting sergeant for the Bay Ridge (Brooklyn) Army and Air Force recruiting office. He also was selected as the "Sports King" of the Brooklyn March of Dimes Ball, held at the Hotel St. George on January 30, 1948. Casey was chosen, the proclamation read, because "his stout-hearted courage in tight spots serves as an inspiration to polio victims in Brooklyn."[12]

Concerning his baseball career, Casey said he felt great and expected to pitch for a few more years. He said he was a little surprised at how well some of the young Dodgers players had done the prior season. Echoing the thoughts of Leo Durocher and others, he predicted Brooklyn would win several pennants within the next few years. "We have a very good chance to repeat next year," he said. He dismissed the Giants because of their lack of pitching but expected the Braves to be much tougher. As for St. Louis, he believed their pitching had been inconsistent and overall they had gotten older and slower.[13]

Following the 1947 season, there was much speculation by the press and fans about who would manage the team in 1948—Shotton or Durocher. In an interview with sportscaster Ernie Harwell, Casey said he did not expect Leo Durocher to return in 1948. Leo "doesn't have a chance of ever managing in Brooklyn again," he said. Moreover, Casey doubted if Durocher ever would be in baseball again. "If he does," Casey predicted, "I think it will be on the West Coast."[14]

Yet, in late January, the likelihood of Durocher returning took on an aura of inevitability. At a dinner held by the New York baseball writers for Shotton at Toots Shor's Manhattan restaurant, a gathering place for sports figures and entertainers, Shotton announced he would never manage again. "Nobody should manage the Dodgers except Leo Durocher," he told attendees, who included his boss and friend Branch Rickey. "If he could have got the breaks I had got he would have had the pennant sewed up in July."[15]

Shotton said everyone on the club had helped him, while singling out Casey.

"I don't know what I would have done without Hugh Casey," he said. "I used to wake up screaming at night, dreaming that Casey had been injured. He was always sticking his neck out of the dugout, begging me to let him go in and pitch."

Toastmaster Roscoe McGowen of the *New York Times* asked Casey to say a few words. "Shotton was more than just the manager of the Dodgers," said Casey, the only team member present. "He was a father to the players. I could see some of 'em grow into men under his guidance. I saw that happen myself."[16]

At 34, he and Arky Vaughan (36) were the oldest members of the team. Branch Rickey had signed Casey to his 1948 contract in February, but Vaughan's status was still in doubt. Rickey had a lot of young players full of potential, but he worried about the lack of veterans. "Six years ago we had ten 12-year men. We may start the 1948 season with just one—Hugh Casey. It's a young club. Casey's age, for instance, is nine years more than the club average."[17] (Vaughan eventually did sign for his final big-league season.)

In the end, Rickey brought Durocher back to manage the Dodgers in 1948. Meanwhile, Shotton became the first pennant-winning manager to not return to his club since Rogers Hornsby of the Cardinals in 1927. The Dodgers held spring training at Ciudad Trujillo in the Dominican Republic. After 10 days of fishing in Florida, Casey arrived in camp on March 3. As he had throughout his career, he looked a bit heavy around his midriff. "It isn't anything. Only about 10 pounds," he said. "I'll sweat that off in a hurry."[18]

Casey made his first pitching appearance of the spring on March 16, throwing three strong innings against Montreal. As the team's oldest and most experienced pitcher, he had served the past two years as a mentor and teacher to the younger members of the staff. That role increased in 1947, under Shotton. Rex Barney, the 23-year-old right-hander noted for his dazzling fastball and lack of control, had been his pet project. Thus, as pleased as he was with his performance that afternoon, he was even more pleased about Barney, who had pitched an effective first three innings.

"There's still a lot of work to be done," said Casey, clearly delighted, but still cautious. "He has enough natural stuff to breeze his fastball and curve past the batters and leave 'em hanging when he pulls the string with his change of pace."[19] He predicted that by July, Barney would be a consistent winner.[20]

Casey was generous with his advice to young pitchers. One morning, Sam Lacy, of the *Baltimore Afro-American*, was having breakfast with Dan Bankhead, a black pitcher who had been with the club briefly in 1947. "That's one prince of a fellow," Bankhead said to Lacy when he spotted Casey coming into the dining room, continuing,

> Do you know that he taught me a whale of a lot about pitching the short time I was with the club last year. He came over to me one day

in Brooklyn and told me what I was doing wrong with my fastball. Then a short time later in Boston, he spent an entire afternoon teaching me a changeup. All the fellows have treated me nicely, but Casey, Bobby Bragan, and Carl Furillo have been particularly swell.[21]

Bankhead may or may not have known he was praising three of the players who had, to some degree, originally been opposed to playing with blacks.

24

FALLING, LITERALLY AND FIGURATIVELY

During the March 25 morning workout in Ciudad Trujillo, Casey experienced severe pains in his back and groin that forced him to leave the practice field. Dr. Gerard Kasper dismissed the early speculation that Casey was suffering from appendicitis or a hernia. It was nothing so serious, said Dr. Kasper. It was likely the result of the pulled leg muscle that had been bothering him the past few days and all that was needed was a week of rest.

Casey had started only one game in 1946, and none in 1947, and did not figure to start any in 1948. Yet, Durocher started him in several exhibition games, including Casey's final preseason appearance, sometimes allowing him to go as long as five innings.

Durocher had used Casey as a starter against the Yankees for three innings three days earlier, but on Opening Day, at the Polo Grounds, he was back where he was most comfortable—in the bullpen. Rex Barney, his star pupil, who had earned the start, pitched six innings, allowing three runs. He left with a 5–3 lead, to which the Dodgers added two more runs.

Casey relieved Barney in the seventh and was no better than adequate. The Giants reached him for three hits, two walks, and two runs in his three innings of work. In the ninth, a worried Durocher went to the mound; he seemed close to making a pitching change but stayed with Casey. The Giants, having already scored two in the inning, had the tying run at third base with two outs, when Casey struck out Walker Cooper to nail down the victory.

In the top of the seventh, Spider Jorgensen had pinch-hit for catcher Gil Hodges. When Casey came on in the last of the seventh, his battery-mate was Roy Campanella, in his major-league debut.

Casey was even worse in his third 1948 appearance, the first game of a May 2 doubleheader at Shibe Park. Brooklyn had given Barney a 6–0 lead, but in the fourth inning, by which time he had walked six Philadelphia batters, Leo called on Casey. The early call was a significant change from 1947, when Shotton rarely used him before the seventh inning. Casey was in and out of trouble but was unscored on until the seventh, when the Phillies scored three runs. They added three more in the eighth before Durocher replaced him with Ralph Branca.

Five days later, in Chicago, Casey looked more like his old self. The Cubs had scored five runs in three innings against Joe Hatten and Willie Ramsdell. Johnny Van Cuyk blanked them in the fourth, but when Brooklyn tied the score in the top of the fifth, Durocher made another early call for Casey. Hugh held the Cubs scoreless in the remaining five innings in a game the Dodgers won, 9–5. Brooklyn had only eight hits in the contest, but Cubs pitchers walked 14 and Cubs fielders made three errors. Rookie Preston Ward's sixth-inning bases-loaded triple was the key blow for the Dodgers.

On March 6, the Dodgers had traded second baseman Eddie Stanky to the Boston Braves to open the spot for Jackie Robinson. That left an opening at first base, which Ward won based on the promise he had shown during spring training. In June, with the Dodgers struggling, Durocher shook up the lineup. Ward had not shown the power expected of a first baseman and was sent to Mobile of the Southern Association. Gil Hodges, who had been doing most of the catching because of an injury to Bruce Edwards, was shifted to first base, and Campanella was recalled from St. Paul, where he had been the American Association's first black player, to become the everyday catcher.

After a few moderately effective appearances, Casey was awful again at home against Boston on May 17. He was the fourth and worst Brooklyn pitcher in a game in which the Braves scored 12 runs on 18 hits. Casey entered the game in the eighth inning and allowed 5 hits, 3 walks, and 7 runs (5 earned), while getting just a single out.

The next day the Cardinals came in for the start of a three-game series, their first visit of the season. Pummeling an unsettled Brooklyn pitching staff, they swept the three games by a combined score of 31–14. Stan Musial, on his way to his greatest season, had 11 hits in 15 at-bats in the series.

In the middle game, a 14–7 pasting, Casey was only slightly less awful than he had been two days earlier. He replaced Clyde King in the fourth inning with the bases loaded and one out. He walked the first batter he faced and then gave up a bases-clearing double to Nippy Jones, followed by Ralph LaPointe's run-scoring double. Casey, who had not retired a batter, was replaced by Erv Palica.

LaPointe's double "started discriminating customers home, while others wondered about Casey," noted the *Brooklyn Eagle*. "That was his second futile fireman stint in succession, and the innkeeper hasn't really been sharp this year."[1]

The Cardinals margin of victory in the third game was even greater, 13–4, a game that again brought out the decade-long antagonisms between these teams. Casey turned in yet another poor performance. He relieved Joe Hatten in the sixth inning and gave up four runs, all earned, in three innings. His recent poor performances may have been behind the fastball he threw that beaned Cardinals catcher Del Rice in the eighth inning, although Casey denied any harmful intention.

Fortunately, Rice was not seriously hurt thanks to his wearing a batting helmet and the blow being a glancing one. Casey was among the first to reach Rice and later visited him in the Cardinals dressing room.

"I was trying to pitch him close to his letters," Casey said. "The ball wasn't more than an inch or so inside. Rice must have turned his head or was looking for a curve."[2]

Immediately after Rice hit the ground, Cardinals manager Eddie Dyer was on the field demanding that umpire Art Gore eject Casey from the game. Gore denied that request, which so enraged Dyer that he was the one who ended up being ejected.

"You're a better pitcher than that," he said to Casey upon leaving, but he chose not to make a statement to the press after the game.[3] Gore's statement was that he was not a mind reader and did not see anything wrong in Casey's pitch; however several Cardinals claimed that Casey had earlier thrown at the heads of Rice and Enos Slaughter, and had drilled Whitey Kurowski in the back. "This looks like the revival of 1946, when Brooklyn kept knocking down our hitters until I thought someone would get killed—and still we beat 'em 16 out of 24 games," Dyer said.[4]

On Sunday, May 23, the Dodgers lost their eighth-consecutive game to fall into last place, nine games behind the Cardinals. Before the game, they learned that on Saturday evening Casey had fallen down the steps in his apartment over the restaurant, injuring his back. Casey said he was going downstairs to get some orange juice.

Even in an era when athletes' personal foibles were less discussed in the press, Casey's heavy drinking was no secret. The idea that he fell down the steps in a search for orange juice was laughable, unless it was to add it to his vodka. Again, not likely; Casey was a whiskey drinker.

Carl Furillo told author Peter Golenbock,

> Casey was basically a nice guy, but sometimes he could be real mean and sarcastic. He was southern, moody. Sarcastic and moody. He'd be friends with you one time, and even if you went out with him the night before, went out to dinner with him or did him a favor, the following day, if things didn't go right on the field, he'd chew you out like you were a piece of dirt.
>
> And he was one guy who liked to drink. Hell, yeah. We would go to Boston, and he would have a little handbag, and a normal guy would have a little handbag and a toothbrush or maybe a shirt or something. Not him. He'd have two quarts of whiskey in it. If he needed a shirt, he'd buy one up there. Oh, he went through money like water. He always had a pocketful of money.[5]

Suspecting he had fractured some ribs, Casey called Dr. Dominic Rossi, the team's physician, who took him to Swedish Hospital in Brooklyn's Crown Heights section for x-rays. There were no broken bones, according to the x-rays, but there was a severe internal bruise, and Casey was sent home. Later it was discovered he indeed had fractured a couple of ribs.

The Dodgers were down to six healthy pitchers, one fewer than Branch Rickey thought necessary but two fewer than they had been carrying. One bright spot was the expected return of Harry Taylor. Taylor, surprise star of the 1947 team as a rookie, had been out since having his appendix removed on April 29. "We need Taylor," said Durocher, "and don't tell me that's a gross understatement. I know it."[6]

When doctors predicted that it would take at least 30 days for Casey to heal, the Dodgers placed him on the 60-day disabled list. The open roster spot allowed Durocher to recall right-handed knuckleballer Willard Ramsdell. On June 8, Ramsdell turned in a performance that had Durocher satisfied he had found a replacement for "fat Hugh Casey," as the wire services were calling him. Ramsdell pitched six-and-a-third scoreless innings in Brooklyn's 6–5 win at Cincinnati.

Durocher said for Casey to contribute when he returned in July he would have to lose weight, something he always had trouble doing. Casey had been having a terrible season before his injury, fueling speculation he would soon retire. He had given up 23 runs and 32 hits (13 for extra bases) in 18 and two-thirds innings. More and more, Durocher was using him when the outcome of the game was no longer in doubt.

Casey's story about falling down the steps at home on Saturday evening lasted for a few days until it was learned that he had been given a speeding ticket in New Jersey that Sunday morning. He had been stopped at 9:35 a.m., for going 65 miles an hour in a 40-mile-per-hour zone on Route 6 in the town of Pine Brook. He was taken before Judge Miriam R. Waxberg and fined $25, but that was not the end of it. Casey appeared to be drunk and was sporting a large bandage on his head. He told the judge he had banged his head earlier that morning and was in great pain. He said he had been speeding to get to a doctor's office for medical treatment of the wound.[7]

The next day, Judge Waxberg clarified what had happened, taking issue with what the newspapers had printed. "He had not been drinking," she said. "His head was not bandaged," as the story said. "But I noticed as he left the courtroom he was in pain and had difficulty entering his car. One foot seemed to be bothering him."[8]

In 1949, a version of the story in the *New York Times* suggested that the bandage on Casey's head had resulted from a "brawl with a [New Jersey] state trooper over the manner in which he was driving an automobile."[9]

Yet another twist to the Casey injury story—speculation really—showed up in several newspapers in late June. A newspaper in Pines Plain, a Dutchess County suburb of New York, printed a disjointed, imagined scenario in which Casey's injury had been the result of being beaten by several Cardinals players.

"Recall a few weeks back," the story began,

when the St. Louis Cards were on an eastern trip and playing a game against Brooklyn when Hugh Casey, on the mound for the Dodgers, hit Kurowski and Del Rice of the Cards? . . . Prior to that game Hugh had been hit quite hard in his role as a relief pitcher for Brooklyn. . . . Then in this game when the Cards Kurowski and Rice hit the dirt in one inning and a couple of innings later he hit Kurowski . . . Rice was hit in the head but was saved from serious (possibly fatal) injury from the head guard which he was wearing. . . . This brought a bitter protest and denunciation by Dyer, Cards manager. . . . Casey was supposedly a good control pitcher. . . . The next day or two, the Dodgers announced that Casey was on the disabled list for 60 days, for Hugh had fallen and injured himself in his home. . . . This conflicted with reports from the New Jersey Police when they arrested Casey for speeding. . . . Could the true story have been quite different from what the Dodgers told? It is quite possible the Card players had beaten up Casey after the game. . . . Naturally Durocher would have to keep such a story a strict secret, for the eagle eye of Chandler is always watching every move of Leo. . . . We just wonder, that's all.[10]

Brooklyn fans had been grumbling all season, mostly about Rickey. They were unhappy with higher ticket prices and the trading away of Stanky to Boston, and allowing the beloved Dixie Walker to leave for Pittsburgh. (Walker remained the National League's player representative, with Casey replacing him as the Dodgers representative.)

Rickey claimed he had received only a dozen letters critical of the Walker deal. "They were without exception from people who liked Dixie," he said. "I understood all of the letters. I might have written them myself if I'd been in the public's place. I like Dixie too. But all of them were tempered and friendly. Nothing like the violent communications I received when I traded Dolph Camilli."[11]

Yet, when Walker and the Pirates made their first visit to Ebbets Field on May 21, with the Dodgers in the midst of their eight-game losing streak, Brooklyn fans welcomed Dixie home with a day in his honor. His old friend, Judge Sam Leibowitz, presented him with a new car during a pregame ceremony. Leibowitz expressed what many fans were thinking. "The place doesn't look the same since you've gone, Dixie," he said.[12]

Even *Time* magazine weighed in on the disenchantment among Dodgers fans:

In Brooklyn last week, two Pittsburgh sportswriters grabbed a cab after the ballgame. They asked the cab driver what he thought of his Dodgers. The elaborately bored driver replied curtly, "In Brooklyn we're even turning off the television sets."

The day before, Ebbets Field had been three-quarters empty. That day [May 23], it had an unusually small Saturday crowd of 12,821. In effect, the Dodgers were being boycotted.

Why? Why had the fans suddenly soured on last year's pennant-winning heroes? A week earlier, after an eight-game losing streak, the Dodgers had descended into the National League cellar. But that wasn't the main reason—even though it just about eliminated them from the pennant race.

The slow chill from the Brooklyn fans began before the season opened, when the Dodger brain trust traded away two of Brooklyn's favorite heroes: Dixie Walker and Eddie Stanky.

The article continued,

Another blow was a boost in admission prices. But mostly the fans grumbled to each other that baseball games in Ebbets Field no longer even looked very much like baseball: The games dragged, the pitching was terrible, the Dodger lineup was forever shifting and changing, team morale was drooping.

Last week nervous manager Leo ("The Lip") Durocher left the dugout and went back to directing his club from the first-base coaching line. He promptly got booed by the Brooklyn fans—those who were still going to games. What fans kept asking each other as they milled out of the exits: Will Leo finish out the season on the first-base line? Or even in Brooklyn?[13]

Casey was scheduled to come off the disabled list on June 24. To get himself back into pitching form, the Dodgers approved his appearance in several games for Max Rosner's Brooklyn Bushwicks. The Bushwicks were a semipro team that played in Dexter Park, in the Woodhaven section of Queens, just across the county line from Brooklyn. Casey's first game for the Bushwicks was a July 2 night game against the New York Black Yankees. He pitched the first five innings, allowing two runs and three hits, but was tagged with the loss in the Black Yankees' 3–2 win.

Casey came back to start the second game of the July 4 doubleheader against the Staten Island Drillers, pitching four scoreless innings and allowing just one hit. Three days later he was the winning pitcher, tossing five innings and yielding one run against the Queens club. This was not the major leagues, but he seemed to be throwing freely without any lingering effects from his injury.

An even bigger test came on July 11, when he faced the powerful Baltimore Elite Giants, who had won the first half of the pennant race in the Negro National League. Casey passed the test with an outstanding performance, allowing a single run in his five innings. He followed that with four and two-thirds strong innings in a July 14 exhibition game against the American League-leading Cleveland Indians. The charity event drew close to 65,000 to Cleveland's home park, Municipal Stadium, and featured two scoreless innings by Indians pitcher Satchel Paige, in which he retired all six batters he faced.

Few people were aware that this would be the last game Leo Durocher would manage for Brooklyn. On July 16, with the fifth-place Dodgers in Cincinnati, Branch Rickey and Giants owner Horace Stoneham shocked the baseball world with the announcement that Durocher would replace Mel Ott as manager of the Giants and Burt Shotton would return to Brooklyn to replace Durocher. New York baseball fans were especially stunned by the moves, which forced them to reevaluate long-held feelings and loyalties.

The players on both teams were equally stunned. "We hated the Dodgers. He [Durocher] was our worst enemy," recalled Giants second baseman Bill Rigney. "Everybody in those days hated Durocher," said outfielder Willard Marshall. "He was peppy and arrogant, and got everybody a little teed off."[14]

The reactions of the Dodgers players ranged from Jackie Robinson's joy, to Pee Wee Reese's disappointment, to Ralph Branca and Gene Hermanski's indifference, and everything in between.

"I love playing for Shotton," Robinson said. "I can't wait to see him. It's going to be a lot different." Robinson, who had clashed with Durocher after reporting overweight at spring training, pointed out a major difference between the two men. "When Shotton wants to bawl out a player he takes him aside and does it in private. . . . If Leo has something on his mind you hear it right there—out loud and in front of anyone who's around. But they're both great managers," he added.

"I've always been a Durocher man, you know," said a regretful Reese. "Leo didn't want to lose at any game he played, and I liked that. If he rode me—and he did pretty hard sometimes—I could take it, and I think any player who can't doesn't belong up here." Reese thought Shotton was better than Durocher with young players. "Burt is a good manager, no mistake about that," he concluded.

Branca said it made no difference to him. "You play as hard for one as the other. You play to win for either manager." Hermanski's view was much the same. "Don't make much difference to me," he said. "Who's pitching against us? That's more important."[15]

25

CASEY AND THE DODGERS PART WAYS

Harry Taylor had been struggling all season, looking nothing like the pitcher he had been in 1947. On July 19, Rickey demoted him to the St. Paul Saints of the American Association. To replace Taylor, he called up 21-year-old right-hander Carl Erskine, who had compiled a 15–7 record with the Fort Worth Cats of the Texas League. "The boy's got the finest change of pace I've ever seen," Rickey said. "His fast ball [*sic*] isn't so terribly fast. I would say that he's a little faster than Vic Lombardi. But he mixes 'em up like Vic to good advantage. It's all a question of poise if he can pitch for the Dodgers."[1]

Most teams at that time did not employ a pitching coach. Young pitchers relied on the older, experienced pitchers for counsel and advice. Erskine recalled years later that soon after he joined the Brooklyn club, Casey, the team's unacknowledged pitching coach, offered him two pieces of advice.

"Hey kid. Welcome to the big leagues," he said, continuing,

> Let me tell you. There's hitters in this league that hit .340 every year. Now, I've never seen you pitch. I don't know if you throw overhand, sidearm, underhand—I don't know what you pitch. They're going to hit you just like they hit the rest of us. So my advice—bear down on the .220 hitters and the weak guys ahead of the good hitters. They're going to get their hits, but keep those weak sisters off the base.

The second piece of advice he offered was as follows:

> The things in this league you can't change: the weather on the day
> you're pitching, the park you're pitching in, and who's umpiring. . . .
> Forget all that stuff. You have no control over it. Control what you
> have control of. Keep your fastball where you want it. Keep your
> curveball down. Kid, you'll win some games.[2]

Casey, fully recovered from his injury, rejoined the Dodgers on July 24.
The team was in second place, five games behind Boston; nevertheless,
Rickey believed the addition of Erskine and the return of Casey would
make Brooklyn the league's best team. Hugh made his first appearance
the next day in Brooklyn's 7–6 win at Pittsburgh. He pitched one scoreless inning, as did winning pitcher Erskine in his major-league debut.

"Hugh Casey was very good to me as a rookie," Erskine remembered, adding,

> Oddly enough he gave me that advice my first day in the big leagues
> during batting practice at Forbes Field. I was in the bullpen that day
> and was called in to relieve Casey in the eighth inning, two runs
> behind. I finally got out of the inning, Shotton pinch hit for me, we
> scored some runs, and I got my first big-league win.[3]

Ernie Harwell, a rookie announcer with the club in 1948, also had fond
memories of Casey. In his book *The Babe Signed My Shoe*, he remembered him as a "big, boisterous guy with a cigar in one hand and a
scotch in the other."[4] Harwell writes of a fishing trip in Brooklyn's
Sheepshead Bay the day before a big series with Boston. On board with
Harwell were Casey and rookies Erskine and George Shuba. The trip
had been Casey's idea, and while he puffed on a cigar and drank Scotch,
the other three were getting more and more seasick.

After Casey snagged a 100-pound marlin, the men finally headed
back to shore. "Hey you guys," he said, "if any of you want that marlin,
I'll give it to you." No one wanted any part of it. "Thanks, Hugh,"
Erskine said. "You caught the fish. It should be yours. Besides, you've
got a restaurant here in Brooklyn where you can put that marlin on
display."[5]

On July 26, the Dodgers were at Ebbets Field to play the Giants in
Leo Durocher's return to Brooklyn. Expectations of a managerial chess
game between Leo and Burt Shotton ended when the Giants scored
five runs off Preacher Roe and Hank Behrman in the first inning. Casey

pitched a mop-up ninth inning in Brooklyn's 13–4 loss, giving up New York's final two runs.

He did better against Pittsburgh a few days later. Coming on in the seventh inning in a game in which the Pirates had a comfortable lead, he gave up five hits and a run in three innings. Fans have short memories. The fans had been booing their longtime savior throughout the year, and the boos were very much in evidence when he took the mound that day.

It was more of the same on August 2, when the Dodgers lost at home to Chicago, 4–2, in 11 innings. Left-hander Johnny Schmitz went the distance for the Cubs to record his eighth consecutive win over Brooklyn. Rex Barney went the first eight innings for the Dodgers, with Casey taking over in the ninth. Again, he was ineffective. He walked Roy Smalley, the number-eight hitter, to lead off the inning. Then, after Schmitz sacrificed Smalley to second base, he walked Phil Cavarretta. Shotton quickly brought in Paul Minner, who retired the next two batters without surrendering a run.

The Dodgers, who trailed the Braves by 10 games in early July, had reduced their deficit to one game when the teams met in an August 21 doubleheader. In front of a full house at Ebbets Field, the Dodgers jumped on Johnny Sain for five first-inning runs and held on to win the first game, 8–7. The win moved them past Boston into first place. But the Braves regained the lead when Warren Spahn won the second game, 2–1.

Brooklyn fell to five games behind on August 25, but the team vaulted into first following a four-game sweep at St. Louis at the end of the month. Casey had his best game of the season on August 29. The Cardinals had scored two runs in the home ninth to tie the score at 4–4, when Casey relieved Barney with Musial, the potential winning run, on third. He fanned Don Lang to send the game into extra innings. The Dodgers scored two runs in the 10th, and Casey overcame a single and a Pee Wee Reese error to get the next two batters and earn the win, his first since May 7.

The Dodgers won a doubleheader against the Cardinals the next day, with Casey getting a save in the opener. With the four-game sweep of the Cardinals, Brooklyn was one and a half games ahead of the Braves. But nine losses in their next 12 games while Boston was winning nine of 12 dropped them from contention and to an eventual third-place finish.

Overall, it had been an unsatisfying season for the fans, as reflected in a drop in attendance of more than 400,000. They continued to blame Rickey for getting rid of Eddie Stanky and Dixie Walker. Outfielder Tommy Holmes, of the pennant-winning Braves, spoke of how important the acquisition of Stanky was to his team. "I think Dixie Walker's shift to the Pirates hurt the Dodgers too. If Stanky and Walker stayed with Brooklyn all season it would have been a lot tougher for us to win," he declared.[6]

Shotton did not agree. When asked if having Walker and Stanky would have made the difference in the season, he defended his old pal and boss, Rickey. "Stanky and Walker just didn't fit into his plans for the Dodgers of the future," he said.[7]

On September 12, Casey pitched two scoreless innings in a loss against the Giants. It was his final appearance as a Dodger. Rickey was looking to make room for youth, and just before the season ended, traveling secretary Harold Parrott announced that the team had given unconditional releases to its two oldest players, Casey and Arky Vaughan.

Vaughan was hoping to obtain a job as a manager in the Pacific Coast League. That did not happen, although he did play the 1949 season with the PCL's San Francisco Seals. Casey, meanwhile, had jumped the gun on Parrott by announcing the night before that the Dodgers were planning to release him. He did so in Charleston, South Carolina, where he had stopped to visit friends on the way to a fishing vacation in Jacksonville, Florida. He planned to return to Brooklyn after his vacation and continue running his tavern.

Casey predicted he would sign with the Giants for the 1949 season, reuniting him with Leo Durocher. "I've always been a Durocher man all the way through," he said.[8] "I hinted about a job to Durocher, and he said 'any time.'"[9]

The groundwork for a Casey move to the Giants had been laid on September 23, when the Dodgers made their final visit to the Polo Grounds. Before the game, Casey, already aware that he would be released, paid Durocher a visit. The two men discussed the condition of Casey's arm and back, and the possibility of his playing for his former skipper in 1949.

"I know what Casey, in good physical condition, can do," said Durocher. "He told me his arm was as strong as ever, but that he had been unable to throw hard because of his back," which he thought would be healed by the time of spring training. Durocher continued,

> When a man like Casey comes along, and it costs no more than railroad fare to Phoenix to have a look at him, it's well worth that. If he's able to go at top speed for two innings at a stretch next year, I'd much rather take chances on him than some youngster who blows hot and cold. If Casey can't make it he'll know it and so will I—and nothing will be lost. [10]

Meanwhile, there was speculation that Casey would end up with the Yankees if Bucky Harris were retained as manager. After Harris led the Yankees to the world championship in 1947, his first season, the club fell to third place in 1948. That was all the reason general manager George Weiss needed to fire Harris and replace him with Casey Stengel.

On October 7, the *New York Sun* published a report from the *Florida Times-Union* that ended the speculation about Casey's future. According to the *Times-Union*, Casey, who was on that fishing vacation in Jacksonville, told friends he had accepted an offer from Pittsburgh Pirates general manager Roy Hamey to join the Pirates in 1949. [11]

Four days later came the official announcement that Casey had signed as a free agent with Pittsburgh, joining ex-Dodgers Dixie Walker, Kirby Higbe, Stan Rojek, Vic Lombardi, and Ed Stevens, who were now members of the Pirates. His salary was reported at $15,000, with a $20,000 bonus. The famous Brooklyn Sym-phony had made a recording of the poem "Leave Us Go Root for the Dodgers, Rogers," with Casey, a throaty baritone, doing the vocal. [12] But his sale to Pittsburgh came shortly before the recording was to be released, and it never did see the light of day.

Hamey foresaw Casey playing much the same role he had filled in his glory years in Brooklyn. "Casey will bring up the rear," he said. "We want him for those eighth and ninth innings." [13] Kirby Higbe had filled that role for Pittsburgh in 1948, but as a starter in his years with the Dodgers, Higbe had been rescued from many tough situations by Casey.

After the Pirates turned him into a late-inning reliever, he had cracked, "Casey should see me now." Higbe's 10 saves were third in the league in 1948, but Hamey thought he needed help. "Casey will be great for two- or three-inning chores," he said.

Higbe was thrilled to have his old friend and roommate as a teammate again. "Get Casey," he said. "I'll start the games, and he can finish 'em."[14]

Hamey was questioned about how the 35-year-old Casey fit into the Pirates youth movement. "We've got to fill in as best we know how until our young gang develops on the farms," he explained, "and we need savvy fellows like Casey to stay as close to the top as possible."[15]

Rickey and Shotton had begun to sour on Casey in 1948, and that feeling was returned. Beginning in the spring of 1948 and carrying through the season, Casey had made statements indicating his unhappiness with the Dodgers. At one point he said he no longer cared about baseball because his restaurant was bringing him more money than baseball did.

He had thrived under Shotton in 1947, often praising the way the manager had used him. Yet, he was unhappy when Shotton replaced Durocher in July. He had decided to leave the Dodgers following the July 26 game against the Giants, when Shotton called on him in a game that was hopelessly lost—in the ninth inning, with Brooklyn losing by seven runs.

"What did he think of doing," Casey said in his bar following the game, "making a fool of me? What did he have to send me into the game at that point for?"[16] In addition to his pride being wounded, Casey expressed displeasure with the team's youth movement in 1948. He predicted Brooklyn would be a second-division team in 1949.

"That youth stuff can be overdone," he said, suggesting the trading away of Eddie Stanky and Dixie Walker had cost the Dodgers the pennant. "Kids are great, but you need tried competitors to close in on a pennant. If we had Walker's bat in the stretch and the drive and will to win of Stanky, we would have won," he said. "This last Brooklyn team was different than any others I've seen in the last 10 years. They just weren't aggressive and didn't hustle like Brooklyn teams always have . . . through the years. They'd munch candy bars on the bench . . . laugh . . . and kid around," he complained. "You don't win pennants with that approach to the game."[17]

With the exception of Pee Wee Reese and Jackie Robinson, Casey said, most of the Brooklyn players were "pretty good, but not outstanding." He was happy to be joining so many of his former teammates who were now with the Pirates. He related, "Dixie called me first and told me how fine it was with the Pittsburgh people, and Hamey called me about eight times. 'Come in with us, Hughie. We're going to win the pennant next year if we have to buy every ballplayer in the United States.'"

In mid-November, Casey followed his fishing trip to Florida with a hunting trip to Maine, where he shot a deer one day and a 200-pound black bear another. Meanwhile, he continued to attend charity events in Brooklyn as if he were still a member of the Dodgers. One was a highly anticipated January 17 bowling match at Fitzsimmons Bowling Lanes, former Dodger Freddie Fitzsimmons's bowling alley at 120 Empire Boulevard.

On January 21, 1949, Casey, Tommy Brown, and Hank Behrman of the Dodgers, Sid Gordon of the Giants, and Bert Adler, manager of Toomey's Diner at 252 Empire Boulevard, took on a group of five women representing Toomey's Ladies League. The proceeds raised from this event went to the Cardiac Fund.

Following a last-place finish in 1947, the Pirates, under first-year manager Billy Meyer, had finished a surprising fourth in 1948. Looking at his 1949 team at spring training in San Bernardino, California, Meyer judged them to be 25 percent better overall and the pitching staff to be 40 percent better. He expected the newcomers to his pitching staff— Murry Dickson, Cliff Chambers, Bob Muncrief, Bill Werle, and "even the old-timer, Hugh Casey"—to give the club a big boost.

Meyer stated, "I figure to use Casey for an inning or two to finish up our games when he's needed, and I think he can do the job for us."[18] He added that having Casey would free Kirby Higbe to return to his role as a starter or long reliever.

Throughout spring training, Meyer was effusive, perhaps hyperbolically so, in his praise for Casey. "The best pitcher I've ever seen. I've never seen anyone like him," he said. "He is in control of the situation every time he takes the mound. A manager doesn't have to worry about his getting free with bases on balls. That's what makes him a great relief pitcher."

Meyer told a story about a 12-inning game against the St. Louis Browns earlier in spring training. "Well, let me tell you something about Casey that day. He came into the game in the ninth after the Browns had tied the score." Meyer remembered how Casey had fallen behind, 2–0, and then ran the count to 3–2 before retiring the batter.

"'Never worry about me out there, Bill,' said Casey. 'I just wanted to find out if I still could do it. That's why the first two pitches I threw were balls. I was just testing myself to see whether or not I could still throw the ball where I wanted.'" Meyer smiled and said, "He's always been like that. The best pitcher I've ever seen."[19]

26

THE PIRATES AND THE YANKEES

Casey made his debut with the Pirates at Forbes Field on April 22, 1949, in the team's home opener. He entered the game in the ninth inning, with two on and two out, and Pittsburgh leading Cincinnati, 5–4. He got the third out by fanning Dixie Howell to save Bill Werle's first major-league win. Two days later, he pitched the final three innings of the first game of a doubleheader against the Reds, allowing two runs, including the game-winner in the 10th.

On May 18, Casey picked up his third save of the season, preserving Bob Muncrief's victory over the Giants. In doing so, he lowered his earned run average to 2.08, which then ballooned to 4.15 after a May 21 home game against the Braves. The Pirates, behind Murry Dickson, had led in that game, 2–0, after seven innings. But in the eighth the Braves erupted for eight runs. Dickson allowed two and left with two runners on, both of whom eventually scored. Casey, his replacement, faced three batters—two of them former Dodgers teammates—and allowed three runs. Eddie Stanky walked, Alvin Dark doubled, and Pete Reiser hit his first home run of the season.

Before the June 5 game at Ebbets Field, Casey was marveling at a home run teammate Ralph Kiner had hit in a game at Braves Field. Kiner had emerged as the game's greatest home-run hitter. For seven consecutive years beginning in 1946, his rookie season, he would lead or tie for the National League lead in home runs.

"You know the Boston ballpark," Casey said. "Well, this fellow tees off and hits one over the fence, over the bleachers, and over the scoreboard in left field, and darned near over the light standard above the scoreboard. If he hit a ball that far here in Brooklyn," Casey added, "it would clear the roof of the left-field stands."[1]

Kiner did hit a home run that afternoon, his 13th of the season. His 10th-inning blast, off Rex Barney, landed in the upper deck in left-center field. The blow was not as prodigious as the one at Boston, but it gave the Pirates a 5–4 win and dropped the Dodgers to third place.

In early May, during the Pirates' first visit to Ebbets Field, Casey had treated the entire team to dinner at his restaurant, although manager Billy Meyer had not used him in either of the two games. He made his first appearance at Ebbets Field in a Pittsburgh uniform on the night of June 6, replacing Bob Chesnes in the eighth inning following Duke Snider's leadoff home run. Don Newcombe, making his fourth start since being called up in May, was breezing to a 5–1 win. Casey pleased his old fans by striking out Roy Campanella and Newcombe, then getting Pee Wee Reese on a fly ball.

He had been mostly effective in the month since that awful May 21 outing against Boston, but things began going downhill in a home game against the Giants on June 18. Casey relieved Elmer Riddle at the start of the eighth inning, with the Giants ahead, 2–0. In two innings, he gave up three runs on four hits and two walks, which increased New York's lead to 5–0, and negated the four runs the Pirates scored in the last of the ninth. The *Brooklyn Eagle* called his performance "rather wretched."[2]

Casey was wretched again in a home game against the Dodgers on June 26. Newcombe won the game easily, 15–3, aided by a 10-run seventh inning. Casey was charged with three runs (although all were unearned) in two-thirds of an inning pitched in the disastrous seventh. After giving up a two-run triple to Carl Furillo during the inning, he hit Jackie Robinson on the knee.

Robinson and Casey exchanged words after the incident, but there were no repercussions. "Sure, Casey threw at me," Robinson told sportswriter Sam Lacy of the *Baltimore Afro-American*. "Maybe it was deliberate, I don't know . . . but it didn't have to be because of my color . . . Casey throws at anybody."[3] For black fans, who thought Casey was trying to hurt Robinson, Lacy pointed out that while a beanball is thrown at a player's head, Jackie was hit just above the knee.

According to New York's leading black newspaper, the *Amsterdam News*, manager Burt Shotton said Casey hit Robinson deliberately, a charge neither Casey nor Pirates management denied. The paper called for Commissioner Happy Chandler to expel Casey from baseball, but the incident was quickly forgotten.[4]

All was quiet between Casey and Robinson when Pittsburgh played a three-game series at Ebbets Field on July 19–21. Meyer used Casey in each of the games, two of which the Pirates lost. In the first game, Casey had the shortest outing of his career—throwing only one pitch. He replaced Rip Sewell in the last of the ninth inning of a tie game with the bases loaded and no one out. Bruce Edwards, his former battery-mate, bounced a grounder between drawn-in infielders for a game-winning single.

He pitched one inning in the next game, won by Pittsburgh. He gave up one run, also driven in by an ex-teammate. Facing Carl Furillo with two on and two out, Casey motioned right fielder Wally Westlake to move closer to the foul line. Westlake moved a few steps but not enough to catch Furillo's line-drive double, which landed a few feet fair.

In the series finale, Casey again allowed the game-ending hit. Brooklyn had tied the game in the ninth inning with a run against Bill Werle and had Edwards, the potential winning run, at second base. Dodgers manager Burt Shotton replaced the left-handed-hitting Gene Hermanski with right-hand-hitting Luis Olmo. Meyer countered by replacing left-hander Werle with Casey. Olmo ripped a low line drive to center field. Dino Restelli tried for a shoestring catch, but the ball hit off his foot and Edwards came home with the game-winner. As in the first game, Casey's official line showed zero innings pitched, one batter faced, and one hit allowed.

While he could not have known it, Casey had pitched the final game of his career at Ebbets Field. Two weeks later, on August 4, at Forbes Field, he made his final National League appearance. Fittingly, it was against the Dodgers. He pitched the final three innings of what was an 11–3 Brooklyn blowout.

The Pirates had suffered injuries to their two first basemen, Johnny Hopp and Ed Stevens, forcing manager Meyer to look for a replacement. He found him in a player whom he had managed in the Yankees' farm system, purchasing Jack Phillips from the New York club.

The Pirates now needed to clear a roster spot, and Casey, two months short of his 36th birthday, was the choice to go. On August 6, the Pirates announced they were seeking waivers to give him his unconditional release. He left with a 4–1 record, 5 saves, and a 4.66 ERA in 33 games.

Overall, it had been an unsatisfying season for the Pirates. Much had been expected of them after their fourth-place finish in 1948; but they languished in the second division for most of the season, before finishing a disappointing sixth.

Casey ended his nine-year NL career with a 74–42 record and a 3.41 ERA in 339 games. Although he had been the league's foremost relief pitcher for much of his career, he had only 54 regular-season saves, a reminder of how different the role of a "fireman" was when saves were not an official statistic. Thirty-one of Casey's saves had come in the two seasons he was the NL leader: 13 in 1942 and 18 in 1947. No NL saves leader has led with fewer than 20 since 1961, when Pittsburgh's Roy Face and San Francisco's Stu Miller each had 17.

Casey's fastball was gone, but he still knew how to pitch. Surely, some team could use him. The Yankees, under first-year manager Casey Stengel, were in a tight pennant race with the Boston Red Sox and were the team most often mentioned. Johnny Mize, picked up by the Yankees from the Giants in midseason, suggested to Stengel that the Yankees sign his longtime antagonist.

Stengel was initially resistant to the idea. "I am not interested in Hugh Casey," he said, when asked about a report he had offered him a job. "I would not consider releasing anybody to make room for Casey," he added.[5] But Stengel soon had a change of heart, and on September 4, the Yankees signed Casey as a free agent.

Stengel was aware that Casey had not pitched in a month but felt if he were in shape, he would be a big help to the team down the stretch. The Yankees located Casey, who was on a fishing tour somewhere near Rice Lake, Wisconsin, and told him to report to the team in Philadelphia the next day. Casey was now a teammate of Joe Page, his fellow reliever with whom he had dominated the 1947 World Series.[6] Casey "should be the answer to our pitching problem," Stengel said. "Page could sure use some help."[7]

Although Casey had not done any pitching since the Pirates released him, Stengel had him warming up in the seventh inning of the second game of the Labor Day doubleheader against the Athletics at Shibe Park but did not use him.

Casey made his American League debut against Boston on September 9, at Yankee Stadium. He allowed two unearned runs in two innings, a game the Red Sox won, 7–1, to cut the Yankees' lead to a game and a half.

The winning pitcher was Ellis Kinder, who won his 19th game of the season and his ninth in a row. Kinder's performance against New York that afternoon led Casey to call him the best right-hander in the game. "I pick him over Don Newcombe of the Dodgers," Casey said, referring to Brooklyn's sensational rookie. "Newcombe is stronger and younger, and will develop, but right now, I'd say Kinder is the best right-hander in Major League Baseball today."[8]

The Yankees went into their September 18 home game against Cleveland leading Boston by two and a half games. Stengel, George Weiss's surprise choice to replace Bucky Harris as manager, had done a superb job maneuvering around the many injuries the club suffered to stay ahead of the favored Red Sox. In this game, Vic Raschi was touched for three runs in the first inning and removed after the second inning. Stengel used Ralph Buxton for one inning, Casey for three, and Page for three. That trio held the Indians scoreless the rest of the way, while the Yankees scored seven runs off Al Benton and Early Wynn.

In his second appearance as a Yankee, Casey allowed two hits and was credited with his first American League win. It would be his final major-league victory. Casey had assumed he would be pitching four or five innings, but as he went out for his third, Stengel, wholly committed to Page, said, "This is your last. Give them everything."[9] He struck out Bob Kennedy, got Thurman Tucker to fly out, and finished with a flourish by fanning Jim Hegan.

Casey made his final big-league appearance at Washington on September 23, and it was one of his worst. The Yankees used six pitchers and the Senators four in the first game of a doubleheader won by Washington, 9–8, in 10 innings. The score was tied, 1–1, when Casey came in to pitch the seventh inning. He allowed five runs on two hits and three walks, while retiring just two batters.

In a late-season interview with J. G. Taylor Spink of *Sporting News*, Casey spoke of his hopes for the World Series and the man he considered the game's best reliever—his new teammate Joe Page. Casey was hoping that Stengel would include him on the Yankees' World Series roster should they get there. He thought it would be terrific if the Yankees could meet the Dodgers again.

"What a thrill it would be for me to pitch in a Series this time for the club I faced so often in the 1947 classic!" he said, continuing,

> However, I won't be too finicky. I will settle for another shot at the Cardinals [St. Louis was again battling Brooklyn for the NL pennant]. I sure owe them a few punches. Not that I am taking it for granted that Casey Stengel would call on me if we land in the Series and trouble developed. There happens to be on this club a left-hander named Joe Page, who most likely is the greatest southpaw relief specialist in the history of baseball. [10]

On the final weekend of the season, the Red Sox came to New York leading the Yankees by one game with two to play. A split was all they needed, but the Yankees won both games—and the pennant. The Dodgers had also won the pennant that Sunday, which many Brooklynites, as they did in 1947, celebrated at Casey's restaurant.

"Colored and white Dodgers fans drank champagne on Hugh Casey, the ex-Dodger, now making his third World Series, this time with the New York Yankees," wrote Lacy in the *Baltimore Afro-American*. "An impromptu on-the-house party was staged at Casey's Chop House in Flatbush shortly after the two races had been decided Sunday evening." [11]

Lacy had jumped the gun. Casey would not be pitching in the World Series, but he did foresee one of his former Dodgers teammates giving the Yankees trouble. "[Preacher] Roe is a pitcher who will bother the Yankees," Casey said. "The sort of stuff Roe throws is not what they like. They're fastball hitters. But the Ol' Preach, when he's right, is pretty tough." [12]

Casey's analysis could not have been more incisive. Roe shut out the Yankees, 1–0, in Game Two, but that was Brooklyn's only win. Although Casey was not eligible for the Fall Classic, the Yankees generously made him one of seven men to get one-quarter shares of the Series money.

A few days after the Yankees victory, Stengel was discussing his personnel plans for 1950. He said he would definitely retain Johnny Mize but was less sure about keeping veteran outfielders Charlie Keller and Johnny Lindell, and pitcher Fred Sanford. He was also noncommittal about retaining Casey. "If he wants to stay with us he will be welcome," Stengel said. "But he will have to get into condition. He was much too heavy this past month."[13] A day later, on October 13, one day before his 36th birthday, the Yankees gave Casey his unconditional release.

"Dodger fans always felt that Old Hughie, a fat man whom everybody loved, belonged in Brooklyn no matter where his baseball business took him," writes the *Brooklyn Eagle*'s Harold C. Burr, who had covered Casey during his years with the Dodgers. "It was at Ebbets Field that he achieved his greatest triumphs, even his greatest heartaches."

"He knew how to pitch and had no patience with the modern rookie who thinks he knows it all," added Burr.

There is nothing unusual about players at or nearing retirement complaining about the so-called modern players. It has been part of the game for as long as new players have come along to replace the old. Casey's assessment of the newer pitchers was representative of those sentiments. "I used to sit by the hour on the Cub bench and watch Lon Warneke pitch," he said, recalling his rookie year of 1935. "Nowadays the kids out in the bullpen turn their backs on the ballgame to beg candy from the bleacher crowd."[14]

In that late-season interview with Spink, Casey, always ready to talk about relief pitching, had listed the attributes that he thought made a great reliever.

"To begin with, he must have a rubber arm, the kind that never gets sore and can take it day after day. . . . You have to be cool, calm, and collected. You can't be the excitable sort." And, Casey continued, "a top-flight relief pitcher has to have guts plus. He has to carry the fight to the enemy." He told Spink the things he had listed were embodied in Page. "He is a big, strong man, with the kind of arm you seldom see. He likes his job, he oozes confidence. . . . Page loves to get into a real fight . . . . If you don't like a fight, you just can't succeed at relief work." While it went unremarked, Casey surely could have been describing himself in his prime.

Spink asked Casey to compare the style of play in the two leagues. "In this league, they hit away more," Casey replied. "In the National League, you walk two or you get hit for a couple, and the game is stopped and you are gone. In the American League, there is greater confidence in the pitcher." He thought umpires gave pitchers the low strike in the NL and the high strike in the AL. Casey also said he believed Ted Williams to be the greatest batter of all time. "Stan Musial is a marvelous hitter, too, but he will go after a bad ball. Williams won't. He has marvelous sight and wonderful judgment."[15]

27

A PENNANT AND A PATERNITY SUIT

As he had for the past few years, Casey spent most of his time during the offseason in Brooklyn. Throughout the fall and winter of 1949–1950, he continued to join with other players residing in the New York area to speak at and bowl in charity events. He also made a major business decision, which would not turn out well. Shortly before Christmas, he bought out his partner Rose Buery's half interest and became sole owner of Hugh Casey's Steak and Chop House. But earlier in December, a managerial change that had taken place in Georgia would allow him to continue to devote most of his time to baseball.

On December 5, 1949, Atlanta Crackers president Earl Mann announced at the minor-league meetings he had signed Dixie Walker to succeed Cliff Dapper as manager of his Double-A club in the Southern Association.

"We are happy to have Dixie back in Dixie," Mann said. "This is a great opportunity for me," said Walker. It is what I have always wanted to do when my playing days were at an end."[1]

Walker hoped to use the Atlanta job as a stepping-stone to a managing job in the big leagues. During his 18-year big-league career, he had played under Joe McCarthy with the Yankees, Mickey Cochrane and Del Baker with the Tigers, Jimmy Dykes with the White Sox, Leo Durocher and Burt Shotton with the Dodgers, and Billy Meyer with the Pirates. His greatest success had come under Durocher, but he said he had no particular managerial model in mind. "I hope I have learned something from each of them that will help me as a manager," Walker commented.[2]

One thing he had learned was the importance of a strong pitching staff. Thus, in late February, Dixie headed to Buchanan, Georgia, where he convinced former Brooklyn teammate Whit Wyatt to be his pitching coach.

The 42-year-old Wyatt had been operating a farm and an insurance office in his hometown since retiring. His last active season was with the 1945 Phillies, when he went 0–7, but he had been the ace of the Dodgers staff in the early 1940s. "The Boston Braves," said Mann, in referring to Atlanta's new major-league affiliation, "are tickled to get Whit into the system."[3] Two days after signing Wyatt, Walker went after another former Brooklyn teammate. He drove to Atlanta to visit Casey, who he believed could still be an effective pitcher, at least at the Double-A level.

After several days of negotiations with Mann, Casey signed a contract to pitch in 1950, for the team he broke in with in 1932. For the Atlanta-born Casey, this would be his third stint with the Crackers. He had gone 0–3 for them as an 18-year-old in 1932, and 8–6 two years later.

"I talked it over with manager Dixie Walker, and he wanted Casey on his staff," Mann revealed. "He plans to use Hugh strictly for relief purposes and thinks he will be able to help our club this season."[4]

The "fat fireman from Flatbush," as an *Associated Press* writer called him, would be reunited with two friends who were not only former Brooklyn teammates, but also fellow Georgians. When he was asked about leaving his restaurant, Casey said, "I recently bought out my partner in the Hugh Casey restaurant in Brooklyn and have hired a manager to run the place for me."[5]

During spring training, Casey lived on a Florida Gulf Coast beach, near Pensacola, the site of the Crackers training camp. One afternoon, after rain had forced the team's workout to be cancelled, Casey and fellow pitcher Norman Brown decided to go fishing. It almost cost them their lives.

Casey and Brown were two and a half miles out on Pensacola Bay when the boat's motor died. They switched to rowing with oars as a way to get back home, but a strong wind coming from the mainland made it impossible to control the vessel. It took them three hours to return to shore, and when they did it was at a point several miles south of where they had started.

The Coast Guard had just begun searching for them when they reported their safe arrival. Casey missed the next day's practice because of an upset stomach, but according to Brown, "He just hasn't gotten over that scare."[6]

In a March 22 intrasquad game, Casey gave up a prodigious home run to 18-year-old third baseman Eddie Mathews that wowed everyone present. (Mathews, a future Hall of Famer, hit 32 home runs for the Crackers in 1950.) On April 7, Casey pitched the last five and two-thirds innings against his old club when Brooklyn played an exhibition game at Atlanta's Ponce de León Park. The Dodgers scored three runs against him, including long home runs by Duke Snider and Gene Hermanski.

Later that month, an affidavit filed in a New York courtroom would set in motion a series of events that would haunt Casey the rest of his life. Hilda Weissman, described by the *Brooklyn Eagle* as a tall, pretty brunette, filed the affidavit in Manhattan Special Sessions Court. The 25-year-old Weissman named Casey as the father of her son, Michael, born on November 2, 1949, at Brooklyn's Beth-El Hospital. She claimed Casey had "swept her off her feet" in February 1949, telling her he loved her and promising to divorce his wife and marry her.[7]

Weissman said Casey had struck up a conversation with her in January, when she and a group of girlfriends visited his restaurant, and Casey invited them for a future dinner date. Several more dates followed, always in the company of her friends. One of the dates was a night of bowling at Fred Fitzsimmons's bowling alley, not far from Ebbets Field.

According to Weissman, one night in February, Casey asked her to go out with him minus her friends, which she did. After visiting several nightspots, he invited her to go with him to a Brooklyn hotel. She agreed and added she did so a second time. Hilda claimed it was on one of those nights she became pregnant, although she never told Casey about the pregnancy, nor did she tell him of Michael's birth. The child, who was "blond and blue-eyed just like his daddy," was currently living with Weissman and her parents.[8]

Weissman's paternity suit claimed that Casey had failed to support the child and that she was indigent. A bench warrant, signed by Special Sessions justice Frederick L. Hackenberg, was issued for Casey's arrest, with bail set at $500. On April 7, Weissman's lawyer, Harry Heller, sent a registered letter to the restaurant and received a receipt for its acceptance but no response from Casey. He said he called the restaurant and asked that the letter be forwarded to Casey in Atlanta. Heller added that he had called Casey the day before the affidavit was filed and spoke to Mrs. Casey, who told him Hugh was on a fishing trip. He insisted he had been trying for two weeks with phone calls and registered letters to track down Casey in Georgia, but Casey had ignored them.

"I know the girl," Casey said. "She used to hang around the ballpark and the ballplayers in Brooklyn, and came into my bar and grill once in a while. But that's all."[9]

Players sleeping with "groupies," as they called them, was widespread and had long been part of baseball's shadier side. The reaction of Brooklyn outfielder Al Gionfriddo, who called Weissman "crazy for ballplayers," was typical. "Shit," Gionfriddo said, "she screwed just about every ballplayer in the country. . . . It could have been anybody's baby."[10]

Weissman, a department store salesgirl, said Casey told her she was the only one of his many female fans he had ever dated. "He told me he was separated from his wife, to whom he had been married twice, that I was the only other woman he had ever gone out with during his 10 years with the Dodgers, and that he was going to get a divorce and marry me."[11] Although Casey and Kathleen often lived separate lives, there is no evidence they ever divorced.

Casey was home in Atlanta recuperating from the flu when he heard about the paternity charge. "I know nothing about the matter," he said. "Someone on one of the press services just called me, and I just finished talking with the manager of my place in Brooklyn. I plan to talk to my New York attorney later on. I have seen Miss Weissman around my place of business and at the ballpark a number of times," he admitted, "but I have never been out with her socially."[12]

Casey said an attorney had approached him when he was in New York in December and January, and told him he had a son in a home there. "I told him I had no children, and he said I had a son in a home and he was going to sue me for nonsupport. I told him that he'd better make sure of himself before suing me, that someone was going to get hurt in the matter. That was the last I heard of it until now."

In addition to his personal troubles, or perhaps because of them, Casey had not been pitching well. His poor spring and early season performances lent credence to those who had labeled him a "has-been." The 36-year-old veteran was hit hard in his first two exhibition appearances against major-league teams, including the embarrassing outing against the Dodgers.

When Casey, after recovering from the flu, got off to a slow start in the regular season—an 0–2 record, 6 innings pitched, 9 hits, and 4 walks—fans began grumbling that he was there only because of his friendship with Dixie Walker.

Whoever thought that, wrote Furman Bisher of the *Atlanta Constitution*, did not know Walker. "[He] is a man who is not to be influenced by friendships when it comes to winning or losing."[13] Walker believed Casey would regain his old form and had been buoyed by Hugh's last outing, a short but effective one against New Orleans. Casey eventually did turn it around, and by mid-July Dixie had the Crackers in first place.

"He walks as if treading on fresh eggs," is how Bisher described Casey's coming in from the bullpen. He said Casey had the necessary requirements for a relief pitcher: good control, a good sinker, and a rubber arm. While those requirements are necessary, they are not sufficient. There is a mental and psychological component to being a good relief pitcher, and Casey was solid in both departments. He seemingly never got ruffled, and he was able to put a bad effort behind him and come out fresh the next time he was called upon.

"I never had too much fastball," Casey told Bisher, continuing,

> I kept it low, got it over, made 'em hit it into the dirt. People talk about me walking in with my head down. I do that because I got the picture in my mind. I know how many are out, how many on base, and who's up, the next two or three men.
>
> It's all in the frame of mind, I think. You make up your mind you're gonna make a batter hit to one side or the other. You have the infield covered that way, you pitch the batter that way, and it works out.[14]

Cardinals outfielder Harry Walker, at Ebbets Field with his team for a series against Brooklyn, was happy for his older brother's success with Atlanta. "Nobody thought Dixie had a chance to win when he took the job of manager," Harry said. (A preseason poll of sportswriters had picked the Crackers for the second division.) "But he's got his kid team right up there fighting for a pennant. I would like to see him make it. I sure would like it."[15]

"Casey has been a big help," Dixie said of his old teammate in early August. "He's no different from when we were at Brooklyn. He's eager to work, and he's always looking over at me when one of our pitchers gets into trouble."[16]

Walker, temporarily short of pitchers, even started him in one game. On August 21, after 41 relief appearances for the Crackers, Casey made his first start of the season. It was also his first start since July 15, 1946, when he failed to survive the first inning against St. Louis. He pitched into the sixth inning in defeating the Mobile Bears, 4–2. The win raised his record to 10–4.[17]

"I would like to see him make it," Harry Walker had said of Dixie and the Crackers, and make it they did, finishing four games ahead of the Birmingham Barons. The Crackers won four straight over the Memphis Chicks in the first round of the Southern Association playoffs but were ousted four games to one by the Nashville Vols in the finals.

To no one's surprise, Dixie Walker was named the Southern Association's manager of the year. As Bisher reminded everyone, the club had been written off before the season as the "biggest collection of has-beens and never-will-bes ever assembled at Ponce de León Park."[18] The consensus among prognosticators was that they were, at best, a sixth-place team.

With his 10–4 record and team-leading 45 games pitched, Casey had been a major contributor to the team's success. If the paternity suit had affected his work, it did not show, at least outwardly. Still, he was well aware that when the season ended a court date was waiting for him.

The decree came on October 24. He was ordered to report for trial in Manhattan's Special Sessions Court on November 30, 1950. On that day and in that place, he would face charges brought by Hilda Weissman that he was the father of her son Michael. Casey, who had been released into the custody of his attorney, Aaron Goldstein, had surrendered to the court the previous day and pleaded not guilty to Judge Frederick L. Hackenberg. He was granted his request for a bill of particulars and a blood test to determine paternity.[19]

At the trial, which actually took place during Christmas week, Hilda—as the New York tabloids were calling her—testified she had met Casey at his restaurant and had four trysts with him. The first time was in January 1949, at Brooklyn's Hotel St. George, and lasted about an hour. The three other meetings were in January and February. Hotel records showed that Casey had registered at the St. George on two of those dates.

Hilda had originally listed Robert Abrams as Michael's father on the child's birth certificate, but when asked about it under cross-examination, she admitted it was a fictitious name. She also said she kept her condition from Casey until after the baby was born. Kathleen Casey, who had flown in from Atlanta to stand by her husband, said she had complete confidence in his "absolute morality" and believed there was no basis for the "preposterous charge."[20]

Gordon J. McNabb, an Atlanta-based real estate broker and a close friend of Casey's, testified in the pitcher's defense. McNabb said that on February 12, 1949, one of the dates Miss Weissman said Casey was with her, he was actually with him in Atlanta discussing an amusement park Casey was considering buying.

"How do you remember it was February 12?" Justice Hackenberg asked.

"Why because it was Lincoln's birthday," replied McNabb.

"Do you celebrate that birthday down there?" Hackenberg asked.

"Well, no we don't," answered McNabb.

Hackenberg smiled and asked the Atlantan who won the war.

"The South won the war," said McNabb, setting off some laughter in the courtroom.

Casey got additional help from George Callan, owner of the Raleigh restaurant, at 91st Street and Fourth Avenue in Brooklyn. Weissman had claimed that she had dined with Casey at the Raleigh. "No, she was never in my restaurant," Callan testified. "I think I would remember the lady if she had been."[21]

Following three days of hearings, the three judges of the Special Sessions Court took 15 minutes to rule unanimously that Casey was the father of Weissman's son.[22] Why such a quick ruling? In the days before matching DNA could test paternity, blood tests were sometimes used for that purpose, as they were in this case. But while they were not fully reliable, the judges evidently found them convincing enough to rule in Weissman's favor.

As such, Casey was obligated to pay $20 a week to support the child. That may seem a piddling amount to the modern reader, but the average family income in New York City in 1950 was $5,105, which was a resounding 20.5 percent higher than the national level. [23] One could get a loaf of bread for 12 cents and a gallon of milk for 82 cents. A gallon of gas cost just 20 cents in 1950, and a letter could be mailed for three cents. That $20 would be the equivalent of roughly $200 in 2016. [24]

Casey continued to insist he knew Weissman only as a customer at his restaurant. He swore he was home in Atlanta with his wife on the night of February 11, 1949, the night Weissman had identified as the night they were intimate in a room at Brooklyn's Hotel St. George. "We'll fight on to establish the truth," said Casey's wife, who had backed him throughout this ordeal. [25]

Kathleen had also testified that she was with Casey on February 12, 1949. She said she had met him on the night of the 11th and spent two days with him. Weissman claimed she had spent the night of the 11th and the morning of the 12th with Casey at the Hotel St. George. "My feelings toward Hugh have not changed in the slightest by the verdict," Kathleen said. [26]

Harry Heller, Weissman's lawyer, said he would apply at once to have Casey's name put on the baby's birth certificate. Meanwhile, Aaron Goldstein, Casey's lawyer, promised that the case would be carried as high in the courts as possible. He announced he would apply for a suspension of the temporary support order pending an investigation by the Probation Bureau and an appeal.

Upon hearing the verdict, Hilda cried in happiness, "for my child's sake."

"I have the highest regard for Casey," said Heller. "He's a fine person. I hope someday he will be proud of his son and that the boy will pitch for Brooklyn." Casey just frowned when he was told what Heller had said.

Meanwhile, Casey steadfastly continued to proclaim his innocence. "Deep down in my heart—and I know it is the truth—I never had anything to do with the girl. My wife and I will fight this as long as we can, to establish the truth." Kathleen continued to defend her husband

and express her belief in his innocence. "I know that he is not guilty of being the father of this child," she said.[27]

Kirby Higbe, Casey's longtime friend and roommate, wrote his auto-biography, *The High Hard One*, which was self-serving and probably not reliable. Nevertheless, and keeping that in mind, he had this to say about Casey as a faithful husband.

Figure 27.1.   Hugh Casey's son, Michael. *Courtesy of Michael Kocijan.*

"Old Case loved his wife, I know for sure because I roomed with him for six years," Higbe wrote. "I never saw him with another girl, which was unusual for ballplayers. I have come into our room many a night to find him sitting up reading a Western magazine and sipping a big water glass full of whiskey."[28]

On January 30, 1951, Justice Hackenberg entered the permanent order directing Casey to pay Hilda $20 a week for the support of their son, Michael. Casey was also assessed $102.50 for hospital costs.

During the afternoon, Hilda gave the tabloids something else to titillate their readers. She disclosed that her last name was no longer Weissman; it was now Weinstein. She had married Philip Weinstein on January 11, 1951, and was living with him in the Coney Island section of Brooklyn. Furthermore, said Hilda, Weinstein wanted to adopt the baby. Casey's lawyer, Aaron Goldstein, said a new trial of the paternity suit would be sought on the basis of this new evidence.[29]

Young Michael was never adopted by Philip Weinstein, nor did Hilda's marriage to Philip last. The couple divorced less than 10 years later. Hilda later married Oreste Mario Kocijan, a refugee from Yugoslavia, with whom she had a daughter, but Kocijan too never adopted Casey's son. Still, Michael took his last name, and it was as Michael Kocijan that he has lived his life, including 20 years in the United States Air Force, before retiring as a master sergeant. Pictures of the 6-foot-3 Michael further testified to the likelihood that he is Hugh Casey's son. In 1981, Los Angeles Dodgers president Peter O'Malley mailed to Michael Casey's 1947 World Series ring, which the team had purchased from a collector.[30]

28

A WONDERFUL GUY WHO NEVER HURT ANYONE—BUT HIMSELF

The year 1951 had not started well for Casey. As if he did not have enough problems dealing with the paternity suit, he received more bad news the day following Judge Hackenberg's permanent order. On January 31, Joseph P. Marcelle, a collector from the Internal Revenue Service for the First District in New York, filed a tax lien against Kathleen and Hugh in Brooklyn Federal Court. The government was seeking $6,759.36 for unpaid income tax, interest, and penalties for 1949. The action surprised Casey, who said his auditor had handled the dispute, and he had been informed he had until February 19 to settle it.[1] Ironically, Marcelle was forced to resign in October 1951, for fraudulently understating income and overstating expenses. He was subpoenaed to appear in front of Congress and was part of a corruption probe that eventually made the IRS part of the civil service.[2]

Professionally, however, Casey had high hopes for the new year. Dixie Walker wanted him back in Atlanta, but Casey had been encouraged by his fine 1950 season with the Crackers and felt he should be returning to the major leagues. Determined to catch on with a big-league club, he traveled to several training camps in Florida to audition for a job. Although no club was impressed enough to have him on its Opening Day roster, Casey refused to give up. In late April, after the season had begun, he worked out and pitched batting practice at Ebbets Field in a final effort to catch on with the Dodgers.

"I'm down to 213, feel great, and may sign a contract this week," he told the *Atlanta Constitution*. "Of course the final decision rests with manager Chuck Dressen."[3] (Dressen had replaced Burt Shotton after the 1950 season.) Casey was still property of the Crackers, but owner Earl Mann had given him permission to seek a deal with a major-league franchise.

After one session of pitching batting practice, he reported his arm was as strong as it ever had been. On May 2, he spoke at a father–son night at the Bushwick Jewish Center, where he told the crowd he expected to be back with the Dodgers "within a few weeks."[4] Casey may have deluded himself into thinking this; the Dodgers had given no indication they had any interest in signing him.

While waiting for the call that never came, he signed to pitch for the semipro Hartford (Connecticut) Indians. On May 13, he pitched for Hartford in the first game of a doubleheader against the Bushwicks at Dexter Park, allowing two runs and four hits in five innings.

Casey had hinted that if he could not pitch in the big leagues, he would retire and devote himself to running the restaurant. By now it had become apparent, even to him, that he no longer had the necessary skills to be a major-league pitcher. But, in truth, he was not ready to retire to the life of a restaurant owner. There was always the possibility of returning to the Crackers. So when he traveled to Atlanta in late June to attend to some personal business, he would investigate the possibility of pitching for the Crackers in the second half of the season.

At this point, Casey's plans for the future seemed totally disjointed. A few hours before he left Brooklyn for Atlanta, he told Ben Gould of the *Brooklyn Eagle* he was preparing to form a softball team. He told Gould he would pay for the uniforms and equipment, and planned to have his team play a series of games for the benefit of the Police Athletic League.[5]

"I've got a bunch of pretty good players lined up," he said, "including Marius Russo."[6] Russo, a year younger than Casey and retired from baseball, had been the winning pitcher in Game Three of the 1941 World Series, in which Casey had been the loser.

Meanwhile, the Dodgers, under Dressen, and the rival Giants, managed by Dressen's former boss, Leo Durocher, had just completed a three-game series in which many pitches had whizzed by very close to opposing batters' heads. The incidents had been serious enough to lead National League president Ford Frick to issue a warning to both teams.

Casey, who had been through a few beanball wars of his own, weighed in. "I'm telling you this beanball trouble between the Dodgers and the Giants is a serious thing," he told Ed Danforth, sports editor of the *Atlanta Journal*.[7] "The trouble about knocking a batter down, and I mean pitching so close to his head he must fall away from it, is that the pitcher doesn't always do it intentionally," he said. "I ought to know because I've brushed a few back from the plate myself. A pitcher's got to when a guy is digging in close up there and hitting the ball back around your ears."[8]

The Caseys, who lived at 950 Ponce de León Avenue in Atlanta, were going through another one of their separations, so Hugh was staying downtown at the Atlantan Hotel. He had been depressed of late, and shortly after midnight on July 3, he called his close friend Gordon McNabb, the real estate dealer who had testified at his paternity hearing, instructing him to come to his hotel. "You'll see me, but I won't see you," he told McNabb.[9]

Those ominous words alarmed McNabb, who understood them to mean that Casey was getting ready to kill himself. He rushed to the hotel in an attempt to prevent the suicide, but at 1:00 a.m., just before he reached Casey's door, he heard the sound of a shotgun being fired. Casey had used a 16-gauge shotgun to fire a blast into his neck. McNabb was 30 feet away, in the hallway, when the shot was fired.

McNabb ran down to the lobby, where he got bellboy William Mobley and a police officer, J. M. Bagwell, to return to the room. The men removed the hinges from the locked door and entered the premises. They found Casey, wearing a shirt and pants, face down on the floor, with the telephone and the shotgun about a foot away. The body was taken from the Atlantan Hotel to the Patterson Funeral Home.

Officer Bagwell said he picked up the receiver and asked the hotel operator for the number Casey had been connected with. He dialed that number, and Mrs. Casey answered. Kathleen said she thought she heard a shot but thought he was just trying to frighten her.[10]

Kathleen told police she had been on the phone with him for 15 minutes. Her husband had been threatening suicide, she said. "I begged and pleaded with him not to do it. I tried to tell him that was for God to do and not for him to do. But he said he was ready to die . . . that this was his time. He was just as calm about it as if he was about to walk out on the ballfield and pitch a game."[11]

She blamed it on the December 1950 paternity suit ruling against him. She told Lieutenant Clarence Fleming of the Atlanta police that Casey's last words were, "I am completely innocent of those charges."[12] She said he had threatened suicide several times since the paternity suit was filed. But, she claimed, the "paternity suit had nothing to do with our separation except for the nervous state of mind it had put him in."[13]

In their telephone conversation, Kathleen said, Casey told her he had felt "all dead inside" since the outcome of the paternity hearing. She quoted him as saying, "I've felt that way since all the embarrassment I went through and the embarrassment I had to drag you through." But, he added, he was "never any more calm than I am right now."[14]

She said the paternity suit had really troubled him, and he kept returning to it in conversations with her. "I can't eat or sleep since going through all the embarrassment. And I had to drag you through it, too, but I swear with a dying oath that I am innocent," he had said.

Kathleen, who had testified on his behalf at the hearing, said that she reassured him of her faith in his innocence and urged him to remember it was "for God to decide when a man must die." What he seemed to feel most was that this was his first year out of baseball, she said, adding that he had expressed some concern because his restaurant was not doing as well as he had hoped.[15]

Mobley, the bellboy, offered another possible reason for Casey's suicide. He said the pitcher told him he was going to kill himself because a doctor had told him he had only 10 days to live because of a leakage in his heart. Casey had said something similar to Gordon McNabb, but Kathleen said he had never complained to her about a leakage, although she knew he was "sick at heart" because of the court's ruling.

The news of Casey's death, at age 37, shocked the baseball world; particularly hard hit were his former teammates and his many fans in Brooklyn. The front-page headline of the *Brooklyn Eagle* that day, a day when the United Nations agreed to a Communist proposal for a conference to discuss a proposed cease-fire in the war in Korea, was, "Hugh Casey Kills Himself." The headline, in capital letters, was spread across all eight columns of the paper.[16]

Casey's tavern was the gathering place for many of his friends and regulars the next day. They raised their glasses in a final toast to a "wonderful guy who never hurt anyone—but himself." No one was putting any coins in the jukebox, and most were too sad to look at the big portrait of Hugh that hung over the cash register.

Bartender Lou Mollinelli had spent a good part of the day answering phone calls from Casey's friends and teammates, who were playing in Boston. The callers had two questions: "Why did he do it?" and "Where can we send flowers?"

One patron told of Casey's visit to the bar a few days earlier. Casey had been telling everyone about the new softball league he was planning to organize when he was interrupted by a phone call. He appeared excited after he hung up and said he had to get down to Atlanta as soon as possible.[17]

Max Rosner, owner of the Bushwicks and a longtime friend of Casey's, said that just two weeks earlier Casey had spoken to him about the possibility of using Dexter Park for a softball game. "He called me from his tavern and wanted me to come down and talk it over," Rosner revealed. Rosner told Casey he was too busy at the time, but "if he got the game organized he was welcome to the park any Tuesday night he wanted it." Rosner said Casey seemed in good spirits, but he never heard back from him.[18]

"I can't believe it happened," said Charlie Dressen, who, back in 1939, had advised Larry MacPhail to draft Casey from Memphis. "He must have had terrible trouble, because the guy I knew was all heart and could face anything," Dressen added. Pee Wee Reese, Casey's former teammate and current captain of the Dodgers, said, "I was very close to Casey, after our experience together in the war, in the South Pacific, and I can hardly believe this happened to my friend Hugh. Why, he was the guy we all relied on in the clutch. He never failed us."[19]

"I'm very sorry, very sorry—it's all so terrible," said the former Hilda Weissman. "It's a shame he had to commit suicide. We feel sorry for him. He must have been a very unhappy man," added her husband, Philip Weinstein.[20]

Funeral services for Casey were held at Atlanta's Spring Hill Chapel, on Independence Day. From there, his body was taken to the Atlanta suburb of Buckhead, Casey's birthplace, where he was buried in the

Mt. Paran Baptist Church Cemetery, not far from the sandlots where he first learned to pitch. Nearby were the graves of his parents, several siblings, and his maternal grandfather, Civil War veteran James Franklin Burdett.

Ballplayers past and present attended, as did sportswriters and fans.[21] Dixie Walker and Whit Wyatt were among the pallbearers, as was Casey's close friend, Gordon McNabb. Furman Bisher and Ed Danforth, sports editors of the *Atlanta Constitution* and the *Atlanta Journal*, respectively, were honorary pallbearers, and members of the Atlanta Crackers formed an escort.

Dr. Charles L. Allen, of Grace Methodist, and Reverend C. D. Reagan, of Mt. Paran, officiated at the funeral services. With Mrs. Casey looking on, Dr. Allen referred to the pressure the paternity suit had placed on Casey. "You never know what is in a man's mind at such a time," he said. "But I think Hugh believed that he had been knocked out of the box, unjustly perhaps, and he didn't want to go back to the bench."[22]

In addition to his wife, Casey was survived by two sisters, three brothers, and several nieces and nephews. The lien of $6,759.36 filed against Casey in January for taxes, interest, and penalties owed for 1949 had not yet been paid.[23]

Hugh "had always been moody, and his nerves were shot to pieces," Kathleen said the day after his suicide. She repeated her feeling that he never recovered from the guilty verdict in the paternity suit. "His dying words were, 'I'm innocent,' and I believe him." She said she had again left Hugh, several weeks prior, but the couple planned yet another reconciliation. They had spoken for two hours a week earlier, which was the last time she saw him.

"I begged and pleaded with Hugh not to do it," Kathleen said, continuing,

> but since that trial he couldn't eat, sleep, or think straight anymore. When we went back to Brooklyn after Atlanta won the pennant last year, he wasn't able to concentrate on his bar and grill business. I helped him, and we went through the ordeals of the trial.
>
> Six weeks ago, I decided that it might be better if I left Hugh, so I came home, got a job, and didn't hear from him anymore until last week. He called me Wednesday morning, wanted to see me, and I told him certainly. He met me that night, talked for two hours, and

seemed terribly gloomy. I told him, "Hugh, you know I've loved you since I was 12 years old, always have and always will."

She said that if he could pull himself together she would rejoin him in Brooklyn.[24]

McNabb related his conversation with Casey that night, when he had hinted at what he was going to do. "He was laughing during the conversation but sounded desperate," McNabb remembered.

McNabb had spent a lot of time with Casey since Hugh's arrival a week earlier. "He was dejected Wednesday," McNabb recalled, "but seemed in fine spirits Saturday, when I saw him for the last time. Wednesday, he told me that his doctor told him he had an incurable disease and he couldn't pitch anymore."[25]

One New York newspaper described Casey as a "sort of 20th-century Huckleberry Finn," who had "enshrined himself among such Dodger heroes as Zach [sic] Wheat, Dazzy Vance, Babe Herman, and Dixie Walker."[26]

Casey had earned a reputation as a pitcher who was at his best when things were rough, which is why his suicide came as a shock to many. Jesse Outlar, of the *Atlanta Constitution*, recorded several players' reactions.

"I can't believe it," said Whit Wyatt. "Casey was the calmest guy I've ever known. I pitched with Hugh for seven years. It's unbelievable. A few weeks earlier, Casey had said to 'tell old Dix I may be down there about July if he really needs me.'"

Dixie Walker was as unbelieving as Wyatt. "I actually thought we might have Casey and Wyatt pitching on the same club again. Remember, we were talking about it in Memphis Monday. When I called him a few days ago, he told me things were going amazingly well. He never seemed to get excited." Walker remembered the night in 1947, when Casey had struck and killed a blind man with his car. "Most men would have gone to pieces," Walker said, "but not Hugh. He was as calm as though he had been making that long walk from the bullpen."

Dodgers president Walter O'Malley said, "Mention of Casey always stirs memories of the 1947 World Series. Hughie rescued Dodger pitchers in six of those seven games against the Yankees and won one of them with one pitch. I've talked with him several times this summer, and it's hard to realize he's gone."

"Most of the Dodgers knew Hugh well," said Harold Parrott, Dodgers traveling secretary. "His steak house is only a short distance from Ebbets Field, and many of the boys dropped in to see Hugh. . . . They all feel bad about it. Ole Case was the favorite player with the players, when he was a Dodger."

Kirby Higbe had been Casey's roommate and one of his closest friends when they were with Brooklyn. "There never was a better fellow," Higbe said. "I roomed with him for four years and never saw him ruffled for a minute."

Sid Scarborough, Casey's friend for more than 20 years, remembered him as a brash, confident man, with the utmost confidence in himself. "He was that way when we played sandlot ball," Scarborough recalled. "It is most amazing to me that Casey, of all the people I know, would reach the end of the line this way."

Neil Baldwin Jr., who played football with Casey at Monroe A&M and Tech High, remembered him as a happy-go-lucky teenager. "He loved to hunt and fish and play ball, when he was a kid. He wasn't such a hot football player, but he could throw that baseball."[27]

29

REMEMBERING HUGH CASEY

As the shock of Casey's death began to wear off, some of the reporters who knew him attempted to put his career and life in perspective. The *Brooklyn Eagle*'s Tommy Holmes, who covered Casey for most of the pitcher's career, paid tribute to his old friend a few days after his passing. To Brooklyn fans, Casey was more than a name in a box score, he wrote. His steak house made him a fixture in the neighborhood.

"Thousands of people met him and knew him," noted Holmes. "It is safe to say that most of these had that friendly feeling toward the big, moonfaced fellow with the easygoing air, the soft Southern drawl, and the ready, somewhat shy, smile."[1]

Bob Cooke remembered how kind the pitcher was when the *New York Herald Tribune* columnist was in his first year covering the Dodgers. The team was in Atlanta, when Casey, aware that Cooke was looking for a story to write, invited him to his hotel room.

He had long forgotten the story, wrote Cooke, but he did recall the glass of corn whiskey Casey had poured him. "You can't get this stuff up north where you come from," Casey had said. "It's the stuff that made Georgia famous."[2]

Furman Bisher, of the *Atlanta Constitution*, remembered Casey for his toughness:

> He'd as soon knock you down with his high, hard one as to spit in your eye. If he ever had a soft spot he never allowed it to be exposed to opponent or public. He belonged in another era, in the days of filed spikes and spitballs, and Ty Cobb slicing up Buck Herzog. In

this brawling setting, the strong-backed Casey frame would have looked ever so much more at home. The cud in his cheek and the cold steel in his eyes belonged in one of those pancake caps with the horizontal stripes.

Bisher wemt on to discuss the problems former ballplayers faced when they dropped out of the spotlight and the "public ceased to regard him as an individual" and just "one of the mob who lost his job." Casey, of course, had his restaurant, Bisher said, but that too was in financial trouble.[3]

In 1968, sportswriter Edgar Munzel asked Leo Durocher, who was then managing the Cubs, about some of the relief pitchers he had managed during his career. The greatest one he ever had, said Durocher, was knuckleballer Hoyt Wilhelm, with the New York Giants of the early 1950s. But Leo also had praise for Casey.

"Casey was a different type," he chuckled. "He was mean and ornery. The first pitch would be right here," Leo said, while moving his hand under his chin. "And if you said something the next one would be here," pointing behind his head. "Then he'd break a curve over the plate."[4]

"He wasn't embarrassed to knock you off of the plate!" said Wally Westlake, a former National League outfielder with Pittsburgh and St. Louis. "In fact that whole Dodger pitching staff was that way. I guess they put that into their minds in the minor leagues. I faced him several times. He probably did to me like he did to everybody else, stick the bat up your butt." Westlake did have one pleasant memory of his duels with Casey. "I hit my first grand slam off of him," he recalled. "It was in Ebbets Field, hit a line drive to left field. Ebbets was a hitter's paradise, and a pitcher's nightmare!"[5]

A week after Casey's death, Commissioner Chandler announced that Hugh's widow, Kathleen, would receive a pension of $100 a month for the next 12 years from Major League Baseball's player fund. Chandler said, "It's part of the fund's plan to pay pensions to the beneficiaries of any eligible player who dies before he reaches 50."[6]

That fund provided $100 a month to players with at least 10 years of major-league service when they reached age 50. Chandler also announced that Ruth Bonham, the widow of Ernie Bonham, also would be getting a pension. Hers would be $90 a month because Bonham had played only nine years. Casey and Bonham had been teammates on the

1949 Pirates. The 36-year-old Bonham died of intestinal cancer on September 15 of that season.

For the first time in years, Casey was absent that November from the group of major leaguers who hunted deer in the Maine woods in late fall. Gone but not forgotten; a group of his former hunting buddies, at the suggestion of Joe Page, set up a memorial to him. An annual award would be made to the outstanding sportsman-athlete from Milo (Maine) High School, the town closest to where the hunters would gather. The school's principal and athletic director would select the recipient.[7]

Casey, who always had a plug of tobacco in his left cheek during ballgames, was a "mean, rough man," remembered Dodgers broadcaster Red Barber, adding.

> It's an old line in baseball, but I truly believe that if it meant something in a ballgame, Casey would not only knock his own mother down with a pitch, he would have hit her in the head. He did not care for man or devil. He didn't even care for himself, as he proved several years later, after he was out of baseball, when he stuck a shotgun in his mouth, pulled the trigger, and blew himself into eternity.[8]

While Barber claimed that Casey had stuck a shotgun in his mouth, other sources differed. According to the *New York Herald Tribune*, he had fired a blast into his neck.[9] And the *Brooklyn Eagle* wrote he had shot himself in the throat.[10]

A quarter-century after Casey's death, Barber described him as a "big man with a large stomach. He had rosy apple cheeks. He spoke slowly and softly in his Georgia accent. But he had become a killer in a baseball game by strolling in from the bullpen and then cold-bloodedly getting opposing batters out." In Barber's view, Casey was a troubled man, consumed by doubts and fears, but he kept them mostly hidden. On the road, Barber said, he would get into bed and read comic books while smoking his big cigars and drinking whiskey from water glasses, minus the water.[11]

Leo Durocher hinted at another possible hidden flaw in Casey's makeup. In his autobiography, *Nice Guys Finish Last*, he reflected on Casey's breakdown in the 1941 World Series:

I don't know whether Casey had grown mentally weary from the long, pressure-packed season or whether there was a latent instability in him that had been brought to the fore. Or whether he simply made a couple of very bad pitches at a very bad time. Except for that one stretch, he always seemed at least as stable as the average player, and I know he had all the guts in the world.

But, Durocher concluded, "The only other thing I can tell you about Hugh Casey is that a dozen [*sic*] years later he committed suicide. Stuck a gun in his mouth and pulled the trigger."[12]

Casey, a 1991 inductee to the Georgia Sports Hall of Fame, had been the NL's best reliever during the 1940s and a memorable presence in two World Series against the Yankees. Yet, almost a decade after his death, he was remembered not for his relief pitching, but for the same physical characteristic to which so many writers had referred during his career—his weight.

On a cold February afternoon in 1960, a construction company began the demolition of Ebbets Field, a project that would take 10 weeks to complete. The storied ballpark was being razed to make room for a middle-income housing project.

Two hundred spectators and several former players—pitchers Carl Erskine and Ralph Branca, and catchers Otto Miller and Roy Campanella—attended the ceremony. Miller had caught the first game played there, on April 9, 1913, and Campanella had caught the last, on September 24, 1957.

Gay Talese, who covered the story for the *New York Times*, described the crane that moved slowly out to center field, writing, "When it reached the 376-foot mark, the workman swung back on this iron ball painted white to resemble a baseball. It came spinning toward the wall, and, after a few shots, there was a hole the size of Hugh Casey."[13]

NOTES

I. THE BLOOD OF THE OLD SOUTH

1. Ed Burns, "War of '61 Starts New War on Cubs," *Sporting News*, 8 August 1935.
2. "Letter Solves the Shooting of Bill Jurges," *Chicago Tribune*, 7 July 1932.
3. Bob Ray, "Sac Rookies in Bow Here," *Los Angeles Times*, 21 April 1936.
4. Thomas Bourke of St. Petersburg, Florida, provided me with the genealogical data. Mr. Bourke is former chief of the microforms division at the New York Public Library.
5. "James F. Burdett Dies at Age of 94," *Atlanta Constitution*, 24 February 1934.
6. In the South in those years, the conflict was usually referred to as the "War of Northern Aggression."
7. Ernie Harwell, "Casey, Given Dinner and Gun by Home-Town Friends, Takes 'Shot' at Wisecracks at Mickey Owen," *Sporting News*, 6 November 1941.
8. Harwell, "Casey, Given Dinner and Gun by Home-Town Friends."
9. J. G. Taylor Spink, "Looping the Loops," *Sporting News*, 11 June 1947.
10. Harold C. Burr, "Size of Squads Bewilder Casey on 18th Training Trip," *Brooklyn Eagle*, 3 March 1947.
11. Spink, "Looping the Loops."
12. Tom Knight, "Uncle Robbie and Hugh Casey," *Baseball Research Journal* (1993): 106.
13. Clarence Greenbaum, "Uncle Robbie Was Casey's First Sponsor," *Brooklyn Eagle*, 3 July 1951.

14. Ralph McGill (1898–1969) won the Pulitzer Prize for editorial writing in 1959.

15. Ralph McGill, "Hugh Casey's 'Blood Starter,'" *Atlanta Constitution*, 7 October 1947.

16. McGill, "Hugh Casey's 'Blood Starter.'"

17. Harold Parrott, "Big Hugh Casey, Dodgers' Legacy from Uncle Robbie, Watches His Diet in Effort to Weigh in with 20 Wins," *Sporting News*, 28 March 1940.

18. Spink, "Looping the Loops."

19. "Minors Coming up to Majors in '35," *Sporting News*, 14 February 1935.

20. Burr, "Size of Squads Bewilder Casey."

21. Parrott, "Big Hugh Casey, Dodgers' Legacy from Uncle Robbie."

2. A SENSE THAT GOOD TIMES WERE COMING TO BROOKLYN

1. Harold Parrott, "Durocher Plans to Use Stars against Cards, *Brooklyn Eagle*, 18 September 1939.

2. J. G. Taylor Spink, "Looping the Loops," *Sporting News*, 11 June 1947.

3. Harold Parrott, "Big Hugh Casey, Dodgers' Legacy from Uncle Robbie, Watches His Diet in Effort to Weigh in with 20 Wins," *Sporting News*, 28 March 1940.

4. "Cy Found Hugh Casey a Merry Companion," *Sporting News*, 24 February 1968.

5. Parrott, "Big Hugh Casey, Dodgers' Legacy from Uncle Robbie."

6. Spink, "Looping the Loops."

7. Quoted in Richard Applegate, "The Battle of the Hatfields and the McCoys," in *Mound City Memories in St. Louis*, edited by Robert L. Tiemann (Phoenix, AZ: Society for American Baseball Research, 2007), 89.

8. Richard Bartell and Norman L. Macht, *Rowdy Richard* (Berkeley, CA: North Atlantic Books, 1987), 311.

9. Roscoe McGowen, "Spirit of Dodgers Pleases Durocher," *New York Times*, 11 March 1939.

10. Lyle Spatz, *Dixie Walker: A Life in Baseball* (Jefferson, NC: McFarland, 2011), 57.

11. Tommy Holmes, "Accent on Pitching as Dodgers Announce Early Program," *Brooklyn Eagle*, 4 January 1939.

12. Tommy Holmes, ".500 in Exhibitions Will Mean Flock's on Rise," *Brooklyn Eagle*, 10 March 1939.

13. Ernie Harwell, "Casey, Given Dinner and Gun by Home-Town Friends, Takes 'Shot' at Wisecracks at Mickey Owen," *Sporting News*, 6 November 1941.

14. "Hugh Casey Called a Second Mathewson," *Brooklyn Eagle*, 18 June 1939.

15. Tommy Holmes, "Hugh Casey Impressive in Victory over Pirates," *Brooklyn Eagle*, 5 June 1939.

3. BROOKLYN'S BEST PITCHER

1. Herbert Goren, "Dodgers Pin Hope on Pitcher Casey, *New York Sun*, 14 June 1939.

2. Roscoe McGowen, "Dodgers Stay Third by Two Points by Rallying to Check Cards, 8–3," *New York Times*, 16 June 1939.

3. "Meet Those Amazing Dodgers, Face to Face," *Brooklyn Eagle*, 8 July 1939.

4. Leo Durocher, with Ed Linn, *Nice Guys Finish Last* (New York: Simon & Schuster, 1975), 118.

5. Bill Wise, "Dixie Does All Right," *Sport Pix*, June 1949.

6. Robert Rice, "The Artful Dodger," *PM*, 8 August 1943.

7. Tommy Holmes, "Dodgers' Road Efforts Hindered by Raw Deals," *Brooklyn Eagle*, 31 July 1939.

8. Tommy Holmes, "Casey Emerges Hero of Battle of St. Louis," *Brooklyn Eagle*, 1 August 1939.

9. Saves did not become an official statistic until 1969. Saves for prior years were awarded based on the 1968 rule, as cited by Baseball-Reference. A relief pitcher earned a save when he entered the game with his team in the lead and held the lead for the remainder of the game, provided that he was not credited with the victory. A relief pitcher could not be credited with a save if he did not finish the game unless he was removed for a pinch-hitter or pinch-runner. When one or more relief pitchers qualified for a save according to the provisions of this rule, the official scorer would credit the save to the pitcher he judged to have been the most effective.

10. "New York Dodger Stunt—Twin-Bill Televised," *Sporting News*, 31 August 1939.

11. Jonathan F. Light, *The Cultural Encyclopedia of Baseball* (Jefferson, NC: McFarland, 1997), 724.

12. "Dodgers Series Cut Is $22,050," *Brooklyn Eagle*, 16 October 1939.

13. "Brooklyn Dodgers Are Given Bonuses," *Syracuse Herald-Journal*, 9 November 1939.

14. Harold Parrott, "Casey Says He'll Win 20 for Dodgers Next Year," *Brooklyn Eagle*, 30 September 1939.

15. Harold Parrott, "Big Hugh Casey, Dodgers' Legacy from Uncle Robbie, Watches His Diet in Effort to Weigh in with 20 Wins," *Sporting News*, 28 March 1940.

16. Dick Farrington, "Fanning with Farrington," *Sporting News*, 26 October 1939.

17. Harold Parrott, "Both Sides," *Brooklyn Eagle*, 2 December 1939.

18. Lou E. Cohen, "Markes Rolls 639, with 233 High Game, in Inter-Club League: Hugh Casey, Dodger Pitcher, Hits 630 to Star in Team Match," *Brooklyn Eagle*, 25 November 1939.

19. Harold Parrott, "Both Sides."

20. Harold Parrott, "Big Hugh Casey, Dodgers' Legacy from Uncle Robbie."

4. A LEGITIMATE PENNANT CONTENDER

1. Tommy Holmes, "Lippy Leo Talks up Team as It Stands," *Sporting News*, 14 December 1939.

2. John Martin, "Knee O.K., Wyatt Looks Forward to Great 1940 Season," *Brooklyn Eagle*, 15 January 1940. This article originally appeared in the *Atlanta Journal*.

3. Harold Parrott, "Big Hugh Casey, Dodgers' Legacy from Uncle Robbie, Watches His Diet in Effort to Weigh in with 20 Wins," *Sporting News*, 28 March 1940.

4. Parrott, "Big Hugh Casey, Dodgers' Legacy from Uncle Robbie."

5. Harold Parrott, "No Beer in Casey's Contract," *Brooklyn Eagle*, 28 February 1940.

6. Jimmy Wood, "Sportopics," *Brooklyn Eagle*, 15 March 1940.

7. Tommy Holmes, "Casey Seen as Dodgers' Big Winner This Year," *Brooklyn Eagle*, 6 March 1940.

8. "Casey May Be Ace in Sophomore Year," *Brooklyn Eagle*, 27 March 1940.

9. Parrott, "Big Hugh Casey, Dodgers' Legacy from Uncle Robbie."

10. The Dodgers sent Red Evans (September 1, 1939) and Art Parks (February 24, 1940) to the Red Sox to complete the trade.

11. Charles C. Alexander, *Breaking the Slump: Baseball in the Depression Era* (New York: Columbia University Press, 2002), 244.

12. "Reese Glad He's Sold to Brooklyn Club Now," *Hartford Courant*, 20 July 1939.

13. "Brooklyn in $75,000 Deal for Reese," *Sporting News*, 27 July 1939.

14. Roscoe McGowen, "Reese Impressive at Shortstop in His First Drill with Dodgers," *New York Times*, 20 February 1940.

15. Roscoe McGowen, "Hamlin Accepts $12,000 Dodger Contract with $3,000 Bonus Clause," *New York Times*, 21 February 1940.

16. Grantland Rice, "Rice Nominates Diamond Stars for Coming Pennant Races," *Baltimore Sun*, 15 April 1940.

17. Tommy Holmes, "Casey Takes Assignment in His Stride," *Brooklyn Eagle*, 18 April 1940.

18. Holmes, "Casey Takes Assignment in His Stride."

19. The nine consecutive wins to start a season tied a post-1893 major-league record set by the 1918 Giants.

20. Tommy Holmes, "'No-Hitter' Spurs Dodgers in Drive for Record Today," *Brooklyn Eagle*, 1 May 1940.

21. Tommy Holmes, "Dodgers Relax after Pinning Back of Ears," *Brooklyn Eagle*, 8 May 1940.

22. Unidentified clipping from Casey's Hall of Fame file, 16 May 1940.

5. BEANBALLS, SPIKINGS, AND RHUBARBS

1. "Flock Air-Minded—with Exceptions," *Brooklyn Eagle*, 8 May 1940.

2. "Flock Air-Minded—with Exceptions."

3. Tommy Holmes, "Unrestricted War on at Ebbets Field," *Brooklyn Eagle*, 21 May 1940.

4. Roscoe McGowen, "Casey, Shoulder Ailing, Is Sent by Dodgers to Visit Specialist," *New York Times*, 12 June 1940.

5. Medwick batted .374, with 31 home runs and 154 runs batted in. No National League player has won the Triple Crown since.

6. "Medwick Deal Brings Joy to Flatbush," *Washington Post*, 14 June 1940.

7. Enos Slaughter, with Kevin Reid, *Country Hardball: The Autobiography of Enos "Country" Slaughter* (Greensboro, NC: Tudor, 1991), 52.

8. Louis Effrat, "Medwick Injured by Pitched Ball as Dodgers Lose," *New York Times*, 19 June 1940.

9. Paul Green, "Whitlow Wyatt," *Sports Collectors Digest*, 28 March 1986.

10. J. G. Taylor Spink, "'Pass Bean Ball Rule in N.L.'—Ducky; Frick Favors Helmets," *Sporting News*, 27 June 1940.

11. "Medwick Says He Knew of No Cardinal Threats," *New York Times*, 20 June 1940.

12. "Medwick Says He Knew of No Cardinal Threats."

13. Donald Honig, *Baseball When the Grass Was Real: Baseball from the Twenties to the Forties, Told by the Men Who Played It* (New York: Coward, McCann & Geoghegan, 1975), 196.

14. Spink, "'Pass Bean Ball Rule in N.L.'"

15. Slaughter, *Country Hardball*, 52–53.

16. Tommy Holmes, "'Dustings-Off' May Fire New Spark in Flock," *Brooklyn Eagle*, 19 June 1940.

6. CASEY FUELS A FEUD WITH THE CUBS

1. J. G. Taylor Spink, "'Pass Bean Ball Rule in N.L.'—Ducky; Frick Favors Helmets," *Sporting News*, 27 June 1940.

2. "Still Dusting Dodgers," *Brooklyn Eagle*, 14 July 1940.

3. Richard Farrington, "Fanning with Farrington," *Sporting News*, 18 July 1940.

4. "Pilots Dislike Helmets," *Sporting News*, 18 July 1940.

5. Jonathan Weeks, *Mudville Madness: Fabulous Feats, Belligerent Behavior, and Erratic Episodes* (Lanham, MD: Taylor Trade, 2014), 103.

6. Jack Kavanagh, "A Dodger Boyhood," in *Baseball History 3: An Annual of Original Baseball Research*, edited by Peter Levine (Westport, CT: Meckler, 1990), 127.

7. Tommy Holmes, "Brooklyn Bolsters Pitching with Cash," *Sporting News*, 8 August 1940.

8. Tommy Holmes, "Scrappy Flock Meet the Cards with Dander Up," *Brooklyn Eagle*, 20 July 1940.

9. "Gallagher, Passeau Fined for CHI Brawl," *Brooklyn Eagle*, 21 July 1940.

10. Tommy Holmes, "Dodger Hopes Hurt By Feud Setback," *Brooklyn Eagle*, 3 August 1940.

11. Harold Parrott, "Casey's Poor Form Mystifies Dodgers," *Brooklyn Eagle*, 15 August 1940.

12. Tommy Holmes, "Dodgers Still See Selves Very Much in Pennant Race," *Brooklyn Eagle*, 9 September 1940.

7. BUILDING A CHAMPION

1. Ed Hughes, "Ed Hughes' Column," *Brooklyn Eagle*, 21 March 1941.

2. Tommy Holmes, "Casey Seems Old Self," *Brooklyn Eagle*, 2 April 1941.

3. Tom Meany, "Loyal Watchers Daffy about Dodger Flag Chances," *Sporting News*, 20 March 1941.

4. Harold Parrott, "Hamlin and MacPhail Just Like This Once Again," *Brooklyn Eagle*, 11 February 1941.

5. Roscoe McGowen, "Dallas Set Back by Brooklyn, 5–1," *New York Times*, 4 April 1941.

6. Roscoe McGowen, "Dodger Chief Sees Reiser in Big Role," *New York Times*, 16 February 1941.

7. Pat McDonough, "Dodgers Need Comebacks," *New York World-Telegram*, 31 March 1941.

8. *Time*, 21 April 1941.

9. John Lardner, "Frank McCormick Comes Out of Fall Hibernation," *Hartford Courant*, 19 December 1940.

10. Harold Parrott, "Two Walkers in Bow to Palpitating Public," *Brooklyn Eagle*, 22 April 1941.

11. Tommy Holmes, "Reiser May Return to Action in Week," *Brooklyn Eagle*, 24 April 1941.

12. Holmes, "Reiser May Return to Action in Week."

13. Tommy Holmes, "Pitching Enables Dodgers to Match Their 1940 Record," *Brooklyn Eagle*, 30 April 1941.

14. *Time*, 26 May 1941.

8. CASEY THE WORKHORSE

1. Tommy Holmes, "Frick Likely to Nix Dodger Bleat on Cubs," *Brooklyn Eagle*, 20 May 1941.

2. Holmes, "Frick Likely to Nix Dodger Bleat on Cubs."

3. J. G. Taylor Spink, "Looping the Loops," *Sporting News*, 11 June 1947.

4. Ernie Harwell, "Casey, Given Dinner and Gun by Home-Town Friends, Takes 'Shot' at Wisecracks at Mickey Owen," *Sporting News*, 6 November 1941.

5. Robert W. Creamer, *Baseball in '41: A Celebration of the Best Baseball Season Ever—in the Year America Went to War* (New York: Penguin, 1991), 153.

6. Creamer, *Baseball in '41*, 203.

7. "Bill Terry Selects Brooklyn to Win N.L. Pennant Race," *Syracuse Herald-Journal*, 9 July 1941.

8. Tommy Holmes, "Dodgers' Dixie Trio Counts Out Jealousy," *Brooklyn Eagle*, 8 July 1941.

9. "Fitz's Team Tops Lavagetto Squad in Bowling Match," *Brooklyn Eagle*, 16 July 1941.

10. John Kieran, "Sports of the Times," *New York Times*, 24 July 1941.

11. Roscoe McGowen, "Brooklyn Victor with 12 Hits, 8–5," *New York Times*, 23 August 1941.

12. Louis Effrat, "'Could Have Sold 200,000 Tickets for Double Bill,' Mac-Phail Says," *New York Times*, 25 August 1941.

13. *Time*, 8 September 1941.

14. Rob Neyer and Eddie Epstein, *Baseball Dynasties: The Greatest Teams of All Time* (New York: W. W. Norton, 2000), 172.

15. Lyle Spatz, *Dixie Walker: A Life in Baseball* (Jefferson, NC: McFarland, 2011), 86.

16. Donald Honig, *Baseball When the Grass Was Real: Baseball from the Twenties to the Forties, Told by the Men Who Played It* (New York: Coward, McCann & Geoghegan, 1975), 92.

17. "Casey, Varipapa Defeat Reiser, Wasdell on Alleys," *Brooklyn Eagle*, 27 August 1941.

9. NATIONAL LEAGUE CHAMPIONS

1. Bill Borst, "Showdown in St. Louis," in *The National Pastime: A Review of Baseball History*, vol. 11, edited by the Society for American Baseball Research (Phoenix, AZ: Society for American Baseball Research, 1991), 63–64.

2. Tommy Holmes, "Dixie Walker Comes Back to the Majors," *Brooklyn Eagle*, 11 December 1952.

3. Roscoe McGowen, "Herman Snaps Tie," *New York Times*, 14 September 1941.

4. Thomas Liley, "Whit Wyatt: The Dodgers' 1941 Ace," in *The National Pastime: A Review of Baseball History*, vol. 11, edited by the Society for American Baseball Research (Phoenix, AZ: Society for American Baseball Research, 1991), 47.

5. J. G. Taylor Spink, "Always Something Doing with Dixie," *Sporting News*, 25 December 1941.

6. Rudy Marzano, *The Brooklyn Dodgers in the 1940s: How Robinson, MacPhail, Reiser, and Rickey Changed Baseball* (Jefferson, NC: McFarland, 2005), 63.

7. Tommy Holmes, "Durocher Is Fined $150 for Squawk," *Brooklyn Eagle*, 19 September 1941.

8. Richard Goldstein, *Superstars and Screwballs: 100 Years of Brooklyn Baseball* (New York: Dutton, 1991), 215.

9. George Kirksey, "Dodgers Are Champions Collectively, Individually," *Brooklyn Eagle*, 26 September 1941.

10. Red Barber, "Ernest Hemingway and the Tough Dodger," *New York Times*, 14 November 1976.

11. Quoted in Marzano, *The Brooklyn Dodgers in the 1940s*, 67.

12. Lyle Spatz, *Dixie Walker: A Life in Baseball* (Jefferson, NC: McFarland, 2011), 93.

13. *Time*, 6 October 1941.

14. Tommy Holmes, "Dodgers Tip Lid and Flatbush Tosses Hats in Flag Celebration," *Sporting News*, 2 October 1941.

15. Leo Durocher, with Ed Linn, *Nice Guys Finish Last* (New York: Simon & Schuster, 1975), 129.

16. Ron Fimrite, "The Play That Beat the Bums," *Sports Illustrated*, 20 October 1997.

17. Peter Golenbock, *Bums: An Oral History of the Brooklyn Dodgers* (New York: G. P. Putnam's Sons, 1984), 70.

18. *Time*, 6 October 1941.

19. Liley, "Whit Wyatt," 47.

20. Quoted in W. C. Heinz, "The Rocky Road of Pistol Pete," in *The Baseball Reader: Favorites from the Fireside Books of Baseball*, edited by Charles Einstein (New York: Lippincott & Crowell, 1980), 166.

21. Bill James, *The New Bill James Historical Baseball Abstract* (New York: Free Press, 2001), 207.

22. In 1890, the Brooklyn Bridegrooms of the National League and the Louisville Colonels of the American Association met in an early version of a postseason championship. Each team won three games, with one ending in a tie.

23. "Casey Finds Link between Infield, Yank D. P. Mark," *Brooklyn Eagle*, 30 September 1941.

24. "Hugh Casey Has Reunion with Kin, Here to See Relief Ace Strut Stuff," *Brooklyn Eagle*, 3 October 1941.

25. James L. Kilgallen, "Pa, Ma Walker Root for Dixie in First Series," *Brooklyn Daily Eagle*, 1 October 1941.

26. *Time*, 6 October 1941.

27. Bill Roeder, "Owen Dropped the Strike: The Horror of the '41 Series," *New York World-Telegram/New York Sun*, 23 September 1953.

10. A DRAMATIC WORLD SERIES ENDS
A MEMORABLE SEASON

1. "Day's Delay Asked in Start of Series," *New York Times*, 17 September 1941.

2. Ron Fimrite, "The Play That Beat the Bums," *Sports Illustrated*, 20 October 1997.

3. Harold Parrott, "Casey Fails Fitz, Blowing Two Plays," *Brooklyn Eagle*, 5 October 1941.

4. Parrott, "Casey Fails Fitz."

5. Bill Roeder, "Baseball," *New York World-Telegram*, 6 September 1947.

6. Roscoe McGowen, "Dodgers Gloomy over Fitz's Fate," *New York Times*, 5 October 1941.

7. Harold Parrott, "Both Sides," *Brooklyn Eagle*, 1 December 1941.

8. "MacPhail Is Dissatisfied," *New York Times*, 5 October 1941.

9. Harold Rosenthal, "Series Classic: Owen's Missed Third Strike in '41," *Sporting News*, 23 October 1976.

10. "Henrich Says He Didn't Know Ball Escaped," *New York Herald Tribune*, 6 October 1941.

11. Richard Goldstein, "Tommy Henrich, Yanks Star, Dies at 96," *New York Times*, 2 December 2009.

12. Tommy Henrich, with Bill Gilbert, *Five O'clock Lightning: Ruth, Gehrig, DiMaggio, Mantle, and the Glory Years of the NY Yankees* (New York: Carol, 1992), 124.

13. Shirley Povich, "This Morning," *Washington Post*, 6 April 1943.

14. Leo Durocher, with Ed Linn, *Nice Guys Finish Last* (New York: Simon & Schuster, 1975), 130.

15. Charles Dunkley, "'Always Happens to Us!' Dodgers Wail," *Los Angeles Times*, 6 October 1941.

16. Rosenthal, "Series Classic."

17. Deacon Phillippe of the 1903 Pittsburgh Pirates and Christy Mathewson of the 1911 New York Giants lost successive games, but not on consecutive days.

18. Christopher Bell, *Scapegoats: Baseballers Whose Careers Are Marked by One Fateful Play* (Jefferson, NC: McFarland, 2002), 37.

19. Harold Parrott, "Both Sides," *Brooklyn Eagle*, 6 October 1941.

20. Lee MacPhail, "A Year to Remember, Especially in Brooklyn," in *The National Pastime: A Review of Baseball History*, vol. 11, edited by the Society for American Baseball Research (Phoenix, AZ: Society for American Baseball Research, 1991), 43.

21. "Henrich Says He Didn't Know Ball Escaped."

22. Joe Trimble, "Fans Don't Spare Saddened Owen," *New York Daily News*, 6 October 1941.

23. Shirley Povich, "This Morning," *Washington Post*, 8 October 1941.

24. Trimble, "Fans Don't Spare Saddened Owen."

25. Charles Dunkley, "'Lord Must Be On Yanks' Side,' Walker Fears," *Atlanta Constitution*, 6 October 1941.

26. Andrew Paul Mele, *A Brooklyn Dodgers Reader* (Jefferson, NC: McFarland, 2004), 56.

27. Leo Durocher, *The Dodgers and Me: The Inside Story* (Chicago: Ziff-Davis, 1948), 108.

28. Harold Parrott, "Lad Raids Penny Bank to Buck up Mickey," *Brooklyn Eagle*, 6 October 1941.

11. THE PITCH THAT GOT AWAY

1. Rudy Marzano, *The Brooklyn Dodgers in the 1940s: How Robinson, MacPhail, Reiser, and Rickey Changed Baseball* (Jefferson, NC: McFarland, 2005), 69.

2. J. G. Taylor Spink, "Looping the Loops," *Sporting News*, 28 September 1949.

3. Tommy Holmes, *The Dodgers* (New York: Macmillan, 1975), 89.

4. Richards Vidmer, "Down in Front," *New York Herald Tribune*, 8 October 1941.

5. Harold Parrott, "Both Sides," *Brooklyn Eagle*, 6 October 1941.

6. Harold Rosenthal, "Series Classic: Owen's Missed Third Strike in '41," *Sporting News*, 23 October 1976.

7. Joe Trimble, "Fans Don't Spare Saddened Owen," *New York Daily News*, 6 October 1941.

8. Information provided by David Vincent, the official scorer for the Washington Nationals.

9. John Snow, "'Held Glove Sideways,' Explains Mickey Back on His Goatless Farm," *Sporting News*, 16 October 1941.

10. Norman L. Macht, "Why Did Mickey Miss the Ball?" in *The National Pastime: A Review of Baseball History*, vol. 11, edited by the Society for American Baseball Research (Phoenix, AZ: Society for American Baseball Research, 1991), 44–45.

11. Dan Daniel, "Over the Fence," *Sporting News*, 16 October 1941.

12. Parrott, "Both Sides."

13. Leo Durocher, with Ed Linn, *Nice Guys Finish Last* (New York: Simon & Schuster, 1975), 129.

14. Paul Green, "Whitlow Wyatt," *Sports Collectors Digest*, March 28, 1986.

15. Donald Honig, *Baseball When the Grass Was Real: Baseball from the Twenties to the Forties, Told by the Men Who Played It* (New York: Coward, McCann & Geoghegan, 1975), 138.

16. Bill Roeder, "Owen Dropped the Strike: The Horror of the '41 Series," *New York World-Telegram/New York Sun*, 23 September 1953.

17. H. I. Phillips, "Casey in the Box," *New York Sun*, 6 October 1941.

18. Ernie Harwell, "Casey, Given Dinner and Gun by Home-Town Friends, Takes 'Shot' at Wisecracks at Mickey Owen," *Sporting News*, 6 November 1941.

19. Ben Gold, "Casey Denies Threat to Quit," *Brooklyn Eagle*, 7 November 1941.

20. Harwell, "Casey, Given Dinner and Gun by Home-Town Friends."

21. Ernie Harwell, "'Welcome Means More to Me Than Beating Yankees,' Says Dodger Ace, Stirred by Tribute," *Sporting News*, 23 October 1941.

22. Harwell, "Casey, Given Dinner and Gun by Home-Town Friends."

23. Harwell, "Casey, Given Dinner and Gun by Home-Town Friends."

12. A MEMORABLE NIGHT WITH
ERNEST HEMINGWAY

1. "Hugh Casey May Be Next Great Ball Player Lost to the Army," *Washington Post*, 22 January 1942.

2. "Mrs. Hugh Casey Seeking Divorce," *Atlanta Constitution*, 11 February 1942.

3. "Hugh Casey May Be Next Great Ball Player Lost to the Army."

4. Tommy Holmes, "Casey Tries again in Poundage Dep't," *Brooklyn Eagle*, 22 January 1942.

5. "Higbe Refuses to Join Dodgers on Havana Plane," *Chicago Tribune*, February 19, 1942.

6. Tommy Holmes, "Dodgers Repel Old Foes on New Arms and Counter-Blows," *Sporting News*, 5 March 1942.

7. Donald Honig, *Baseball When the Grass Was Real: Baseball from the Twenties to the Forties, Told by the Men Who Played It* (New York: Coward, McCann & Geoghegan, 1975), 152–55, and Steven P. Gietschier, "Slugging and Snubbing: Hugh Casey, Ernest Hemingway, and Jackie Robinson—a Baseball Mystery," *Nine: A Journal of Baseball History and Culture* 21, no. 1 (Fall 2012): 20–21.

8. Red Barber, "Ernest Hemingway and the Tough Dodger," *New York Times*, 14 November 1976.

9. Tommy Holmes, "'Juan Law' Saves Dodgers in Cuban Departure," *Brooklyn Eagle*, 10 March 1942.

10. "Call for Casey!" *Brooklyn Eagle*, 26 April 1942.

11. Tommy Holmes, "Wyatt Not Worried over Sore Shoulder," *Brooklyn Eagle*, 29 April 1942.

12. Roscoe McGowen, "42,822 Tickets Sold for Contest, but Attendance Is Put at 34,000," *New York Times*, 9 May 1942.

13. Harold Parrott, "Both Sides," *Brooklyn Eagle*, 9 June 1942.

14. Harold Parrott, "Brooks' Extra Edge Lies in Experience," *Sporting News*, 11 June 1942.

15. Bob Broeg, "The '42 Cardinals," *Sport* 7 (July 1963): 43.

16. Honig, *Baseball When the Grass Was Real*, 197–98.

17. Duke Snider, with Phil Pepe, *Few and Chosen: Defining Dodger Greatness across the Eras* (Chicago: Triumph, 2006), 57.

13. BECOMING A FULL-TIME RELIEF PITCHER

1. Leo Durocher, with Ed Linn, *Nice Guys Finish Last* (New York: Simon & Schuster, 1975), 118.

2. Roscoe McGowen, "Dodgers Stay Third by Two Points by Rallying to Check Cards, 8–3," *New York Times*, 16 June 1939.

3. Hugh Fullerton Jr., "Grimm Knows How to Direct Paul Erikson," *Syracuse Herald-Journal*, 14 May 1943.

4. Bob Broeg, "The '42 Cardinals," *Sport* 7 (July 1963): 40.

5. Richard Applegate, "The Battle of the Hatfields and the McCoys," in *Mound City Memories: Baseball in St. Louis*, edited by Robert L. Tiemann (Phoenix, AZ: Society for American Baseball Research, 2007), 89.

6. Bob Broeg, *One Hundred Greatest Moments in St. Louis Sports* (St. Louis: Missouri Historical Society Press, 2000), 69.

7. Broeg, "The '42 Cardinals."

8. Tommy Holmes, "Durocher Can Say It Again for Casey," *Brooklyn Eagle*, 17 July 1942.

9. Tommy Holmes, "Reiser Out of Action for Several Days," *Brooklyn Eagle*, 20 July 1942.

10. Peter Golenbock, *Bums: An Oral History of the Brooklyn Dodgers* (New York: G. P. Putnam's Sons, 1984), 78.

11. J. G. Taylor Spink, "Looping the Loops," *Sporting News*, 11 June 1947.

12. Tommy Holmes, "Casey Injury Disturbs Dodger Strategists," *Brooklyn Eagle*, 24 July 1942.

13. "Wants Bullpen Phone," *Sporting News*, 23 July1942. Quoting a Dick McCann article in the *New York Daily News*.

14. Arthur E. Patterson, "Dodgers' 19-Hit Barrage Routs Braves, 11–1," *New York Herald Tribune*, 20 August 1942.

15. Tommy Holmes, "Newsom Deal Gives MacPhail Signal for an 'I-Told-You-So,'" *Brooklyn Eagle*, 2 September 1942.

16. *New York World-Telegram/New York Sun*, 12 March 1953.

17. Stephen D. Boren and Thomas Boren, "The 1942 Pennant Race," *National Pastime* (journal for the Society for American Baseball Research) 15 (1993): 134.

18. "Newsom, Senators, Bought by Dodgers," *New York Times*, 31 August 1942.

19. Boren and Boren, "The 1942 Pennant Race," 134.

20. Tommy Holmes, "Dodgers Didn't Lose Flag—Cards Won It," *Brooklyn Eagle*, 28 September 1942.

21. Shirley Povich, "This Morning," *Washington Post*, 6 April 1943.

22. "Give Those Dodgers a Big Hand," *Sporting News*, 17 September 1942.

14. YOU'RE IN THE NAVY NOW

1. "Fireman Hugh May Join Coast Guard," *Brooklyn Eagle*, 2 November 1942.

2. "Hugh Casey Headed for U.S. Coast Guard," *New York Sun*, 5 January 1943.

3. Tommy Holmes, "Pee Wee Reese, Hugh Casey Enlist in Navy," *Brooklyn Eagle*, 31 January 1943.

4. Roscoe McGowen, "Webber Slated for No. 1 Relief Job on Dodgers' 11-Man Pitching Staff," *New York Times*, 18 March 1943.

5. Harold Parrott, "Both Sides," *Brooklyn Eagle*, 22 March 1943.

6. "Dodgers Beat Army Nine, 12–8; Clash with Red Sox Here Today," *New York Herald Tribune*, 3 April 1943.

7. Shirley Povich, "This Morning," *Washington Post*, 3 April 1943.

8. Eddie Robinson, with C. Paul Rogers III, *Lucky Me: My Sixty-Five Years in Baseball* (Dallas, TX: Southern Methodist University Press, 2011), 25.

9. "Casey Hurls No-Hitter for Norfolk Air Team," *New York Herald-Tribune*, 27 April 1943.

10. "Navy Cloudbusters Nip Norfolk in the 8th, 3–1," *New York Herald Tribune*, 31 May 1943.

11. Stanley Woodward, "In the Rickey Manner," *Baseball Digest*, July 1950.

12. Al Figone, "Larry MacPhail and Dolph Camilli," *National Pastime* (journal for the Society for American Baseball Research) 14 (1994): 108.

13. Tommy Holmes, "More Trouble Due, Dodgers Only Face N.L.'s Top Pitcher," *Brooklyn Eagle*, 8 July 1943.

14. Robert L. Tiemann, *Dodger Classics* (St. Louis: Baseball Histories, 1983), 174.

15. Harold Parrott, "Both Sides," *Brooklyn Eagle*, 23 August 1943.

16. Arthur E. Patterson, "Dodger Revolt Lapses after Players Meet," *New York Herald Tribune*, 12 July 1943.

17. Patterson, "Dodger Revolt Lapses after Players Meet."

18. Clifton Blue Parker, *Big and Little Poison: Paul and Lloyd Waner, Baseball Brothers* (Jefferson, NC: McFarland, 2003), 173.

19. Roscoe McGowen, "Dodgers Revolt against Durocher," *New York Times*, 11 July 1943.

20. Harold Parrott, "Both Sides," *Brooklyn Eagle*, 12 July 1943.

21. "Sailors Have World Series of Their Own," *Syracuse Herald-Journal*, September 8, 1943.

22. Tom Ferguson, "Dodger Casey Keeps Airmen in Navy Series," *Sporting News*, 23 September 1943.

23. William B. Mead, *Even the Browns: The Zany, True Story of Baseball in the Early Forties* (Chicago: Contemporary Books, 1978), 122–23.

24. Noel Hynd, *The Giants of the Polo Grounds* (New York: Doubleday, 1988), 331.

15. BASEBALL ENTERS A NEW ERA

1. Ben Gould, "Athletes in Uniform," *Brooklyn Eagle*, 30 September 1944.

2. William B. Mead, *Even the Browns: The Zany, True Story of Baseball in the Early Forties* (Chicago: Contemporary Books, 1978), 195.

3. "'True World Series' with the Cardinals Sought for Navy Team in Pacific Area," *New York Times*, 10 October 1944.

4. "'True World Series' with the Cardinals Sought for Navy Team in Pacific Area."

5. Peter Golenbock, *Bums: An Oral History of the Brooklyn Dodgers* (New York: G. P. Putnam's Sons, 1984), 89.

6. Bob Considine, "On the Line with Considine," *Washington Post*, 12 October 1944.

7. Considine, "On the Line with Considine."

8. *Time*, 9 April 1945.

9. Manager Durocher had played 18 games in 1941, and would play in two in 1945. Owen would enter the navy early in the 1945 season.

10. David Jordan, "A Fresh Look at Wartime Baseball," paper delivered at the 1991 SABR convention in New York City.

11. Lyle Spatz, *Dixie Walker: A Life in Baseball* (Jefferson, NC: McFarland, 2011), 136–37.

12. Quoted in "Casey Eyes Return to Dodger Hurling," *New York Times*, 24 April 1945.

13. "Casey Hurls All-Stars to Pearl Harbor Win," *Brooklyn Eagle*, 27 September 1945.

14. "Where Have You Been?" *New York World-Telegram*, 19 March 1946.

15. Sgt. Dan Polier, *Yank*, 10 March 1944.

16. *Syracuse Herald-Journal*, 10 December 1945.

17. "No Good from Raising Race Issue," *Sporting News*, 6 August 1942.

18. Harvey Frommer, *Rickey and Robinson* (New York: Macmillan, 1982), 104.

19. Fay Young, "End of Baseball's Jim Crow Seen with Signing of Jackie Robinson," *Chicago Defender*, 3 November 1945.

20. Fay Young, "End of Baseball's Jim Crow," *Chicago Defender*, 3 November 1945.

21. Young, "End of Baseball's Jim Crow."

22. Lyle Spatz, *New York Yankee Openers: An Opening Day History of Baseball's Most Famous Team, 1903–1996* (Jefferson, NC: McFarland, 1997), 195–96.

23. Tommy Holmes, "Salt and Slinging Worry Mr. Rickey," *Brooklyn Eagle*, 22 January 1946.

24. Bob Cooke, "Dodgers Sign Casey, Webber, Lund after Brief Conferences" *New York Herald-Tribune*, 4 March 1946.

25. Roscoe McGowen, "Durocher Selects Herman for Third," *New York Times*, 4 March 1946.

26. Tommy Holmes, "Dodger GIs in Batting Practice," *Brooklyn Eagle*, 6 March 1946.

27. *Time*, 25 March 1946.

28. Robert Weintraub, *The Victory Season: The End of World War II and the Birth of Baseball's Golden Age* (New York: Little, Brown, 2013), 71.

16. THE RETURN OF PEACE BRINGS
THE RETURN OF WARS WITH ST. LOUIS

AND CHICAGO

1. In 1989, the field was renamed Jackie Robinson Ballpark.

2. Roscoe McGowen, "Dodgers Conquer Montreal by 7–2," *New York Times*, 18 March 1946.

3. Bernard Kahn, "Walker's Bat Ices Dodgers' Win; Robinson Plays," *Daytona Beach Evening-News*, 18 March 1946.

4. *Time*, 25 March 1946.

5. "Flatbush Hurling Now Club's Best Asset, Says Lippy," *Brooklyn Eagle*, 15 April 1946.

6. Tommy Holmes, "Hurler Named Head Spins a No-Hitter," *Brooklyn Eagle*, 24 April 1946.

7. Robert Weintraub, *The Victory Season: The End of World War II and the Birth of Baseball's Golden Age* (New York: Little, Brown, 2013), 115. The quote originally appeared in the *St. Louis Post-Dispatch*.

8. Harold C. Burr, "Dodgers–Cubs in 15th Season," *Brooklyn Eagle*, 24 May 1946.

9. Joseph M. Sheehan, "Dodgers Trip Cubs in 13th, 2–1," *New York Times*, 23 May 1946.

10. Tommy Holmes, "Higbe Finds Winning Formula in Walker," *Brooklyn Eagle*, 23 May 1946.

11. Irving Vaughan, "Dodgers Defeat Cubs in 13th Inning, 2–1," *Chicago Tribune*, 23 May 1946.

12. Art Ahrens, "The Old Brawl Game," *National Pastime* (journal for the Society for American Baseball Research) 23 (2003): 5.

13. *New York World-Telegram*, 24 May 1946.

14. Bill Roeder, "Walker–Merullo Bout Seen Top Diamond Brawl," *New York World-Telegram/New York Sun*, 26 July 1954.

15. Leo Durocher, *The Dodgers and Me: The Inside Story* (Chicago: Ziff-Davis, 1948), 236.

16. J. G. Taylor Spink, "Looping the Loops," *Sporting News*, 3 July 1946.

17. Peter Golenbock, *Bums: An Oral History of the Brooklyn Dodgers* (New York: G. P. Putnam's Sons, 1984), 47–48.

18. Dan Daniel, "Dodgers Now Look Like Best Bet for World Series," *New York World-Telegram*, 5 July 1946.

19. Dan Daniel, "Dixie Walker Ascribes Added Power to Change in Bats," *New York World-Telegram*, 8 July 1946.

20. Harold C. Burr, "Dodgers Nursing Five-Game Lead as Western Trip Opens," *Brooklyn Eagle*, 11 July 1946.

17. A RESTAURANT LAUNCHED AND
A PENNANT LOST

1. Robert Weintraub, *The Victory Season: The End of World War II and the Birth of Baseball's Golden Age* (New York: Little, Brown, 2013), 67.

2. J. G. Taylor Spink, "Looping the Loops," *Sporting News*, 11 June 1947.

3. Jimmy Cannon, "Leo Buttons His Lip," *Baseball Digest*, November 1946.

4. Furman Bisher, "The Jury Delivers a Verdict for Casey," *Atlanta Constitution*, 13 July 1950.

5. Leo Durocher, *The Dodgers and Me: The Inside Story* (Chicago: Ziff-Davis, 1948), 246.

6. "Dodgers Robbed!—But It's Only Money This Time," *Brooklyn Eagle*, 19 July 1946.

7. "Flatbush Catching Relief Nears as Soskovic Returns," *Brooklyn Eagle*, 20 July 1946.

8. Harold C. Burr, "Cardinals Leave Town Mumbling at Flock Dusters," *Brooklyn Eagle*, 2 August 1946.

9. George F. Will, "Professional Baseball Players Live Life by 'the Codes,'" *Washington Post*, 4 April 2010.

10. Harry J. Roth, "Bridge," *Brooklyn Eagle*, 2 August 1946.

11. Bob Broeg, "Cards Eye Sweep to Clinch Pennant," *St. Louis Post-Dispatch*, 12 September 1946.

12. In 2015, the King of Tandoor, an Indian restaurant, occupied the site.

13. Ward Morehouse, "Casey's Club for Food, Foam, and Fanning Bees," *Sporting News*, 24 December 1947.

14. "Truck Strikers Strike Out Casey Menu in Opener," *Brooklyn Eagle*, 14 September 1946.

15. *Time*, 7 October 1946.

16. Rob Neyer and Eddie Epstein, *Baseball Dynasties: The Greatest Teams of All Time* (New York: W. W. Norton, 2000), 173.

17. Roscoe McGowen, "Gloom Surrounds Flatbush Rooters," *New York Times*, 2 October 1946.

18. Thomas Oliphant, *Praying for Gil Hodges* (New York: St. Martin's, 2005), 159.

19. Wilfrid Sheed, *My Life as a Fan* (New York: Simon & Schuster, 1993), 139.

20. Jeff Prugh, "Ebbets Field," *Los Angeles Times*, 16 August 1974.

21. Peter Golenbock, *Bums: An Oral History of the Brooklyn Dodgers* (New York: G. P. Putnam's Sons, 1984), 101.

22. Spink, "Looping the Loops."

23. Cannon, "Leo Buttons His Lip."

24. "20 Brooklyn Boy Winners to Dine at A&S Luncheon," *Brooklyn Eagle*, 11 October 1946.

18. A HISTORY-MAKING ADDITION

1. *Time*, 7 October 1946.

2. *Time*, 7 October 1946.

3. Peter Golenbock, *Bums: An Oral History of the Brooklyn Dodgers* (New York: G. P. Putnam's Sons, 1984), 139, 144.

4. Lee Lowenfish, "The Gentlemen's Agreement and the Ferocious Gentleman Who Broke It," *Baseball Research Journal* (journal for the Society for American Baseball Research) 38, no. 1 (Summer 2009): 34.

5. Golenbock, *Bums*, 145.

6. Red Barber, "Leadoff Man," *New Republic*, 4 July 1983.

7. Tommy Holmes, "Scatter Shot at the Sport Scene," *Brooklyn Eagle*, 13 January 1947.

8. Harold C. Burr, "Vaughan Rarin' to Go for Flock," *Brooklyn Eagle*, 11 February 1947.

9. Tommy Holmes, "Where Will Dodgers Train With Robinson?" *Brooklyn Eagle*, 16 July 1946.

10. "Robinson Set to Appear in Ebbets Field," *New York Amsterdam News*, January 11, 1947.

11. Ed Stevens, *The Other Side of the Jackie Robinson Story* (Mustang, OK: Tate, 2009), 40.

12. Roscoe McGowen, "Head, Gregg, Lombardi, Van Cuyk Praised by Durocher for Speed," *New York Times*, 24 February 1947.

13. Harold C. Burr, "Hugh Casey Finally Shows Up in Cuba a Plump 214," *Brooklyn Eagle*, 24 February 1947.

19. BURT SHOTTON REPLACES LEO DUROCHER

1. Harold C. Burr, "Size of Squads Bewilder Casey on 18th Training Trip," *Brooklyn Eagle*, 3 March 1947.

2. "Durocher Says," *Brooklyn Eagle*, 27 March 1947.

3. "Durocher Says," *Brooklyn Eagle*, 6 April 1947.

4. "Durocher Says," 27 March 1947.

5. Jules Tygiel, *Baseball's Great Experiment: Jackie Robinson and His Legacy* (New York: Vintage, 1984), 174.

6. Roscoe McGowen, "Dodgers Shut Out Montreal, 6–0," *New York Times*, 27 March 1947.

7. Irv Goldfarb, "Spring Training in Havana," in *The Team That Forever Changed Baseball and America: The 1947 Brooklyn Dodgers*, edited by Lyle Spatz (Lincoln: University of Nebraska Press/Society for American Baseball Research, 2012), 4.

8. Ed Stevens, *The Other Side of the Jackie Robinson Story* (Mustang, OK: Tate, 2009), 43.

9. Ira Berkow, "The High Hard One," *New York Times*, 11 May 1985.

10. J. Ronald Oakley, *Baseball's Last Golden Age, 1946–1960: The National Pastime in a Time of Glory and Change* (Jefferson, NC: McFarland, 1994), 50.

11. Scott Simon, *Jackie Robinson and the Integration of Baseball* (Hoboken, NJ: John Wiley & Sons, 2002), 106.

12. Leo Durocher, with Ed Linn. *Nice Guys Finish Last* (New York: Simon & Schuster, 1975), 166–67.

13. Roger Kahn, *Rickey and Robinson: The True, Untold Story of the Integration of Baseball* (New York: Rodale, 2014), 119.

14. Tygiel, *Baseball's Great Experiment*, 193.

15. Simon, *Jackie Robinson and the Integration of Baseball*, 136.

16. Jackie Robinson, as told to Alfred Duckett, *I Never Had It Made* (New York: G. P. Putnam's Sons, 1972), 78.

17. Arnold Rampersad, *Jackie Robinson: A Biography* (New York: Ballantine, 1997), 178.

18. Sam Lacy, "From A to Z," *Baltimore Afro-American*, 11 October 1947.

19. Jeffrey Marlette, "The Suspension of Leo Durocher," in *The Team That Forever Changed Baseball and America: The 1947 Brooklyn Dodgers*, edited by Lyle Spatz (Lincoln: University of Nebraska Press/Society for American Baseball Research, 2012), 50.

20. John Drebinger, "Giants Rout Dodgers in Polo Grounds Inaugural; Shotton Brooklyn Manager," *New York Times*, 19 April 1947.

21. Joseph M. Sheehan, "Shotton, 62-Year-Old Veteran, Takes Over as Brooklyn Pilot," *New York Times*, 19 April 1947.

22. "Dodgers to Bowl in Red Cross Benefit," *Brooklyn Eagle*, 29 April 1947.

23. Michael Gaven, "Double Duty Casey," *New York Journal-American*, 25 April 1947.

24. Tom Meany, "Hugh Casey," *Sport*, May 1948.

25. Peter Golenbock, *Bums: An Oral History of the Brooklyn Dodgers* (New York: G. P. Putnam's Sons, 1984), 169.

26. Red Barber, "Leadoff Man," *New Republic*, 4 July 1983.

27. *New York World-Telegram*, 13 September 1947.

20. THE HUGH CASEY THEORY
OF RELIEF PITCHING

1. Harold C. Burr, "Fireman Casey Pulls Dodgers' Bacon Out of Fire for Sixth Time," *Brooklyn Eagle*, 19 May 1947.

2. Burr, "Fireman Casey Pulls Dodgers' Bacon Out of Fire for Sixth Time."

3. Jules Tygiel, *Baseball's Great Experiment: Jackie Robinson and His Legacy* (New York: Vintage, 1984), 183.

4. Jackie Robinson, as told to Alfred Duckett. *I Never Had It Made* (New York: G. P. Putnam's Sons, 1972), 74.

5. "Casey Absolved in Auto Death," *Brooklyn Eagle*, 26 May 1947.

6. Kirby Higbe, with Martin Quigley, *The High Hard One* (New York: Viking, 1967), 63.

7. J. G. Taylor Spink, "Looping the Loops," *Sporting News*, 11 June 1947.

8. E-mail from Bob Hurte, who spoke to Westlake about the home run on 14 February 2016.

9. Charles J. Doyle, "Cheers Drown Jeers as Hank Starts Hitting Home Runs for Bucs," *Sporting News*, 13 August 1947.

21. HOLDING OFF THE CARDINALS

1. Red Smith, "Views of Sport," *New York Herald Tribune*, 19 August 1947.

2. Bob Broeg, "Kurowski Hit Stretch Puts Snap Back into Resilient Redbirds," *Sporting News*, 27 August 1947.

3. *Daily Worker*, 16 September 1947.

4. "Cards Praised by Eddie Dyer," *Baltimore Sun*, 21 August 1947.

5. Sam Lacy, "Charge Spiking of Jackie Intentional," *Baltimore Afro-American*, 30 August 1947.

6. Enos Slaughter with Kevin Reid, *Country Hardball: The Autobiography of Enos "Country" Slaughter* (Greensboro, NC: Tudor, 1991), 111.

7. Sam Lacy, "Leo Reveals Jackie's Trials, Tribulations," *Baltimore Afro-American*, 22 May 1948.

8. Leo Durocher, *The Dodgers and Me: The Inside Story* (Chicago: Ziff-Davis, 1948), 277.

9. Bob Cooke, "Dodgers Beat Pirates, 3–1," *New York Herald Tribune*, 25 August 1947.

10. Jimmy Cannon, "Jimmy Cannon Says," *New York Post*, 6 September 1947.

11. Cannon, "Jimmy Cannon Says."

12. J. G. Taylor Spink, "Looping the Loops," *Sporting News*, 17 September 1947.

13. William Marshall, *Baseball's Pivotal Era, 1945–1951* (Lexington: University Press of Kentucky, 1999), 141

14. Roscoe McGowen, "Dodger Pennant Bid Blocked as Braves Triumph, 8–1," *New York Times*, 21 September 1947.

22. THE MAINSTAY OF THE
1947 WORLD SERIES

1. "Joyful Fans of Flatbush Parade at Midnight, Hail 'Beloved Bums,'" *New York Times*, 23 September 1947.

2. "Joyful Fans of Flatbush Parade at Midnight."

3. Joe Williams, "Casey May Be Better Than Marberry," *New York World-Telegram*, 6 October 1947.

4. Tommy Holmes, "Experience Meets Speed in Series," *Brooklyn Eagle*, 24 September 1947.

5. John Lardner, "Henrich Batting, Casey Pitching Revives Famous Owen Boner," *Atlanta Constitution*, 1 October 1947.

6. Lardner, "Henrich Batting, Casey Pitching Revives Famous Owen Boner."

7. Herb Goren, "Casey Ace Hurler of Dodger's Staff," *New York Sun*, 3 October 1947.

8. Roscoe McGowen, "Silence on Hurler Broken by Shotton," *New York Times*, 3 October 1947.

9. Grantland Rice, "Setting the Pace," *New York Sun*, 3 October 1947.

10. Roscoe McGowen, "Wild Celebration in Dressing Room," *New York Times*, 4 October 1947.

11. **[QU: Article title?]**, *Variety*, 8 October 1947.

12. Tom Hawthorn, "The 1947 World Series," in *Bridging Two Dynasties: The 1947 New York Yankees*, edited by Lyle Spatz (Lincoln: University of Nebraska Press/Society for American Baseball Research, 2013), 279.

13. **[QU: Article title?]**, *Life*, 13 October 1947.

14. Harold C. Burr, "'Miracle' Strikes Flatbush," *Brooklyn Eagle*, 4 October 1947.

15. Deacon Phillippe of the 1903 Pirates, Jack Coombs of the 1910 Athletics, Red Faber of the 1917 White Sox, and Ray Kremer of the 1925 Pirates won successive games but not on consecutive days.

16. India McIntosh, "Barside Chant at Hugh Casey's: 'Championship in the Bag,'" *New York Herald Tribune*, 4 October 1947.

17. Arthur Daley, "Sports of the Times," *New York Times*, 4 October 1947.

18. Roger Kahn, *The Era, 1947–1957: When the Yankees, the Giants, and the Dodgers Ruled the World* (New York: Ticknor & Fields, 1993), 127.

19. Harold C. Burr, "No Rest for Mighty Casey Even Though He's Ailing," *Brooklyn Eagle*, 6 October 1947.

20. Roscoe McGowen, "Outfielder Feted for Mighty Catch," *New York Times*, 6 October 1947.

23. A WORLD SERIES HERO AND A SUCCESSFUL RESTAURATEUR

1. Grantland Rice, "Casey in the Box," *New York Sun*, 6 October 1947.

2. Joe Williams, "Casey May Be Better Than Marberry," *New York World-Telegram*, 6 October 1947.

3. Gus Steiger, "Courage and Control Casey's Series Assets," *New York Mirror*, 24 October 1947.

4. Steiger, "Courage and Control Casey's Series Assets."

5. "Our Dodgers Are Beaten but Unbowed," *Brooklyn Eagle*, 7 October 1947.

6. Bob Broeg, "Broeg on Baseball," *Sporting News*, 26 January 1974.

7. Dan Daniel, "Daniel's Dope," *New York World-Telegram*, 19 September 1949.

8. Mary O'Flaherty, "Hugh Casey's Wife Coddles Cold, Found Series a Strain," *New York Daily News*, 12 October 1947.

9. Ward Morehouse, "Casey's Club for Food, Foam, and Fanning-Bees," *Sporting News*, 24 December 1947.

10. Kirby Higbe, with Martin Quigley, *The High Hard One* (New York: Viking, 1967), 63–64.

11. Morehouse, "Casey's Club for Food, Foam, and Fanning Bees."

12. "Ball King," *Brooklyn Eagle*, 6 January 1948.

13. Morehouse, "Casey's Club for Food, Foam, and Fanning Bees."

14. "Leo Through, Says Hugh," *Sporting News*, 5 November 1947.

15. Harold C. Burr, "Shotton Says He'll Never Pilot Again," *Brooklyn Eagle*, 20 January 1948.

16. Burr, "Shotton Says He'll Never Pilot Again."

17. Harold C. Burr, "Best Guess on Jackie's Pay $15,000, Boost of 200 Percent over '47," *Sporting News*, 18 February1948.

18. Harold C. Burr, "Hugh Casey Arrives, Takes over at Short," *Brooklyn Eagle*, 4 March 1948.

19. Harold C. Burr, "Barney Sparkles as Casey Beams," *Brooklyn Eagle*, 17 March 1948.

20. Rex Barney had his greatest season in 1948. He won 15 games and had 138 strikeouts. Three years later, his big-league career was over at age 26.

21. Sam Lacy, "Wholesome Fellowship among Dodgers' Men," *Baltimore Afro-American*, 20 March 1948.

24. FALLING, LITERALLY AND FIGURATIVELY

1. "Flock Takes Fourth Pasting in Row as Flingers Go through Wringer," *Brooklyn Eagle*, 20 May 1948.

2. "Cards Rekindle Feud on Beanball Charge," *Brooklyn Eagle*, 21 May 1948.

3. "Cards Rekindle Feud on Beanball Charge."

4. "Hannegan Complains to Frick," *Sporting News*, 2 June 1948.

5. Peter Golenbock, *Bums: An Oral History of the Brooklyn Dodgers* (New York: G. P. Putnam's Sons, 1984), 47.

6. "Taylor Will Soon Resume Pitching," *New York Sun*, 24 May 1948.

7. "Jersey Marks Spot, Casey Now Reveals," *Brooklyn Eagle*, 26 May 1948.

8. "Hugh Casey Gets Clean Bill," *Brooklyn Eagle*, 27 May 1948.

9. "Hugh Casey Joins Yank Mound Staff," *New York Times*, 5 September 1949.

10. *Pine Plains Register-Herald* (New York), 1 July 1948.

11. Harold C. Burr, "Flock Fans Support Rickey on Dixie Deal," *Brooklyn Eagle*, 12 December 1947.

12. Joseph M. Sheehan, "Brooklyn Loses to Pirates 8–4, Fall to Seventh Place in Flag Race," *New York Times*, 22 May 1948.

13. *Time*, 31 May 1948.

14. William Marshall, *Baseball's Pivotal Era, 1945–1951* (Lexington: University Press of Kentucky, 1999), 213.

15. "Shotton Promises Action on Players," *New York Times*, 17 July 1948.

25. CASEY AND THE DODGERS PART WAYS

1. Harold C. Burr, "Dodgers Ship Harry Taylor to St. Paul," *Brooklyn Eagle*, 20 July 1948.

2. Fay Vincent, *We Would Have Played for Nothing: Baseball Stars of the 1950s and 1960s Talk about the Game They Loved* (New York: Simon & Schuster, 2008), 146.

3. E-mail from Carl Erskine to the author on 9 February 2015.

4. Ernie Harwell, *The Babe Signed My Shoe*, edited by Geoff Upward (South Bend, IN: Diamond Communications, 1994), 113.

5. Harwell, *The Babe Signed My Shoe*, 114.

6. Ben Gould, "Holmes Home in Triumph," *Brooklyn Eagle*, 29 September 1948.

7. Harold C. Burr, "Shotton Rates Flock Best Team in League," *Brooklyn Eagle*, 27 September 1948.

8. "Casey Says He'll Sign with Giants," *New York Sun*, 28 September 1948.

9. "Casey Sees Himself with Giants in '49," *Brooklyn Eagle*, 28 September 1948.

10. Frank C. True, "Casey to Get Test on Giants," *New York Sun*, 29 September 1948.

11. "Casey Reported a Pirate," *New York Sun*, 7 October 1948.

12. The Dodgers Sym-phony was a musical group of five fans, led by Shorty Laurice, who entertained fans at Ebbets Field. The poem "Leave Us Go Root for the Dodgers, Rogers" was written by Dan Parker, sports editor for the *New York Daily Mirror*.

13. "Casey Joins Pirates after Seven Years as Dodger Hurler," *New York Times*, 21 October 1948.

14. "Higbe and Casey Together Again—with the Pirates," *Sporting News*, 27 October 1948.

15. "Casey Joins Pirates after Seven Years as Dodger Hurler."

16. "Casey Wasn't Happy with Dodgers," *New York Sun*, 29 September 1948.

17. "Dodger Demise Is Predicted," *Baltimore Sun*, 27 October 1948.

18. Les Biederman, "Meyer Marks up Pirates 25 Pct. over Last Year," *Sporting News*, 30 March 1949.

19. "Pirate Manager Pays Hugh Casey High Compliment," *New York Sun*, 13 April 1949.

26. THE PIRATES AND THE YANKEES

1. Tommy Holmes, "Kiner's (Unlucky) 13th Homer Knocks Flock from Top to Third Place," *Brooklyn Eagle*, 6 June 1949.

2. "Giants, on Ropes in Ninth, Win by 5–4," *Brooklyn Eagle*, 19 June 1949.

3. Sam Lacy, "From A to Z with Sam Lacy," *Baltimore Afro-American*, 9 July 1949.

4. *New York Amsterdam News*.

5. "No Room for Hugh Casey on Yankees, Says Stengel," *Sporting News*, 17 August 1949.

6. "Hugh Casey Joins Yank Mound Staff," *New York Times*, 5 September 1949.

7. "Yanks Sign Hugh Casey to Assist Joe Page," *Baltimore Sun*, 5 September 1949.

8. "Kinder Best Right-Hander in Majors, Casey Insists," *Sporting News*, 28 September 1949.

9. Dan Daniel, "Bauer Latest to Aid Bombers in Clutch," *New York World-Telegram*, 19 September 1949.

10. J. G. Taylor Spink, "Looping the Loops," *Sporting News*, 28 September 1949.

11. Sam Lacy, "Big Don May Pitch Two Games in Series," *Baltimore Afro-American*, 8 October 1949.

12. Bob Mack, *Bird Hunting in Brooklyn: Ebbets Field, the Dodgers, and the 1949 National League Pennant Race* (Self-published, 2008), 408.

13. Dan Daniel, "Daniel's Dope," *New York World-Telegram*, 13 October 1949.

14. Harold C. Burr, "Casey Draws Walking Papers from Yankees," *Brooklyn Eagle*, 15 October 1949.

15. Spink, "Looping the Loops."

27. A PENNANT AND A PATERNITY SUIT

1. "Dixie Walker to Manage Atlanta Club," *Hartford Courant*, 6 December 1949.

2. Guy Tiller, "Prospect for Majors: Dixie Walker," *Baseball Digest*, October 1950.

3. "Whitlow Wyatt to Coach Braves' Rookie Pitchers," *Hartford Courant*, 1 March 1950.

4. F. M. Williams, "Hugh Casey to Hurl for 1950 Crackers," *Atlanta Constitution*, 3 March 1950.

5. "Hugh Casey Signs Atlanta Contract," *New York Times*, 3 March 1950.

6. F. M. Williams, "Casey and N. Brown Get Scare Fishing in Bay at Pensacola," *Atlanta Constitution*, 15 March 1950.

7. "Irate Fan Names Casey as Father of Her Child," *Brooklyn Eagle*, 21 April 1950.

8. "Irate Fan Names Casey as Father of Her Child."

9. "Girl Fan Sues Casey as Father of Her Son," *New York Daily Mirror*, undated clipping from Hugh Casey's file at the National Baseball Hall of Fame and Library.

10. Carl E. Prince, *Brooklyn's Dodgers: The Bums, the Borough, and the Best of Baseball* (New York: Oxford University Press, 1996), 80.

11. "Girl Fan Sues Casey as Father of Her Son."

12. "Hugh Casey Denies Paternity Charge," *Atlanta Constitution*, 22 April 1950.

13. Furman Bisher, "The People vs. Casey," *Atlanta Constitution*, 15 May 1950.

14. Furman Bisher, "The Jury Delivers a Verdict for Casey," *Atlanta Constitution*, 13 July 1950.

15. Harold C. Burr, "Governor Studies Flock First Hand," *Brooklyn Eagle*, 26 July 1950.

16. Fred Russell, "Southern Young Man's Loop—with Experience for Spice," *Sporting News*, 9 August 1950.

17. "Casey Makes First Start since '46, Wins for Crax," *Sporting News*, 30 August 1950.

18. Furman Bisher, "Ex-Dodgers Aided Crax to 13th Flag," *Sporting News*, 20 September 1950.

19. "Casey Ordered to go to Bat in Paternity Suit," *Brooklyn Eagle*, 25 October 1950.

20. "Times in Hotel with Casey, Hilda Says at Paternity Trial," *New York Daily News*, 22 December 1950.

21. "Georgia Gent Alibis Casey in Love Suit," *New York World-Telegram*, 28 December 1950.

22. The three judges were Frederick L. Hackenberg, Eugene G. Schulz, and Nathan D. Perlman.

23. "100 Years of Consumer Spending: Data for the Nation, New York City, and Boston," *United States Bureau of Labor Statistics*, http://www.bls.gov/opub/uscs/ (accessed 3 October 2016).

24. $avings.org, http://www.saving.org/.

25. "Casey Calls Ruling Foul, Asks for Relief," *Brooklyn Eagle*, 30 December 1950.

26. "Court Decides Casey Is in Father's League," *New York Daily Mirror*, 30 December 1950.

27. "Ruled Father, Hugh Casey to Continue to Fight," *New York Herald Tribune*, 30 December 1950.

28. Kirby Higbe, with Martin Quigley, *The High Hard One* (New York: Viking, 1967), 63.

29. "Girl Who Won Casey Paternity Suit Is Married," *Brooklyn Eagle*, 30 January 1951.

30. Series of telephone calls and e-mails between Michael Kocijan and the author in March and April 2016.

28. A WONDERFUL GUY WHO NEVER HURT ANYONE—BUT HIMSELF

1. "Tax Lien against Hugh Casey," *New York Times*, 1 February 1951.

2. "Collector Didn't List All Income," *Boston Globe*, 26 October 1951.

3. "Casey Works Out with Brooklyn; May Sign Pact," *Atlanta Constitution*, 30 April 1951.

4. "Returning to Flock, Hugh Casey Tells Bushwick Center," *Brooklyn Eagle*, 3 May 1951.

5. "Casey Planned to Form Brooklyn Softball Team," *Sporting News*, 11 July 1951.

6. "Casey Planned to Form Brooklyn Softball Team."

7. The *Atlanta Constitution* and the *Atlanta Journal* published a joint edition on Sundays.

8. Ed Danforth, "Hugh Casey Says Beanball Brawl between Giants and Dodgers Serious," *Atlanta Journal*, 1 July 1951.

9. "Hugh Casey, Ex-Dodger Relief Star, Ends His Life," *Sporting News*, 11 July 1951.

10. "Hugh Casey Kills Himself," *Brooklyn Eagle*, 3 July 1951.

11. "Hugh Casey, Ex-Dodger Relief Star, Ends His Life."

12. "'Innocent'—Casey Kills Self," *New York Daily News*, 4 July 1951.

13. "Hugh Casey Kills Himself."

14. "Wife on Phone as Hugh Casey Ends His Life," *New York Herald-Tribune*, 4 July 1951.

15. Casey, Ex-Dodger, Is Atlanta Suicide," *New York Times*, 4 July 1951.

16. "Hugh Casey Kills Himself."

17. Joseph Kiernan, "Glum Friends Toast Hugh at His Own Bar," *New York Daily News*, 4 July 1951.

18. "Hugh Casey Ends Life with Shotgun," *New York World-Telegram/New York Sun*, 3 July 1951.

19. Joe King, "Friends Knew Hugh Casey as 'Guy Who Was Kind to All but Himself,'" *Sporting News*, 11 July 1951.

20. Casey, Ex-Dodger, Is Atlanta Suicide."

21. "Casey Buried Near Sandlots Where He Learned to Pitch," *Brooklyn Eagle*, 5 July 1951.

22. Jesse Outlar, "Casey Bids Farewell to Beloved Buckhead," *Atlanta Constitution*, 5 July 1951.

23. Tax liens can be satisfied after death through the filing by the government of a claim with the administrator of the will of the deceased. "U.S. Holds Tax Lien of $6,759 against Casey," *Brooklyn Eagle*, 5 July 1951.

24. Jesse Outlar, "Casey Threatened Suicide for Past Year, Wife Says," *Atlanta Constitution*, 4 July 1951.

25. Outlar, "Casey Threatened Suicide for Past Year."

26. "Hugh Casey Ends Life with Shotgun."

27. Jesse Outlar, "Death of Casey Shocks His Old Diamond Buddies," *Atlanta Constitution*, 4 July 1951.

29. REMEMBERING HUGH CASEY

1. Tommy Holmes, "The Sad Passing of an Old Friend," *Brooklyn Eagle*, 6 July 1951.

2. Bob Cooke, "Another Viewpoint," *New York Herald Tribune*, 8 July 1951.

3. Furman Bisher, "Of Time, Men, and Careers," *Atlanta Constitution*, 16 July 1951.

4. Edgar Munzel, "Cubs' Bullpen Flop Jogs Lip's Memory of Great Relievers," *Sporting News*, 4 May 1968.

5. E-mail from SABR member Bob Hurte from a telephone interview with Wally Westlake, 17 January 2016.

6. "Mrs. Casey Gets Pension," *New York Times*, 11 July 1951.

7. "Top Prep Athlete to Get Hugh Casey Memorial," *Baltimore Sun*, 25 November 1951.

8. Quoted in James D. Hardy Jr., *Baseball and the Mythic Moment: How We Remember the National Game* (Jefferson, NC: McFarland, 2007), 55.

9. "Wife on Phone as Hugh Casey Ends His Life," *New York Herald Tribune*, 4 July 1951.

10. "Hugh Casey Kills Himself," *Brooklyn Eagle*, 3 July 1951.

11. Red Barber, "Ernest Hemingway and the Tough Dodger," *New York Times*, 14 November 1976.

12. Leo Durocher, with Ed Linn, *Nice Guys Finish Last* (New York: Simon & Schuster, 1975), 131.

13. Gay Talese, "Ebbets Field Goes on the Scrap Pile," *New York Times*, 24 February 1960.

BIBLIOGRAPHY

Ahrens, Art. "The Old Brawl Game." *National Pastime* (journal for the Society for American Baseball Research) 23 (2003): 3–6.

Alexander, Charles C. *Breaking the Slump: Baseball in the Depression Era.* New York: Columbia University Press, 2002.

———. *Our Game: An American Baseball History.* New York: Henry Holt, 1991.

Allen, Maury, with Susan Walker. *Dixie Walker of the Dodgers: The People's Choice.* Tuscaloosa, AL: Fire Ant Books, 2010.

Applegate, Richard. "The Battle of the Hatfields and the McCoys." In *Mound City Memories: Baseball in St. Louis,* edited by Robert L. Tiemann, 88–94. Phoenix, AZ: Society for American Baseball Research, 2007.

Barber, Red. *1947: When All Hell Broke Loose in Baseball.* Garden City, NY: Doubleday, 1982.

———. "Leadoff Man." *New Republic,* 4 July 1983.

———, and Robert Creamer. *Rhubarb in the Catbird Seat.* Garden City, NY: Doubleday, 1968.

Bartell, Richard, and Norman L. Macht. *Rowdy Richard.* Berkeley, CA: North Atlantic Books, 1987.

Barthel, Thomas. *The Fierce Fun of Ducky Medwick.* Lanham, MD: Scarecrow Press, 2003.

Bell, Christopher. *Scapegoats: Baseballers Whose Careers Are Marked by One Fateful Play.* Jefferson, NC: McFarland, 2002.

Bjarkman, Peter C., ed. *Encyclopedia of Major League Baseball Team Histories: National League.* Westport, CT: Meckler, 1991.

Bloodgood, Clifford. "The Abnormal Season of '46." *Baseball Magazine,* December 1946.

Boren, Stephen D., and Thomas Boren. "The 1942 Pennant Race." *National Pastime* (journal for the Society for American Baseball Research) 15 (1995): 133–35.

Borst, Bill. "Showdown in St. Louis." In *The National Pastime: A Review of Baseball History,* vol. 11, edited by the Society for American Baseball Research, 63–64. Phoenix, AZ: Society for American Baseball Research, 1991.

Boston, Talmage. *1939, Baseball's Pivotal Year.* Fort Worth, TX: Summit Group, 1994.

Bragan, Bobby, and Jeff Guinn. *You Can't Hit the Ball with the Bat on Your Shoulder: The Baseball Life and Times of Bobby Bragan.* Fort Worth, TX: Summit Group, 1992.

Broeg, Bob. "The '42 Cardinals." *Sport* 7 (July 1963): 40–43.

———. *One Hundred Greatest Moments in St. Louis Sports.* St. Louis: Missouri Historical Society Press, 2000.

———, and William J. Miller Jr. *Baseball from a Different Angle.* South Bend, IN: Diamond Communications, 1988.

Cannon, Jimmy. "Leo Buttons His Lip." *Baseball Digest* 2 (November 1946): 42.

Cantor, George. *World Series Fact Book*. Detroit: Visible Ink Press, 1996.

Charlton, James. *The Baseball Chronology*. New York: Macmillan, 1991.

Creamer, Robert W. *Baseball in '41: A Celebration of the Best Baseball Season Ever—in the Year America Went to War*. New York: Penguin, 1991.

D'Antonio, Michael. *Forever Blue: The True Story of Walter O'Malley, Baseball's Most Controversial Owner, and the Dodgers of Brooklyn and Los Angeles*. New York: Riverhead Books, 2009.

Davis, William C. *Look Away! A History of the Confederate States of America*. New York: Free Press, 2002.

Dewey, Donald, and Nicholas Acocella. *The Ball Clubs*. New York: HarperCollins, 1996.

———. *The Biographical History of Baseball*. New York: Carroll & Graf, 1995.

Dorinson, Joseph, and Joram Warmund, eds. *Jackie Robinson: Race, Sports, and the American Dream*. Armonk, NY: M. E. Sharpe, 1998.

Durocher, Leo. *The Dodgers and Me: The Inside Story*. Chicago: Ziff-Davis, 1948.

———, with Ed Linn. *Nice Guys Finish Last*. New York: Simon & Schuster, 1975.

Echevarría, Roberto González. "The '47 Dodgers in Havana: Baseball at a Crossroads." *1996 Spring Training Baseball Yearbook* 9 (Spring 1996): 20–25.

Eig, Jonathan. *Opening Day: The Story of Jackie Robinson's First Season*. New York: Simon & Schuster, 2007.

Eldridge, Larry. "Why Isn't Pee Wee Reese in the Hall of Fame?" *Baseball Digest* 4 (July 1978): 80.

Erskine, Carl. *Tales from the Dodgers Dugout: A Collection of the Greatest Dodgers Stories*. New York: Sports Publishing, 2014.

Falkner, David. *Great Time Coming: The Life of Jackie Robinson, from Baseball to Birmingham*. New York: Simon & Schuster, 1995.

Figone, Al. "Larry MacPhail and Dolph Camilli." *National Pastime* (journal for the Society for American Baseball Research) 14 (1994): 106–9.

Fimrite, Ron. "The Play That Beat the Bums." *Sports Illustrated*, 20 October 1997.

Freese, Mel R. *The St. Louis Cardinals in the 1940s*. Jefferson, NC: McFarland, 2007.

Frommer, Harvey. *New York City Baseball: The Last Golden Age, 1947–1957*. New York: Macmillan, 1980.

———. *Rickey and Robinson*. New York: Macmillan, 1982.

Gaven, Michael. "What a Load of Rhubarb." *Baseball Digest* 12 (February 1958): 51.

Gies, Joseph, and Robert H. Shoemaker. *Stars of the Series: A Complete History of the World Series*. New York: Thomas Y. Crowell, 1965.

Gietschier, Steven P. "Slugging and Snubbing: Hugh Casey, Ernest Hemingway, and Jackie Robinson—a Baseball Mystery." *Nine: A Journal of Baseball History and Culture* 21, no. 1 (Fall 2012): 12–46.

Gillette, Gary, and Pete Palmer, eds. *The ESPN Baseball Encyclopedia*, 5th ed. New York: Sterling, 2008.

Goldblatt, Andrew. *The Giants and the Dodgers: Four Cities, Two Teams, One Rivalry*. Jefferson, NC: McFarland, 2003.

Goldfarb, Irv. "Spring Training in Havana." In *The Team That Forever Changed Baseball and America: The 1947 Brooklyn Dodgers*, edited by Lyle Spatz, 3–5. Lincoln: University of Nebraska Press/Society for American Baseball Research, 2012.

Goldstein, Richard. *Spartan Seasons: How Baseball Survived the Second World War*. New York: Macmillan, 1980.

———. *Superstars and Screwballs: 100 Years of Brooklyn Baseball*. New York: Dutton, 1991.

Golenbock, Peter. *Bums: An Oral History of the Brooklyn Dodgers*. New York: G. P. Putnam's Sons, 1984.

Gough, David. "A Tribute to Burt Shotton." *National Pastime* (journal for the Society for American Baseball Research) 14 (1994): 99–101.

Graham, Frank. *The Brooklyn Dodgers: An Informal History*. New York: G. P. Putnam's Sons, 1945.

Graham, Frank, Jr. "Greatest Fight on a Ballfield." *Baseball Digest* 2 (June 1953): 45.

Green, Paul. "Whitlow Wyatt." *Sports Collectors Digest* (March 1986): 172–220.

Greene, A. Wilson. *The Final Battles of the Petersburg Campaign: Breaking the Backbone of the Rebellion*, 2nd ed. Knoxville: University of Tennessee Press, 2008.

Hardy, James D., Jr. *Baseball and the Mythic Moment: How We Remember the National Game.* Jefferson, NC: McFarland, 2007.

Harwell, Ernie. *The Babe Signed My Shoe.* Edited by Geoff Upward. South Bend, IN: Diamond Communications, 1994.

Hawthorn, Tom. "The 1947 World Series." In *Bridging Two Dynasties: The 1947 New York Yankees*, edited by Lyle Spatz, 276–81. Lincoln: University of Nebraska Press/Society for American Baseball Research, 2013.

Heinz, W. C. "The Rocky Road of Pistol Pete." In *The Baseball Reader: Favorites from the Fireside Books of Baseball*, edited by Charles Einstein, 162–76. New York: Lippincott & Crowell, 1980.

Henrich, Tommy, with Bill Gilbert. *Five O'clock Lightning: Ruth, Gehrig, DiMaggio, Mantle, and the Glory Years of the NY Yankees.* New York: Carol, 1992.

Higbe, Kirby, with Martin Quigley. *The High Hard One.* New York: Viking, 1967.

Holmes, Tommy. *The Dodgers.* New York: Macmillan, 1975.

Honig, Donald. *Baseball America.* New York: Macmillan, 1985.

———. *Baseball When the Grass Was Real: Baseball from the Twenties to the Forties, Told by the Men Who Played It.* New York: Coward, McCann & Geoghegan, 1975.

———. *The Brooklyn Dodgers: An Illustrated Tribute.* New York: St. Martin's, 1981.

Hynd, Noel. *The Giants of the Polo Grounds.* New York: Doubleday, 1988.

Jackson, Frank. "'Papa' Hemingway vs. 'Fireman' Casey." *Hardball Times*, 31 January 2013.

Jacobson, Sidney. *Pete Reiser: The Rough-and-Tumble Career of the Perfect Ballplayer.* Jefferson, NC: McFarland, 2004.

James, Bill. *The New Bill James Historical Baseball Abstract.* New York: Free Press, 2001.

Kahn, Roger. *The Boys of Summer.* New York: Harper & Row, 1971.

———. *The Era, 1947–1957: When the Yankees, the Giants, and the Dodgers Ruled the World.* New York: Ticknor & Fields, 1993.

———. *Memories of Summer: When Baseball Was an Art and Writing about It a Game.* New York: Hyperion, 1997.

———. *Rickey and Robinson: The True, Untold Story of the Integration of Baseball.* New York: Rodale, 2014.

Kashatus, William. *Jackie and Campy: The Untold Story of Their Rocky Relationship and the Breaking of Baseball's Color Line.* Lincoln: University of Nebraska Press, 2014.

Kavanagh, Jack. "Dixie Walker." *Baseball Research Journal* (journal for the Society for American Baseball Research) 22, no. 1 (1993): 80–83.

———. "A Dodger Boyhood." In *Baseball History 3: An Annual of Original Baseball Research*, edited by Peter Levine, 119–32. Westport, CT: Meckler, 1990.

Knight, Tom. "Uncle Robbie and Hugh Casey." *Baseball Research Journal* (journal for the Society for American Baseball Research) 22, no. 1 (1993): 105–6.

Korda, Michael. *Clouds of Glory: The Life and Legend of Robert E. Lee.* New York: Harper-Collins, 2014.

Krell, David. *Our Bums: The Brooklyn Dodgers in History, Memory, and Popular Culture.* Jefferson, NC: McFarland, 2015.

Langford, Walter M. *Legends of Baseball: An Oral History of The Game's Golden Age.* South Bend, IN: Diamond Communications, 1987.

Levy, Alan H. *Joe McCarthy: Architect of the Yankee Dynasty.* Jefferson, NC: McFarland, 2005.

Light, Jonathan F. *The Cultural Encyclopedia of Baseball.* Jefferson, NC: McFarland, 1997.

Liley, Thomas. "Whit Wyatt: The Dodgers' 1941 Ace." In *The National Pastime: A Review of Baseball History*, vol. 11, edited by the Society for American Baseball Research, 46–47. Phoenix, AZ: Society for American Baseball Research, 1991.

Lowenfish, Lee. *Branch Rickey: Baseball's Ferocious Gentleman.* Lincoln: University of Nebraska Press, 2007.

————. "The Gentlemen's Agreement and the Ferocious Gentleman Who Broke It." *Baseball Research Journal* (journal for the Society for American Baseball Research) 38, no. 1 (2009): 33–34.

Lowry, Philip J. *Green Cathedrals: The Ultimate Celebration of Major League and Negro League Ballparks.* New York: Walker & Company, 2006.

Macht, Norman L. "Does Baseball Deserve This Black Eye?" *Baseball Research Journal* (journal for the Society for American Baseball Research) 38, no. 1 (2009): 5–9.

————. "Why Did Mickey Miss the Ball?" In *The National Pastime: A Review of Baseball History*, vol. 11, edited by the Society for American Baseball Research, 44–45. Phoenix, AZ: Society for American Baseball Research, 1991.

Mack, Bob. *Bird Hunting in Brooklyn: Ebbets Field, the Dodgers, and the 1949 National League Pennant Race.* Self-published, 2008.

MacPhail, Lee. "A Year to Remember, Especially in Brooklyn." In *The National Pastime: A Review of Baseball History*, vol. 11, edited by the Society for American Baseball Research, 41–43. Phoenix, AZ: Society for American Baseball Research, 1991.

Mann, Arthur. "The Truth about the Jackie Robinson Case." *Saturday Evening Post*, 20 May 1950.

Marlette, Jeffrey. "The Suspension of Leo Durocher." In *The Team That Forever Changed Baseball and America: The 1947 Brooklyn Dodgers*, edited by Lyle Spatz, 50–56. Lincoln: University of Nebraska Press/Society for American Baseball Research, 2012.

Marshall, William. *Baseball's Pivotal Era, 1945–1951.* Lexington: University Press of Kentucky, 1999.

Marzano, Rudy. *The Brooklyn Dodgers in the 1940s: How Robinson, MacPhail, Reiser, and Rickey Changed Baseball.* Jefferson, NC: McFarland, 2005.

McGee, Robert. *The Greatest Ballpark Ever: Ebbets Field and the Story of the Brooklyn Dodgers.* New Brunswick, NJ: Rivergate, 2005.

McGowen, Roscoe. "Boss of Bums but Not Bum Boss." *Baseball Magazine*, August 1947.

McKelvey, G. Richard. *The MacPhails: Baseball's First Family of the Front Office.* Jefferson, NC: McFarland, 2005.

McNeil, William F. *The Dodger Encyclopedia.* Champaign, IL: Sports Publishing, 1997.

McPherson, James M. *Battle Cry of Freedom.* New York: Oxford University Press, 1988.

Mead, William B. *Even the Browns: The Zany, True Story of Baseball in the Early Forties.* Chicago: Contemporary Books, 1978.

Meany, Tom. "Dixie Deal Strictly Business." *Baseball Digest* 9 (March 1948): 55–56.

————. "Hugh Casey," *Sport* 5 (May 1948): 27.

Mele, Andrew Paul. *A Brooklyn Dodgers Reader.* Jefferson, NC: McFarland, 2004.

Miller, Patrick B., and David K. Wiggins, eds. *Sport and the Color Line: Black Athletes and Race Relations in Twentieth-Century America.* New York: Routledge, 2004.

Morris, Peter. *A Game of Inches: The Game behind the Scenes.* Chicago: Ivan R. Dee, 2006.

Moss, Robert A. "The Fireman." *NINE: A Journal of Baseball History and Culture* 21, no. 2 (Spring 2013): 125–34.

Nack, William. "The Breakthrough." *Sports Illustrated*, 5 May 1997.

Newsome, Hampton. *Richmond Must Fall: The Richmond-Petersburg Campaign, October 1864.* Kent, OH: Kent State University Press, 2013.

Neyer, Rob, and Eddie Epstein. *Baseball Dynasties: The Greatest Teams of All Time.* New York: W. W. Norton, 2000.

Oakley, J. Ronald. *Baseball's Last Golden Age, 1946–1960: The National Pastime in a Time of Glory and Change.* Jefferson, NC: McFarland, 1994.

Oliphant, Thomas. *Praying for Gil Hodges.* New York: St. Martin's, 2005.

Panaccio, Tim. "How It Was during the War Years." *Baseball Digest* 3 (January 1977): 68.

Parker, Clifton Blue. *Big and Little Poison: Paul and Lloyd Waner, Baseball Brothers.* Jefferson, NC: McFarland, 2003.

Paxton, Harry T. "It's Raining Dollars in Pittsburgh." *Saturday Evening Post*, 8 May 1948.

Pietrusza, David, Matthew Silverman, and Michael Gershman, eds. *Baseball: The Biographical Encyclopedia.* Kingston, NY: Total Sports/Sports Illustrated, 2000.

Porter, David L., ed. *Biographical Dictionary of American Sports: Baseball*, rev. and exp. ed. Westport, CT: Greenwood, 2000.

Powell, Larry. "Jackie Robinson and Dixie Walker: Myths of the Southern Baseball Player." *Southern Cultures* (Summer 2002): 56–70.

Prince, Carl E. *Brooklyn's Dodgers: The Bums, the Borough, and the Best of Baseball*. New York: Oxford University Press, 1996.

Rampersad, Arnold. *Jackie Robinson: A Biography*. New York: Ballantine, 1997.

Reed, Ted. *Carl Furillo: Brooklyn Dodgers All-Star*. Jefferson, NC: McFarland, 2011.

Reese, Pee Wee, with Tim Cohane. "Reese's Own Story." *Baseball Digest* 8 (May 1954): 32.

Rice, Damon. *Seasons Past*. New York: Praeger, 1976.

Ritter, Lawrence S. *East Side West Side: Tales of New York Sporting Life, 1910–1960*. New York: Total Sports, 1998.

Robinson, Eddie, with C. Paul Rogers III. *Lucky Me: My Sixty-Five Years in Baseball*. Dallas, TX: Southern Methodist University Press, 2011.

Robinson, Jackie. *Baseball Has Done It*. Philadelphia: Lippincott, 1964.

———. "Now I Know Why They Boo Me." *Look*, 25 January 1955.

———, as told to Alfred Duckett. *I Never Had It Made*. New York: G. P. Putnam's Sons, 1972.

Shampoe, Clay, and Thomas R. Garrett. *Baseball in Norfolk, Virginia*. Charleston, SC: Arcadia, 2003.

Shapiro, Milton J. *Heroes of the Bullpen: Baseball's Greatest Relief Pitchers*. New York: Julian Messner, 1967.

Shatzkin, Mike. *The Ballplayers*. New York: William Morrow, 1990.

Sheed, Wilfrid. *My Life as a Fan*. New York: Simon & Schuster, 1993.

Silber, Irwin. *Press Box Red: The Story of Lester Rodney, the Communist Who Helped Break the Color Line in American Sports*. Philadelphia: Temple University Press, 2003.

Silverman, Al. *Heroes of the World Series*. New York: G. P. Putnam's Sons, 1945.

Simon, Scott. *Jackie Robinson and the Integration of Baseball*. Hoboken, NJ: John Wiley & Sons, 2002.

Slaughter, Enos, with Kevin Reid. *Country Hardball: The Autobiography of Enos "Country" Slaughter*. Greensboro, NC: Tudor, 1991.

Smith, Ira. *Baseball's Famous Pitchers*. New York: A. S. Barnes, 1954.

Snider, Duke, with Phil Pepe. *Few and Chosen: Defining Dodger Greatness across the Eras*. Chicago: Triumph, 2006.

Solomon, Burt. *The Baseball Timeline*. New York: Avon. 1997.

Spatz, Lyle. *Dixie Walker: A Life in Baseball*. Jefferson, NC: McFarland, 2011.

———. "Managing the 1947 Dodgers: The 'People's Choice.'" *Baseball Research Journal* (journal for the Society for American Baseball Research) 42, no. 1 (2013): 63–66.

———. *New York Yankee Openers: An Opening Day History of Baseball's Most Famous Team, 1903–1996*. Jefferson, NC: McFarland, 1997.

———. "Three Georgia-Born Former Dodgers Lead the Crackers to a Pennant." *National Pastime* (journal for the Society for American Baseball Research) 40 (2010): 69–71.

———, ed. *Bridging Two Dynasties: The 1947 New York Yankees*. Lincoln: University of Nebraska Press/Society for American Baseball Research, 2013.

———, ed. *The Team That Forever Changed Baseball and America: The 1947 Brooklyn Dodgers*. Lincoln: University of Nebraska Press/Society for American Baseball Research, 2012.

Stevens, Ed. *The Other Side of the Jackie Robinson Story*. Mustang, OK: Tate, 2009.

Thorn, John. *The Relief Pitcher: Baseball's New Hero*. New York: E. P. Dutton, 1979.

Tiemann, Robert L. *Dodger Classics*. St. Louis, MO: Baseball Histories, 1983.

Tiller, Guy. "Prospect for Majors: Dixie Walker." *Baseball Digest* 2 (October 1950): 85.

Tygiel, Jules. *Baseball's Great Experiment: Jackie Robinson and His Legacy*. New York: Vintage, 1984.

Van Blair, Rick. *Dugout to Foxhole: Interviews with Baseball Players Whose Careers Were Affected by World War II*. Jefferson, NC: McFarland, 1995.

Vincent, Fay. *We Would Have Played for Nothing: Baseball Stars of the 1950s and 1960s Talk about the Game They Loved*. New York: Simon & Schuster, 2008.

Weeks, Jonathan. *Mudville Madness: Fabulous Feats, Belligerent Behavior, and Erratic Episodes*. Lanham, MD: Taylor Trade, 2014.

Weintraub, Robert. *The Victory Season: The End of World War II and the Birth of Baseball's Golden Age*. New York: Little, Brown, 2013.

Woodward, Stanley. "In the Rickey Manner." *Baseball Digest* 7 (July 1950): 23.

Zachter, Mort. *Gil Hodges: A Hall of Fame Life*. Lincoln: University of Nebraska Press, 2015.

INDEX

Abraham and Straus Department Store, 167
Abrams, Robert, 257
Adams, Ace, 201
Adler, Bert, 241
Aiea Naval Hospital, 135, 138
Aleno, Chuck, 72
Alexander, Grover, 114
Allen, Charles L., Dr., 266
Allen, Johnny, 72–73, 79, 88, 90, 119, 121, 130
Anderson, Alf, 80, 103
Anderson, Ferrell, 157
Appling, Luke, 103
Atlanta Crackers, 5, 7, 8, 17, 251, 252, 253, 256, 261, 262, 266
Atlantan Hotel, 263
Azarewicz, Alex, 188
Azarewicz, Stella, 188

Baker Field (New York), 25
Bagby, Jim, Jr., 3, 103
Bagwell, J. M., 263
Baker, Bill, 57
Baker, Del, 251
Baldwin, Neil, Jr., 268
Baltimore Elite Giants, 232
Bankhead, Dan, 222–223
Barber, Red, 15, 25, 57, 64, 81, 110, 170, 183, 211, 271
Barber, Lylah, 170

Barlick, Al, 58
Barney, Rex, 141, 167, 187, 191, 208, 212, 222, 225, 226, 237, 244
Barr, George, 162
Barron, Red, 103
Bartell, Dick, 16
Beazley, Johnny, 124
Becker, Heinz, 147
Beckmann, Bill, 14
Behrman, Hank, 155, 158, 161, 182, 185, 192, 205, 207, 208, 210, 216, 236
Bell, Rache, 3, 103
Bennett, George, Dr., 41
Bennett, Robert Russell, 64
Benson, Benney S. C., Rev., 163
Benswanger, Bill, 140
Benton, Al, 247
Berra, Yogi, 138, 208, 213
Beth-El Hospital (Brooklyn), 253
Bevens, Bill, 210–211, 216
Birmingham Barons, 12
Bisher, Furman, 266
Bithorn, Hi, 119
Blades, Ray, 42, 133, 182
Block, Cy, 13
Bodie, Gary, 129
Boggess, Dusty, 149
Bonham, Ernie, 93, 270
Bonham, Ruth, 270
Bonura, Zeke, 18
Borowy, Hank, 64, 147

Reagan, C. D., 266
Reardon, Beans, 18, 80, 196, 202
Reese, Pee Wee, xv, 27, 32–33, 34, 35, 40,
    52, 55, 63, 72, 74–75, 83, 84, 88, 93,
    104, 108, 115, 123, 126, 127, 128–129,
    129, 130, 133, 135, 141, 146, 149, 150,
    160, 161, 182, 186, 187, 200, 206, 209,
    237, 241, 244, 265
Reiser, Pete, xv, 31–32, 55, 70, 71, 72, 73,
    75, 77, 79, 83, 84, 90, 93, 100, 121,
    122, 126, 127, 128, 133, 141, 143, 148,
    149, 160, 161, 163, 180, 186, 196, 197,
    205, 206, 211, 212, 243
Restelli, Dino, 245
Reynolds, Allie, 206, 208
Rice, Del, 227, 230
Rice, Grantland, 34
Rickey, Branch, xv, 16, 32, 42, 74, 127,
    130, 131, 132, 133, 134, 136, 139, 140,
    141–142, 143, 145, 146, 148, 160, 165,
    166, 169–170, 170, 171, 171–172, 177,
    178, 179, 180, 181, 185, 187, 197, 219,
    221, 222, 228, 230, 232, 235, 238, 240
Riddle, Elmer, 140, 244
Riggs, Lew, 112, 133
Rigney, Bill, 232
Rizzo, Johnny, 108, 109, 111
Rizzuto, Phil, 84, 88, 90, 94, 98, 129, 133,
    135, 206, 207–208
Robinson, Eddie, 129, 133
Robinson, Jackie, xv, 137, 139, 140, 145,
    147, 169–170, 171, 176, 177, 178, 179,
    180, 183, 185, 186, 187, 197, 198,
    198–199, 199, 202, 219, 226, 232, 241,
    244–245
Robinson, Mary (Ma), 7
Robinson, Wilbert, xv, 5–6, 6–7, 7, 14, 22,
    81
Roe, Preacher, 236, 248
Rogell, Billy, 40
Rojek, Stan, 148, 150, 239
Rolfe, Red, 88, 89, 90, 98, 104
Roosevelt, Franklin Delano, 111, 138
Rosner, Max, 231, 265
Rossi, Dominic, Dr., 228
Rowe, Schoolboy, 136
Rowell, Bama, 181
Roxy Bowling Center, 72
Rucker, Johnny, 103

Rucker, Nap, 35
Ruffing, Red, 84, 87–88
Ruppert, Jacob, 5, 14
Russell, Rip, 23
Russo, Marius, 84, 88, 262
Ruth, Babe, 23, 93, 207

Sain, Johnny, 203, 237
Salvo, Manny, 50
Sanford, Fred, 249
Scarborough, Sid, 268
Schmitz, Johnny, 119, 149, 237
Schoendienst, Red, 196, 197
Schultz, Howie, 151, 160, 172, 180–181
Schumacher, Hal, 35
Sears, Ziggy, 18, 53, 113
Sewell, Luke, 136
Sewell, Rip, 79, 245
Shea, Frank, 206, 207, 212, 216
Shotton, Burt, 133, 181, 182–183, 185,
    186, 187, 197, 200–201, 202, 205, 207,
    208, 210, 211, 212, 214, 216, 218, 219,
    221, 222, 232, 232–233, 236, 237, 238,
    240, 245, 251, 262
Shoun, Clyde, 11, 54
Shuba, George, 179, 236
Shupe, Vincent, 50
Sisler, Dick, 156
Slaughter, Enos, 36, 46, 54, 74, 79, 121,
    127, 148, 151, 156, 160, 162, 197, 198,
    198–199, 199, 202, 227
Smalley, Roy, 237
Smith, Red, 150
Snider, Duke, 244, 253
Snodgrass, Fred, 93
Southworth, Billy, 13, 42, 43, 45, 46–47,
    51, 113, 114, 136, 146, 147, 164
Speaker, Tris, 207
Spring Hill Chapel, 265
Spahn, Warren, 138, 203, 237
St. Johns Hospital (St. Louis), 121
Stainback, Tuck, 17
Stanky, Eddie, xv, 134, 147, 149, 152, 158,
    159, 167, 172, 177, 187, 196, 198, 208,
    209, 211, 211–210, 226, 230, 231, 238,
    240, 243
Stark, Dolly, 24
Staten Island Drillers, 232

ABOUT THE AUTHOR

Lyle Spatz is author of *New York Yankee Openers: An Opening Day History of Baseball's Most Famous Team, 1903–1996*; *Yankees Coming, Yankees Going: New York Yankee Player Transactions, 1903–1999*; *Bad Bill Dahlen: The Rollicking Life and Times of an Early Baseball Star*; *Dixie Walker: A Life in Baseball*; *Historical Dictionary of Baseball*; and *Willie Keeler: From the Playgrounds of Brooklyn to the Hall of Fame*. He is coauthor of *The Midsummer Classic: The Complete History of Baseball's All-Star Game*; *1921: The Yankees, the Giants, and the Battle for Baseball Supremacy in New York*; and *The Colonel and Hug: The Partnership That Transformed the New York Yankees*. Spatz is also chief editor of *The Baseball Records Update: 1993*; *The SABR Baseball List and Record Book*; *The Team That Forever Changed Baseball and America: The 1947 Brooklyn Dodgers*; and *Bridging Two Dynasties: The 1947 New York Yankees*.

Spatz has contributed chapters to *The Dictionary of Literary Biography: Sportswriters*; *The Biographical Dictionary of American Sports: Baseball*; *Jackie Robinson: Race, Sports, and the American Dream*; *Baseball and the "Sultan of Swat": Babe Ruth at 100*; *Deadball Stars of the American League*; *Deadball Stars of the National League*; *Baseball's First Stars*; *The Perfect Game*; *Major League Baseball Profiles: 1871–1900*; *American Sports: An Encyclopedia of the Figures, Fans, and Phenomena That Shape Our Culture*; and *Inventing Baseball*.

His articles have appeared in the *New York Times*, the *Washington Post*, *Total Baseball*, *Baseball Weekly*, *Baseball Digest*, the *National Pastime*, the *Baseball Research Journal*, and the *Baltimore Orioles Offi-*

cial Game Program. In addition, Spatz has presented papers at the Babe Ruth Conference at Hofstra University and the Jackie Robinson Conference at Long Island University. Since moving to Florida in 2002, he has lectured on baseball history to Elderhostel groups and various civic organizations throughout the state.

A member of the Society for American Baseball Research (SABR) since 1973, Spatz has served as chairman of SABR's Baseball Records Committee since 1991. In 2000, SABR presented him with the L. Robert Davids Award, its most prestigious honor. In 2001, the magazine *Diamond Angle* presented him with their F. C. Lane Award in recognition of his excellence in baseball writing, and *Sporting News* presented him with an award for his research related to *The Midsummer Classic*. His book *New York Yankee Openers: An Opening Day History of Baseball's Most Famous Team, 1903–1996* was a finalist for the Seymour Medal, honoring 1997's best book of baseball history. Spatz's book *1921: The Yankees, the Giants, and the Battle for Baseball Supremacy in New York* (coauthored with Steve Steinberg) was the winner of the 2011 Seymour Medal. His books *The Team That Forever Changed Baseball and America: The 1947 Brooklyn Dodgers* and *Dixie Walker: A Life in Baseball* won the 2013 and 2012 Ron Gabriel Award, respectively, for the best book relating to the Brooklyn Dodgers. In 2016, Spatz and Steinberg shared the SABR Baseball Research Award for their work on *The Colonel and Hug: The Partnership That Transformed the New York Yankees*.